T0090419

(An Urgent Appeal To The World Leaders)

It Was Glorious:
Not a Cheap Shot

MOHAMMED D. HUSSAIN

BANGLADESH IS PART OF A GLOBAL FAMILY TOO

SIZE: 55,598 sq. miles
Population: 158 million!

Our history, sovereignty, integrity, and our culture must be protected

The internal and external conspirators must not be forgiven

Our country may be small but our sovereignty is not

The current illegitimate judicial system must not exist

Peace, progress, and prosperity must be ensured

Human right violations must not be tolerated

Corruption and abuse of power must end

Environmental protection is a must

Civilization must not be perished

Justice must be re-established

UN charter must be respected

Order this book online at www.trafford.com
or email orders@trafford.com

Most Trafford titles are also available at major online book retailers.

Printed in the United States of America.

ISBN: 978-1-4269-3693-7 (sc)
ISBN: 978-1-4269-3694-4 (e-book)

Library of Congress Control Number: 2010911499

Our mission is to efficiently provide the world's finest, most comprehensive book publishing service, enabling every author to experience success. To find out how to publish your book, your way, and have it available worldwide, visit us online at www.trafford.com

Trafford rev. 09/16/2010

www.trafford.com

North America & international
toll-free: 1 888 232 4444 (USA & Canada)
phone: 250 383 6864 • fax: 812 355 4082

Greetings!

I welcome you to my writings.

Whoever you are, wherever you are, anywhere in the world, I wish you all the best!

Please read everything I've written and do not leave out any little part of it. I'd like to send a message to the world leaders for the greater cause of our country – **Bangladesh.**

Please always be wise, safe, and sound!

May the force be with you!

Thank you.

Important Notice:

Responses are welcome. You are strictly restricted to modify my writings with inclusion or exclusion or copy out by any means without my consent. Violators will be prosecuted under the copyright law. Any attempt to fabricate, inclusion or exclusion will be dealt seriously with the maximum extent of law.

The cause of my writing is simply to express my views and share with the people of Bangladesh how to protect our national interests from corrupt politicians and bureaucrats. This is now published as a book but some of my writings were shared by e-mail to some of the communities of Bangladesh.

My endeavor is to reach out to the massive scale of the people of Bangladesh all over the world to share their views as well. Indeed, the readers will make up their mind to accept or reject my opinions.

Despite extreme constraint of my time, I have a strong desire to write more, and will do so if I'm encouraged by the readers or if I feel it is necessary to our people. I've already received some enthusiastic responses from those limited readers. My further request is to please go through my writings without missing any little part of it. You may discover the answers of your questions and concerns.

I believe this is ideal for all times and all walks of people — students, teachers, business communities, politicians, bureaucrats, civilians and military authorities, etc.

May the force be with you!

Mohammed D. Hussain

Respected Readers

It's my honor to publish this book for you with my writings. I'm neither a writer nor a poet — but I started to write by my own style, especially for our country Bangladesh and our people. I'm not someone instantly recognizable. I believe my writings will introduce who I am to the readers.

My writings are literally circumstantial. I tried to write the factual issues to ensure that I do not engage myself with frenzy talks. I've highlighted a variety of issues; those are directly related to the consequence of the violations of political, cultural, moral, and ethical codes of our behavior. I've emphasized mostly the importance of the wisdom and moral and ethical values in our life and the consequence of its violations. I've rejected the myths and propagandas and stood for the truth to stop misleading our current and future generations.

In fact, I never tried to write anything until June 2006. Once I started to write, I couldn't give up and continued to do so despite an extremely busy life on foreign soil. I tried to give up, but couldn't, and I really don't know if I'd be able to do so. I believe it is my moral obligation to speak out for the rightful causes. Our freedom fighters picked up the arms for our liberation — why shouldn't I pick up my pen for the cause of our people and our country, (Bangladesh)?

As an ordinary person, I'm neither associated with the political parties of Bangladesh nor do I desire to be so. Occasionally, I attend some cultural functions and I never expose myself to draw any attention of the audience. I always remain quiet in an orderly manner.

I may not be a politician or an activist of any political party, but I couldn't sit back and relax, detaching myself and not expressing my reactions when something happened to my country — whether extremely good or bad! In those circumstances, I couldn't remain silent and started to express my views and reactions. My writings are morally courageous, but quite risky politically. I've taken it as an obligation.

The details of my writings are a combination of some of my writings with my reactions in different circumstances of Bangladesh and I've titled it as, "**IT WAS GLORIOUS: NOT A CHEAP SHOT.**" I hope you will go through my writings at your convenience with feedback containing your reactions in an acceptable manner.

Indeed, I'll honor your valuable suggestions or advice, if any.

Thank you!

Mohammed D. Hussain

Dedication

Firstly, I with great honor would like to remember my parents who raised me with high moral and ethical values. I'm very proud of my family values. My father, Alhaj Ramizuddin Sarker, Houshdi, Daudkandi, Comilla, Bangladesh passed away on September 27, 1978, at the age of about one hundred and my mother Aklima Begum is nearly one hundred. My father was a pretty well-known figure in our area. The early stage of his life was like a fairytale.

Unfortunately, his life was full of tragedy during the later stages of his life, which had a direct impact on my life as well. But I maintained my positive role with great fortitude in those circumstances and never broke down. I was disproportionately the youngest one of my generation. All of my nephews and nieces were much older than me. Naturally, I was very shy and modest but very uncompromising with any unfair practice, which was significantly different from many others.

Secondly, I'd like to dedicate my writings as a tribute to our freedom fighters who've sacrificed their lives, and to other contributors during our liberation war in 1971. I also would like to dedicate my writings to those politicians who played the positive roles for our success and didn't have any selfish desire for their own.

I've never written anything for the massive cause. This is my first writing and I'm too constraint of my time. I spent that limited time with long thought. I'm not worried at all about my success or failure. All I wanted was to express my views on different circumstances of our country with historical references.

I hope the readers will take their time to go through my writings. Maybe to some this will work as political and behavioral theology to correct themselves.

Mohammed D. Hussain

Preface

This book contains a very strong message, not only to the politicians of Bangladesh but also to the rest of the world. Bangladesh is small—but its sovereignty and its population are not! Bangladesh is a part of the global family as well. As a member country of the UN, each and every country should respect its charter, irrespective of size, shape, and power, and must maintain the mutual interest and trust to maintain a peaceful world order.

My writings are quite revolutionary for the greater cause of our country Bangladesh. Indeed, Bangladesh is one of the most densely populated countries in the world. Sadly, the people are suffering miserably because of the corrupt politicians and bureaucrats with the support of some internal and external destructionists. Very few of us have ever tried to write so courageously the cause of the sufferings of the people.

I, on behalf of the ill-fated Bangladeshis, would like to draw the attention of the world leaders, sending a message to them to protect 158 million people of our country, our sovereignty and integrity, our history, and our nation from those destructionists. My bold stand may surprise many—and I'm not free from deadly threats of the dupes of the current atrocious regime.

The recent report of human rights violations in Bangladesh published by the US State Department is clear evidence of the axioms of my writings.

The current controversial prime minister, Sheikh Hasina, is a glaring example of deadly violence. She managed to obtain power by Mafia-style election-2008 under the unconstitutional caretaker government under Dr. Fakhruddin Ahmed and former chief of army staff, General Moeen U. Ahmed.

Her regime has already been the greatest political catastrophe of anytime of our history. The parliament became the epicenter of hostility toward the opposition parties. Freedom of speech was snatched away. They are also targeting those who express their honest opinions, trying to track them down with the false and fabricated allegations.

Her phony slogan “Digital Bangladesh” became the “Disastrous Bangladesh.” She managed to mislead a large number of the people, especially the current generation. Within a very short period of her regime, our country suffered irreparable damage both domestically and internationally. The sovereignty and integrity of our country, border security, our history, our culture, and civilization are challenged. The manmade catastrophic disaster became a common phenomenon.

I believe history is something to learn from as we take lessons of the consequence of the miscalculations of those failed giant politicians of the past. The modern civilized era denies political and judicial absolutism of any nature. Our judicial system lost its sanctity and the justice system is controlled by the current illegitimate regime.

The horrible prime minister Sheikh Hasina is known as an innovator of deadly violence, corruption, and destruction. She has taken an agenda to assault democracy and our true history.

We inherited our glorious history of the liberation of Bangladesh in 1971. But her father, Sheikh Mujibur Rahman, also known as Bangabandhu (BB), dismayed the hopes and aspirations of the people of our newborn Bangladesh because of his abject failure of corrective administration. He was the cause of the historic corruption, nepotism, cronyism, favoritism, and abuse of power. His lifelong political creditability was diminished in less than four years. The continuation of the same style of politics is nothing but the resurrection of the old evil tactics.

The current prime minister has already undertaken to rewrite our history with the denial of the contribution of the real contributors during our liberation war of Bangladesh in 1971. She is trying to write a parody in the name of our history with the obliteration of the name of genuine heroes that our true history can’t deny. This is not only changing history but is also a crime against the sanctity of our nation at large. This is the total betrayal to the life and blood of our martyrs of 1971.

As a patriotic citizen, no one should allow her to continue this Mafia-style administration in the twenty-first century. As a non-politician, I myself couldn't remain silent, and nobody should! We must oust this illegitimate regime to protect our country Bangladesh from further damage likely to occur.

Our nation already suffered unprecedentedly right after she took charge of her evil regime. We lost fifty-seven high-ranking talented army officers in a single day, more than our nation had ever experienced. We didn't lose that many officers, even in our liberation war in 1971.

It was too early for me to pick up arms during our liberation war. Why shouldn't I pick up my pen for the cause of our country and our people now? I believe it is the obligation of all of us to protect the interests of our country, and I've dedicated my writings to the solemn cause of our country and our people.

In conclusion, I would like to request that readers please read everything I have written without leaving out any little part of it.

Thank you.

Long live Bangladesh! God bless our country, our people, and the entirety of mankind at large!

Mohammed D. Hussain

The Essence of my Writings

Aek Sagar rakter binimoya
Banglar shadhinata anle jara
Amra tomader bhulbona...(2)

The above few lines are part of one of the most important songs of our commitment that we will never forget our freedom fighters who have sacrificed their lives for the cause of our liberation. Our freedom fighters sacrificed their lives for the bright future of our nation in which there will be no discrimination, nor exploitation, injustice and violence, etc. The whole song is very much emotional and touchy to everyone's minds and hearts. I started my writings with the essence of this song.

Sadly enough, we need to ask ourselves if we are really doing everything that we promised or are we using that song to place the wreaths as a tribute for their sacrifice on the very special day or occasions only? If we do, are we consistent enough with what we say and what we do? If we don't, why do we make the false commitment? What was the reason to sacrifice their precious lives in 1971? If we make any false commitment, can we consider ourselves as the trusted ones or should we get our expected outcome? Who is making those false commitments? What did we see as the consequence of our broken promises? What else do we need to see as its consequence? Isn't it true that the consequence doesn't forgive anybody as to we believe it or not? If we face any consequence, should we blame others or we should repent ourselves? Should we continue to mislead our people and the generations to come? If we do, what will be the future of our country and our nation?

The whole purpose of my writings is for us to realize what we are doing in the name of politics. Indeed, it is our moral obligation to respect our own words and actions. But with very few exceptions, we are not respectful to our commitments either as a politician or as any other professional. Sadly enough, we lost our conscience and are doing everything for our selfish causes, even though it was proven to be costlier than whatever we achieve in our lives.

We don't need to go too far. Our short history left a lot of examples. But we hardly do care about those consequences. As a result, we pay for it, which we should. But we don't want to agree with the fact. We want to blame others, ignoring the real cause of those costly prices as we pay to achieve our mischievous desires. I have tried my best to write those issues despite my very poor sense of knowledge of the reality as may be viewed by the genius ones.

I'm trying to do mine, but you must do yours. Together, hopefully we all will be able to achieve our goal that we are all dreaming of.

Let's hope for the best and move forward with solemn commitment with necessary actions!

Greetings!

I welcome you to share my views and reactions about the current political crisis of Bangladesh. This book is written with a combination of some of my writings with the expression of my reactions about the political crisis of our country Bangladesh and its direct impact on our people, our country and our nation. As a non-politician, I didn't hesitate to write about the factual issues the way I viewed them. This could be a serious reaction to many radicals who deny the truth and want to establish their corrupt missions.

Our history is not too old but very eventful. Our history started with pain, sufferings, sacrifice, devotions, struggles and immense joy of freedom. Unfortunately, we could not continue to respect the cause of the sacrifice of our freedom fighters and the devotion of each and every citizen of Bangladesh of the year 1971. Most of the problems were created by some of the selfish power-greedy high-profiled politicians and bureaucrats.

Indeed, some of them paid a very serious price for their distrustful behavior. Sadly enough, some of the dedicated and real contributors were also the victims of intrigues of the betrayers and lost their lives. Some of them took the advantage of those crises to change their fortune and caused the immense miseries for the rests. Historically, we are experiencing the horrible tragedies between good versus corrupt. The current crisis is the consequence of all those corruptions and needs to end.

Within a short period of our history of the last thirty-eight years, we have been experiencing the different kinds of corrupt and deceptive administrations; democratically elected government, dictatorship and the unconstitutional cocktails of both civil and military leaders under the latest emergency of the Caretaker Government (CG), the political banditry of the Chief Advisor, Dr. Fakhruddin Ahmed, and the Chief of Army Staff, Gen. Moeen U. Ahmed. The newly current administration of Prime Minister Sheikh Hasina is the resurrection of old failed political absolutism.

The Election-2008 was not the true reflection of the opinion of the majority of our people. The election result was changed by the few for the few. The unconstitutional CG dismayed the hopes and aspiration of the genuine voters. They disfranchised the peaceful and rational voters and allowed to rig the voting system by their own forces. Now our country is paying the price with unimaginable consequences.

Over and over, our people expected some changes that could make a real difference in their lives. All those administrations came with lots of hopeful commitment to root out the corruption and lead us toward the progressive direction of peace, progress and prosperity. But the reality was quite the opposite. Most of them betrayed our people. Some of them genuinely tried to fulfill hopes and aspiration of the people but couldn't survive. Some of them came with a deceptive formula to abuse the power but ended up with painful price as well. Some of the major political criminals still exist and are causing immense problems for the rest of us.

The current political rivalry is the syndromes of those previous iconic leaders. People continued to trust them but didn't get anything as expected.

People didn't make any mistake trusting them for their wishful future. But the distrustful actions of those administrations were the cause of the sufferings of the people beyond measure. People didn't get anything but the false hopes and aspirations like a mirage of peace and progress.

As an ordinary person, suddenly I do not know how I started to react by my writings since June 2006. I tried to give up with a few articles but couldn't. Despite a very busy life on foreign soil, I continued to write in different circumstances and got entangled with no way out.

I decided to continue my writings since June 2006 at the heated time of deadly political turmoil caused by the recent current administration under the leadership of the controversial PM Sheikh Hasina. I have expressed my deepest concerns about our country

Bangladesh and its people. During that period, the people of Bangladesh experienced lot of awful political hostilities with deadly violence.

The constitutional interim Caretaker Government (CG) failed to hold the election due to the extreme form of deadly violence as carried out by the opponents of the outgoing administration of former Prime Minister Begum Khaleda Zia Bangladesh Nationalist Party (BNP). As a result, the CG imposed the emergency prior to the election on January 11, 2007, which has been termed as **1/11.**

The hotchpotch of the army along with some so-called pundits of civic society came to the political field to play the roles of referees to abolish the destructive course of politics of corruption, destruction and violence. People overwhelmingly supported them with the hope of the better future of our nation.

The joint venture of both army and civilian leaders started to play the fake roles in an effort to hold a credible, free and fair election. They were entrusted by the overwhelming majority of the people to change the course of the politics of horror. Their commitment was to hold a credible, free and fair election to end the political turmoil of Bangladesh. But they ended up disgracefully betraying the people.

Sadly enough, the people of Bangladesh have experienced another hypocritical political banditry in our history under the leadership of Dr. Fakhruddin Ahmed and the Chief of Army Staff, General Moeen U. Ahmed. In the beginning, I did have a profound trust in them like the vast majority of the people of Bangladesh. But we all were proven wrong.

I tried my best to express my views in writing based on my observation of the activities of the unconstitutional CG during the administration of their twenty-three months until the election-2008. It may not be well-taken by many readers because of the different political and philosophical views or their monolithic egoism. But I've expressed my reactions for the greater cause of our country, our people and our nation.

In order to put down the controversial process of our Election-2008,

I have added some of my previous writings in the first part of this issue. The second part contains the activities of the emergency administration under The Chief Advisor, Dr. Fakhruddin Ahmed, and the Chief of Army Staff, General Moeen U. Ahmed, along with his advisory members including the Chief Election Commissioner (CEC), Dr. A.T.M. Shamsul Huda. The third part contains some deceptive campaign propagandas in humorous style by all major political parties to send their messages out to the people, especially to the younger generations. The fourth part contains the subsequent actions of the current administration and its consequences.

In my view, the whole process of the election under the unconstitutional CG was fundamentally flawed. They divided our nation in a very damaging way and our nation is now under the serious threat of sovereignty and integrity. They acted as the agents of outsiders. They are fully responsible for all those devastations our nation is facing today. They themselves held the power unconstitutionally with the false commitment to the people and intended to continue as long as they could.

They've re-established the corruption both in civil and army on a wider scale. The magnitude of their corruption is at an all-time higher in the history of Bangladesh. They are known as the most distrustful, destructive and hypocritical group of political gangs in the history of Bangladesh.

They were biased to some violent political parties and protected themselves with hidden mutual interest. They held the controversial election and left our country in a devastating situation. They were also influenced by the external conspirators. The recent horrible rampage of Bangladesh Rifles (BDR), our border security guards on their officers, is another mystery in our history.

It doesn't require being a rocket scientist to understand how all those horrible occurrences are taking place in our country. With the simple analysis of our history of 1972 to August 1975, and some activities of external conspirators in conjunction with our selfish power-greedy domestic politicians, we can understand who could be behind those horrible operations.

Very often, our border security forces BDR and many innocent people are being killed by the Indian BSF. Instead of dealing with this very important issue bilaterally, our current administration is wagging their tails around their masters to please them as the expression of their loyalty. The importance of the sovereignty and integrity of our country is not an issue.

Once again, the resurrection process of BAKSAL is taking place in a paradoxical style, which was demised in 1975. They are serious about how to nullify the Fifth Amendment of our Constitution just to re-establish the dark chapter of BAKSAL. In fact, the Fifth Amendment and abolition of BAKSAL protected the sovereignty and integrity of our country Bangladesh from further damage, likely to happen in 1975. They are inviting their masters with a red-carpet reception opening up the corridor, border, trade and transit facilities, etc.

Our domestic issues, including our defense and intelligence, are being controlled by the external conspirators. It is like an innocent antelope asking for refuge to some hungry hyenas. They are trying to Indialize Bangladesh with the total betrayal to the martyrs of 1971 and the entity of our country Bangladesh. Without the entity, there is no proper identity. We liberated our country Bangladesh from Pakistan not to get sold to India. The excessive control of India over Bangladesh is the direct threat to the sovereignty of our peaceful country Bangladesh and the regional peace.

The current administration doesn't hesitate to betray our nation but they have to be loyal to their masters who influenced to bring them to power. They think they are above our country and its sovereignty. They think they got the mandate of the vast majority of the people in the last unconstitutional mafia-style election where the genuine voters couldn't cast their votes. It is not a mandate! It is a political bandit! The whole election process under **Dr. Fakhruddin was the political banditry and it is constitutionally challengeable.**

In light of the deceptive election process conducted by the CG, there is no legitimacy of the current administration. Any policies and laws passed by this unconstitutionally elected government are automatically invalid under the definition of our constitution.

The genuine opinions of the courageous people are being targeted as their enemies. The real voices are being titled as extremists or terrorists. They are also going after the religious leaders and thinkers, even though they are not destructive at all. They are trying to make up their dirty case against the patriotic citizens and the true believers to remain in power at the cost of the devastating consequence on our country and our nation. Why do they do this? Because they know they lost the popularity and trust of the people for good and forever. They don't have any other means to obtain power without external boost and horrible violence. Besides, they have the secondary foundation in foreign soil. They don't care about our country and our people.

They are even using our great religion "Islam" very negatively to please their master neighbor who is constantly campaigning against our religion, even in the international media. But they never say anything of their own terrorism. We must not compromise with the extremists of any religious and political parties.

Religion is the divine and spiritual sacred issue. All true religions teach us how to treat each other equally and honorably. We must respect all others beliefs rather than going against one another. We shouldn't politicize the religions with provocative behavior. All religions have some extremists and we need to deal with them very appropriately with proper identification.

The Almighty Creator created the universe, and the earth is the only planet for all human beings. In this planet, He also created the other creatures with incredible natural bounty and beauty to enjoy His creations. He, The Creator also created us with different looks and races, not to humiliate each other but to live peacefully with mutual respect, sharing the bounty as He created for all of us and all other living creatures. Amongst all other creatures He created the human being just to worship Him with His prescribed guidelines.

Our Creator

Our Creator created us by Himself of His own
He also created the universe and its beyond.

The earth is the tiny part of His creation
Designed and created with complete living condition.

If we are little thoughtful about His bounty
How could we deny that no one is behind its beauty?

The sky, the sun, the moon and the stars are so beautiful
Even those are untouchable and unreachable too.

The earth is our living place so amazing
Its beauty and bounty are gift of the Almighty.

He is the only Creator and He is the Protector
We human beings and other creatures are living together.

He created us and other living beings with distinctions
The human being is the highest one amongst all others.

Nature is acting with His one single command
The solar system is functioning with no other's command.

The mystery of the entire creation is so wonderful
To know all about His creation is utterly impossible.

We have very few answers of many questions of His creations
Unless we think about the mystery with sound commonsense.

The ignorance and misconceptions are misdirecting for us
Exercising our sound rationale may get some answers.

To believe in One Creator makes lots of sense
Sharing the multiple creators doesn't make any sense.

We as human beings can't go together
How could the multiple creators go altogether?

If they couldn't agree with unifying decision in any matters
What would have been the consequence of the entire universe?

Lots of revelations to all mankind sent by Him
Soon after He created us as human beings!

Human history has been carrying those messages from the beginning
He warned us with lots of instances with the past happenings.

Our life is so short and so uncertain
Why do we make the difference by ourselves as humans?

To claim superiority from one another is so wrong
Knowingly we don't have any control on our own.

Good and evil are His creation as we all know
These are the transformations by our own.

Greediness and selfishness lead to the evils
Goodness and fairness are struggling against all myths.

The peace and misery are the output of our own
Our actions determine what we should really gain.

The rewards and severe punishment are His commitment
Everyone will see their own destiny in the Day of Judgment.

The devout believers will be rewarded by Him
The others will be isolated for severe punishment.

Believing in one Almighty Allah is so true
Anything else sharing with Him is totally untrue.

May Allah forgive me if I'm wrong with anything!
Lead us through Your guidance to follow as a human being.

May Allah make all of us as one of the rewarded ones!
Save the entire mankind and lead us towards the right direction.
–Amen!

Mohammed D. Hussain

Unfortunately, we human beings can't go along and make the difference with each other with self-proclamation of the superiority to one another even though we do not have any control on our own. The fanatics of different beliefs mislead and misguide the people using their own corrupt ideologies in the name of religion. We ourselves create the problems and blame each other, engaging in horrible violence and terrorism.

We are living very peacefully in our country Bangladesh with all other religions with mutual respect and common understanding and didn't destroy their sacred worship places such as temples and churches, etc. But they demolished the centuries-old historic mosque by their terrorists with the support of their own fanatic government of the past. Didn't they attack even the Sikh golden temple of another minority's religion and killed many Sikhs? What did they do with the Muslims in Gujrat? If this is not terrorism, what then is terrorism? If it is, who is the biggest one?

The clamoring of terrorism pointing to others by the Indians against Bangladesh and many other Muslim countries is totally provocative. We do have strong historic and cultural ties with all other religions in our daily life in our country. But they don't. We do not have any lower or higher caste system to dehumanize any human being. But they do.

The real follower of Islam never interferes in others beliefs and do not make any difference based on color, race, and religion. The real Muslims can't treat any human being as the lower or higher class of people. The core message of Islam is **peace,** treating each other equally and justly. The message of compassion, wisdom, tolerance and justice with the rejection of arrogance, hostility, injustice and atrocity are the ways of real Islam.

Besides, Bangladesh itself was fighting the elements of the so-called religious extremists and tried to eliminate them during the administration of BNP. The tougher actions taken against the extremists earned their reputation from the rest of the world under the administration of BNP. But the current PM, then as an opposition leader, was mocking about those actions saying it was drama!

She herself was engaged in the politics of destruction and deadly violence. She inspired her dupes to continue the deadly violence until she achieved her mischievous goal. She also campaigned of the terrorism in Bangladesh very mean-spiritedly to please her masters.

She used the issue of terrorism for egregious political cause in Bangladesh against her opponents. But she didn't realize how much damage it was for our nation in the eyes of the rest of world. Multiple murderers of her own party got shelter to her masters' countries. They are the ones who are using her to damage the image of our country. They are acting as vultures to loot out Bangladesh in all possible means as they did soon after our liberation in 1971 and her last horrible administration. (*See for details* **"Now Is the Time to Pay the Price!").**

Our country may be small but our sovereignty is not. We are willing to strengthen our relationship with any other nation in the world with honest dealings. But we can't be a capitulator to any hypocritical dealers. We can't surrender our fundamental rights as a country or as a nation to any. We can't ask any favor from any known conspirators both nationally and internationally. We don't want to turn back the dark regime of the imperialism of a one-man show from 1972 to August 1975.

We do not want to be isolated from the rest of the world; rather, we want to be one of the great partners of the globalized family as we already are. We don't want to deal with the past horrible ends of our leaders who themselves were responsible for their political consequences. Who started the politics of assassination? Who said where is Siraj Sikder today in mockery-style soon after his assassination?

If anyone kills someone, his or her price becomes due at least at the same magnitude or sometimes greater. Indeed, it is very shocking for any leader to end up with a horrible finish as we've experienced historically. But those were the consequences of their political and moral miscalculations.

The Biggest Political Miscalculations of the Political Giant, BB: Every effect must have cause. The ups and downs or ascending and descending are the results of the systematic process of input and outcome of the behaviors of any leader. BB himself didn't realize what he achieved in his life-long politics! He achieved to the highest level of leadership to lead our nation until March 25th, 1971. But he became very controversial soon after he took over the charge of our hard-earned liberated Bangladesh. He became known as different BB than the BB until March 1971.

He attempted to be the political absolutist and tried to play hardball against his opponents who liberated the country, risking their lives. He believed that his strong personal defense forces (Rakhkhi Bahini) and with the establishment of unpopular BAKSAL with the deepest relationship with profound capitulation to Indira Gandhi could protect him from any potential rebellions. He also had the illusion to be crowned in the twentieth century while we lost millions of lives just to establish the democracy — the land of the rule of law — where the abuse of power, injustice, unfairness, corruption, cronyism, imperialism and totalitarianism will be perished for good and forever.

In fact, soon after he took over the charge of the newborn Bangladesh, we started to experience all those elements under his leadership. He desperately tried to re-establish all those evil practices. The general people and his rebels became very aggressive to stop his unilateral authoritative tendency. As a result, his hardball hit him back so gravely that the people couldn't ever imagine.

During that short period of time, his popularity was declining sharply and he became extremely controversial. People unbelievably started to view BB differently soon after our liberation. The leaders lose ground when he or she loses the popularity and trust of the people. Under his administration, that was exactly the case.

"When wealth is lost, nothing is lost; when health is lost, something is lost; when character is lost, all is lost". – Billy Graham

Unfortunately, BB was in the same situation. He couldn't uphold his creditability and became disoriented himself just because of the greediness of unilateral power. Even his son was very controversial at that time with some scandals. People started to view him differently, which was the worst dilemma as an iconic leader like BB. The creditability of lifelong politics of BB sharply ended up within the short period of 1972–1975. Let me quote the following:

"Nearly all men can stand adversity, but if you want to test a man's character, give him power." – Abraham Lincoln

The Cruelest Assassination of BB Could Have Been Avoided: The assassination of a leader like him along with his all-available family members including his little son Russel was the cruelest in the history of our nation. The wrath of the rebellions was extremely beyond control. The whole horrible tragedy could have been avoided, if he was a bit calculative about the consequence of his political absolutism. His assassinators could have been loyal to him as opposed to becoming his foes. He could have been known as one of the great leaders of our nation without any controversy and divisions as he was until 1971.

How to Protect the Legacy: If we go back in human history, we can see that many of the great leaders left their legacy for the generations to come just by virtue of their greatness. They are no longer with us, but their legacy is still intact historically and will remain so in the future. But many mighty tyrant, sadist, corrupt and totalitarians left very disgracefully in the history of mankind too. They were known as the curse of mankind.

In my writings, I've already mentioned some of the great leaders in the world of modern history. Some of them are universally honored and some of them are disgraced too. The quality makes the difference spontaneously. It doesn't require amplifying with ultrasonic sound of mythical rhetoric to protect the legacy.

The current illegitimate administration is trying to redefine our history and solely protect the legacy of BB. The legacy has to be on the basis of facts and figures, not by the rhetoric. Our liberation wasn't the sole creditability of BB himself but many others as well, especially our people and our freedom fighters! They were the ones who played the hardest part of the role of our independence while he was in jail during our liberation war. Some of them played extraordinary heroic roles, and martyr President Ziaur Rahman was one of them. You might have different political philosophies but our national history shouldn't be radicalized.

What a Great Leader! I must mention another great leader just passed away who was Senator Ted Kennedy of the United States of America. I pay my deepest respect and condolence to his family and all of his well wishers! His legacy is quite unique. He was from one of the fortunate wealthy families. But his family suffered many tragedies. His brother John F. Kennedy was also another great president and was assassinated. He was the youngest president in the history of the United States of America. His other brother, Robert F. Kennedy, was also assassinated while he was running for president.

Ted Kennedy also ran for the presidential election in 1980 but couldn't get elected. Even though he came through a lot of family tragedies, he was known as the lion of senate nearly half a century for forty-seven years. He was a man of accomplishment. He set the record of legislating for so many issues that the history can never forget. He was a very compassionate person and had a loud and passionate voice for the unprivileged people to alleviate their living standards. He was also known as a champion of human rights.

He always fought for the rightful causes and never ever worked for selfish reasons. His other brothers were also remarkably known as one of the great leaders of the United States of America. This is the family who always tried their best to do something for the country and never expected anything from the country. His brother, President John F. Kennedy, famously said, *"Ask not what your country can do for you. Ask what you can do for your country."*

Ted Kennedy was always against the wars. He very passionately and compassionately spoke out for healthcare, immigration reforms for undocumented immigrants and minimum wage raises for the lower income of people just for the humanitarian causes. All immigrants will remember him with great honor and gratitude, even though the bill was not passed by the senate and congress. He had tremendous success to work with his opponents in a bipartisan manner. Senator Kennedy accomplished more than President Kennedy could have done over his lifelong political career.

I wish, if I could express the same or further beyond for BB, certainly I would, if he would have had the same quality of leadership.

What should be the Duty of the Current Generation: The duty of the current generation is just to take a lesson from the true history of the past and move forward. To damage the image is easier than to protect. Some politicians are like gamblers. They earn a lot by chance without genuine quality and lose everything by themselves. That's what happened to most of those corrupt and power-greedy leaders. It is hard to understand their genuine quality until or unless we experience their real actions and behaviors.

The situation under the current administration is very dire for our nation. The genetic form of the current administration is quite clear. The same darkest chapter of Bangladesh has been turned again. The behavior of India towards Bangladesh is the biggest concern for our small country Bangladesh for many reasons. They successfully managed to put one of the most distrustful parties, their loyalists Awami League (AL) and their associates to exert their wishful plan to keep control over our country Bangladesh. By definition, the parties who are acting against the interests and protection of their own country with the conspiracy with outsiders are the **traitors.**

Their masters want to treat us as one of their own states. On the contrary, the AL and their associates know that they can't regain the popularity and trust of the people because of their past horrible administrations. Therefore, they don't care about the country and our people. We need to understand the difference between the traitors and the patriots. We must not be naïve about what the consequence of their leadership would be.

During our liberation war in 1971, we did experience *rajakars* (the collaborators of Pakistan) and now we are experiencing even the worst element of traitors. They impudently rebuke and vilify the real freedom fighters, those who liberated our country Bangladesh in 1971. They are overly emphasizing the contribution of BB only. I'm not in favor of *rajakars* in any way. But if they want to carry out the justice of the thirty-eight-year-old case of *rajakars* they should be prosecuted as the traitors too. They shouldn't have any affair like relationship with the assassinators of martyr President Ziaur Rahman.

If they want to carry out the justice of the assassinators of BB, they should include the assassinators of martyr President Ziaur Rahman too. If they don't know how to praise the greatness of others, how can they ask for their own? Besides, they don't have any greatness at all. They are misleading our current and future generations with a false and fabricated history.

Within a very short period of the current administration, Bangladesh is facing numerous devastating problems, more than our country has ever had. For example, the Bangladesh Rifles (BDR), our border securities crisis, defense and intelligence, border, trade, corridor, transit, sea borders, Talpatti Island occupation by India annexed to Bangladesh, historic water-sharing problems of Farakka Barrage and newly added up with Tipaimukhi Dam, etc. They've already turned our fertile evergreen land to a desert. The biggest water carrier of Bangladeshi rivers — the Padma, the Meghna and the Jamuna —

became untraceable. The water crisis of Bangladesh became a life-or-death issue for our people.

The absolute control of the flow of water of the Ganges and unlawful occupation of Talpatti Island annexed to Bangladesh and very often attacks on our border forces BDR by India are the clear violations of the international law. Our evergreen Bangladesh has already turned to a desert to some extent and over 158 million people of Bangladesh are in great danger due to the manmade problems created by them.

We need to resolve those problems through mutual understanding diplomatically — not by the conspiracy. The drought and flood in Bangladesh are controlled by India alone. This kind of behavior is not only against any country but also against humanity. I'm not a legal expert, but I do believe this is against international law.

The current administration is not dealing with those vital issues for the greater cause of our country. Rather, they like to deal with the frivolous issues of the house of the former PM Begum Khaleda Zia very egregiously. They want to undermine martyr Ziaur Rahman, the very best leader Bangladesh ever had. They want to compare martyr Zia and BB on the same scale. But people don't. Those two leaders left huge differences in the quality of their leadership and personalities.

What should we do? The current administration became loyalists to their lord India disregarding the real issues of the people of Bangladesh. We as the citizens of Bangladesh should demand the immediate oust of the current controversial and unconstitutional illegitimate administration for the greater cause of our country. The protection of the sovereignty of our country is of the utmost necessity for all of us. We need to hold them accountable, including the mafia group of unconstitutional CG before further damage is likely to be met by our nation before it is too late.

The political opposition doesn't mean that you can go against the interests and protection of your own country. If you do, you are not less than the *rajakars* of 1971, and certainly even worse.

The damage already done, in just a few days under their administration, it is beyond our control and we can't afford anymore. If necessary, we must raise those issues to the United Nations to protect the interests and sovereignty of our country. As a member country of the United Nations, we need to resolve those problems through the United Nations if we fail to reach a peaceful solution bilaterally.

In order to do so, we need the capable leadership to represent our country with the rest of the world — not the traitor-like government. The loyalists have no choice but to worship their lords, giving them away everything that we can't afford. This is exactly what they are doing with India as BB did in his lifetime. This was one of the real causes of the downfall of BB in 1975 with such a horrible end.

Quality of Leadership: First, we have to understand what leadership means. The leader must be capable to undertake the responsibilities with accountability, credible to his or her words and actions, seriousness to his or her commitment and most importantly, must be patriot to his or her country. The leader should be compassionate and capable to judge everything with wisdom. He or she must be respectful to his or her opponents with decency and work together for the common cause of the country, even if he or she might have irreconcilable philosophies on some issues.

The leaders themselves should be respectful to the rule of law. They shouldn't be above or beneath the law to apply the same to others. Missing any of those qualities could cause a serious blow not only on their leadership but also for the country at large. The leadership doesn't mean the unilateral decision maker disregarding the rest. But our so-called leaders are exactly opposite. Most of them are arrogant and mischievous. They play their unilateral role with awful behaviors that people can't respect them at all. *"He who is a good ruler must first have been ruled."* - Aristotle

As a consequence, sometimes they pay the excruciating price and blame others. They are good at it because many of our misguided people support their causes and eventually become part of their dupes.

The current administration is exactly following the same tactics and successfully managed to get to power. The consequence we see is the result of our irrational choice made by the people in the last unconstitutional election-2008. In fact, it was not the choice of the rational voters who were disfranchised by **Dr. Fakruddin Ahmed and Gen. Moeen U. Ahmed.**

It is hard to believe if any patriotic citizen can compromise with all those issues as the current administration is dealing with complete surrender to our risky neighbor India. What are we getting out from India through our open borders? We are getting illegal and deadly drugs, weapons, saris, cultural pollution; very often our innocent people and our border guards are getting killed in the border area by Indian BSF, and the deadly AIDS virus, etc.

We are losing our internal stability by the external conspiracy. If we remain silent and still support this administration, we need to ask ourselves who we are! Aren't we betraying our freedom fighters of 1971, our own country and our nation at large?

Please don't get me wrong; I'm neither against any patriots of Bangladeshis nor Indians. But I'm against our leaders who caused us immense tragedies for a peace-loving country Bangladesh. When the whole world is very much concerned about the global environmental disaster, India is acting against the environmental protection of a small country like Bangladesh. I hope the patriotic people of Bangladesh will agree with my concerns. Let's raise our voices and protect our country first. We don't want to be confrontational to any but be amicable to many who respect each other as a country and as a nation with a complete sign of civilization.

We earned our liberation from barbaric Pakistan at the cost of the lives and blood of millions in 1971, to ensure we did not get sold to India. But our current illegitimate administration already is. We are already experiencing the horrible consequences soon after they took over the power with a mafia-style election. As the sensible citizens of Bangladesh, we can't sit back, relax and watch quietly. We need to raise our voices to protect the sovereignty and integrity of our country. As an ordinary citizen, I'm trying my best in my writings with my mighty pen for the greater cause of our country.

I'm following the advice of the current controversial Prime Minister who suggested the writers, journalists and reporters write their views because she believes that the pen is mightier than the sword. This sounds pretty rational and I hope she wouldn't go after me just because I'm strenuously writing my views truthfully.

The loyalists of the current illegitimate administration are threatening me for my fearless voice but I will continue my strong voice no matter what my destiny holds! As an ordinary person, I couldn't do anything remarkable for my country Bangladesh, but I'll leave my loud and clear voice for our country in a very difficult situation, which our country needs the most. I can't hide in the dark hole while my country Bangladesh is being looted by some vultures.

Why I've Picked up My Pen

I've picked up my pen not to be a writer
I've picked up my pen to be a fighter.

I reject the ideas of guns and weapons
I believe in rational thought and reason.

I don't believe in the wall for protection
I believe in the power of wisdom and compassion.

I believe in peace, progress and prosperity
I'm always against the violence and hostility.

We are listed as one of the top corrupt ones in the world
That was not the cause of the sacrifice of the lives in 1971.

We shouldn't forgive those corrupt politicians and bureaucrats
They are the obstacles of our peace and progress.

The violence and destructions are denial of the civilization
To hold them accountable will be our solemn obligation.

The betrayers are the curse of all human beings
They are the causes of all those evils.

Let's move forward to bring them to justice
Let's stand strong against the injustice.

Mohammed D. Hussain

I must acknowledge that I may not be perfect with everything but I'll respect the good advice from the readers and will appreciate their comments with better suggestions, if any.

Caution! I've taken the full privilege of my freedom of speech to express my views in a loud and clear voice. I also understand that my writings could cause serious reactions to many. I will advise the radicals to read my writings thoroughly before you make any stark comment. Do not pick and choose and deny the truth. Before you make any negative comment about my writings, please read "The Comprehensive Rebuttal of the Political Purification of Bangladesh." Please read everything I have written. You may find somehow, somewhere the answers of your questions and concerns. It may treat your chronic disease of the corrupt monolithic views, mythical and superstitious ideas as well. This will also help you to stimulate a sense of your corrective behavior.

Well, please get started. I hope you will enjoy.

Mohammed D. Hussain

Opening Remarks

Before I started to write, I was thinking as an ordinary person what would be the significance of writing of my political views to the people of Bangladesh? Besides, I'm neither a writer nor a politician or famous for anything. I'm just an ordinary person. But we shouldn't forget that our country was liberated in 1971 by the ordinary people, not only by the extraordinary ones. With very few exceptions, the so-called selfish extraordinary ones enjoyed the fruits of our liberation at the devastating cost of our country.

I know that my life has lot of unique stories that could be chosen for movie production, but the political issue was not my object at all. I'm indeed ordinary but my patriotism is not. That's why I have expressed my political opinions in different circumstances.

I'm neither a movie watcher nor a story reader. I hardly watch a complete movie with necessary patience unless it is really a likeable one. The stories the producers make in the films are mostly imaginary. Indeed, those movies are made for entertaining, documentary or educational purposes that could also impact the life of many. There are many true stories in our life are quite incredible and not fictional.

I never thought that I would write something about my life. I tried to recall what happened in my childhood to onward that had devastating impact on my life and how I tried to overcome those situations and what could have happened if it was otherwise.

I have discovered a significant difference in my life than anyone I know. Every child is born as the blessing of the Almighty Creator. They go through the raising process mostly by the parents as the normal way of life, if they are one of the lucky ones; or in rare cases they've to go through otherwise. Being a newborn baby, to the child all fosterers are like their own parents. The ultimate fate of newborn babies is determined by the Almighty Creator Himself.

The fortunate ones get the perfect environment with utmost love and affection, and others have to go through untold misery even before they understand about themselves. Some of them end up with heavenly living conditions and others have to go through unbearable struggles. Some of them lose their parents before or just after they are born, or some may have parents but unknown.

In this mysterious world, we experience a lot of unimaginable circumstances. Most of those vulnerabilities are manmade and easily avoidable, but because of the misjudgment, selfishness, irresponsibility, greediness and jealousy, the human being behaves inhumanely, even with those newborns very unjustly and ruthlessly. As a result, the sinless innocent, helpless and defenseless newborns have to go through untold misery or even death.

In my life, I've experienced something that many of you may not imagine. In fact, I've never seen a second instance of the same or relatively close to my situation. Perhaps my vulnerabilities started before I was born. But I couldn't understand anything until I attained an early childhood. Normally, I forget a lot. But quite amazingly, I couldn't forget something happened in my life; those are not forgettable at all.

My life story could touch the minds and hearts of many of you that could change your illusive and mischievous abusive behavior to those innocent. If that occurs, it will be protective for many unfortunate innocent.

I listen to radio a lot while I drive. I listen to many interesting programs of the writers on different issues. Some of these include the biographies of the rich and famous, and those that are of family, social, educational, occupational, matrimonial, political, bureaucratic, judicial, economical, cultural, religious, and many other aspects.

Although I'm not one of those rich and famous ones, I was thinking about how my life relates to all those aspects with the harsh experiences that I had to go through. I couldn't disintegrate myself from those issues in my life.

My life was intensely impacted due to the unthinkable challenges that I had to face since my childhood. Besides, I've many experiences of realities like many other normally grownup ones too. Having my thoughtful realization in a little deeper, I concluded and set up my mind to write something about myself, which is my autobiography "**Incredible But True!**"

While I was writing my autobiography, I decided to prioritize to write something else that has direct impact on the life of the vast majority of the people of Bangladesh. I couldn't continue to write about myself and thus changed the direction of my writings.

The recent egregious political games played by the current controversial administration forced me to quit from my original issue for the time being, and subsequently I have shifted my writings to another direction. I've decided to write with the title **"It Was Glorious: Not A Cheap Shot."**

Naturally, my writing style is quite different than any other professional and intellectual writers — because I'm different than them. I'm a self-educated person. I tried to express everything I wanted to in my way and hardly did care to be a super ambitious. I could have written in Bangla to reach out to the grass root level of massive Bangladeshis. But due to some unavoidable circumstances, I decided to write in English to reach out to the global communities for the greater cause of our country Bangladesh.

In my autobiography, I've also crossed the boundary of my personal life as I considered it was necessary.

I've touched upon in all those aspects and expressed my views by my actions and reactions with profound struggles that cost a lot, not only on my life but also on others. There are many short stories that have taken place in my autobiography; these are both pleasant and may be controversial to some readers.

My objective was not to undermine or be disrespectful to any, but to respect them all, if they are repentant for their wrongdoings. After overcoming all those horrible experiences, it's not necessary to write against anyone whatsoever. Perhaps, I'd never have done so. I started to write spontaneously considering that this could prevent others not to behave unfairly or exploit those innocent as human beings. I've also stressed the importance of the corrective behavior of the rest of us. I also tried to stress the importance of the necessity to live as a human being with high moral and ethical values.

The Defiance of Core Elements of Peace: Our life is not meant to consume only but also to contribute. Sharing and caring both at the time of happiness and misery strengthen our positive relationships amongst us. We can make our foes our friends and vice versa just by behaving ourselves. The peaceful living is the utmost desire of all human beings. And yet, just for the greediness and selfishness, we choose the path of illusions, hostility and depravity by rejecting the amity, fairness and dignity.

In those circumstances, to restrain them, we should be both tolerant and resistant with wisdom; not by the arms and weapons. Too much capitulation leads us to give up the very fundamental rights as a person, as a society, as a country, as a nation — and in a broader sense, as a human being!

On the contrary, the violators take the opportunity to serve their ironic and ill purposes very smoothly. As a result, we have to deal with many costly consequences. Most of the times, we rebuke and provoke others by forgetting our own actions. Sometimes we get hypnotized by myths and greediness without any rational and moral justifications and radicalize ourselves. As a consequence, we experience some unimaginable horrible ends. Too many aggressive actions and reactions with fanatic ideologies also obstruct to achieve any wishful solutions. It leads us to the disaster.

In light of the political crisis of Bangladesh, suddenly, despite an extremely busy life on foreign soil, I started to react in different circumstances since June 2006 by my writings, which I have titled **"HOW CAN I REMAIN SILENT."** My autobiography **"Incredible But True"** is an added issue that I never took as the prime object.

In spite of my challenging personal experiences, I've expressed my bold reactions against our corrupt politicians, bureaucrats and so-called intellectuals as well. To some, it is praiseworthy and courageous, but to others it is quite disturbing and dubious.

I have added Part II to express my views and reaction on the basis of the activities of the Caretaker Government (CG) since **1/11 (January 01, 2007).** You may find some humorous dialogues, election campaigns made up for our major political party leaders on very critical issues based on the actions that were taken against the politicians by the CG. You may also find some funny and humorous ways of my writings not to get bored. I've also highlighted the characteristics of our current two inept leading leaders.

Some of us believe to write anything negative about our previous leaders, even if it is true, is not right the thing to do. They think that they were our national icons and very high-profiled figures. We shouldn't write or say anything against them even if those are true. Well...I respectfully disagree with that capitulatory perception.

The genetic syndromes of politics of those iconic figures have a significant impact on our current politics and bureaucratic system. We shouldn't follow the distorting ideologies of those high-profiled politicians and bureaucrats. Besides, the true history is the lesson for the rest of us. Concealing any mischievous ideologies for the sake of their dignity is not the true history. It's a parody. It leads us to intensify the misery of the people.

The Dire Consequence of Concealing the Truth: I believe concealing the truth to establish the myths against the facts has dire consequence too and morally it is quite unacceptable. Our history left many examples and still we are facing a lot of horrible experiences politically, bureaucratically, socially, economically, judicially, culturally, etc. As a result, our valued national culture is losing its gravity and sanctity.

Deceptive Documentary: Just a few days ago, on August 15, 2009, the 34th death anniversary of BB was commemorated by the current administration. With all due respect to his leadership, until March

25th, 1971, I would like to express my views as to how deceptive the documentary was as played by the current administration!

In that documentary, the current administration gave a profound impression to the people of all generations that Bangladesh was liberated only because of BB. The rest of the contributors were not even mentioned in that documentary. My question is when and how was the country liberated? Was it for political success only or the liberation war as well? Of course, there was political success but it was futile. The Liberation War was the real success, not the political success only.

What happened during the period of March 25th to December 16th, 1971? Where was BB when he was arrested on March 25th, 1971? Who fought and led that war during our liberation war? I have already mentioned in my writings and I don't want to reiterate the same. Why didn't those crucial roles take place in that documentary? Is this not a deceptive documentary of the history of Bangladesh?

In that documentary, they didn't show or mention anything about the administrative dismal failures of BB after the post-liberation. The reason I don't need to analyze is because that was the downfall chapter of BB. Our liberation was not an easy one that was accomplished by only one single person and the rest of them who actively took part and led the liberation war and fought in the war-field until our glorious victory was not significant at all!

Who did have the major contribution during our liberation war? Why were their names and sacrifices not mentioned in that documentary? What would likely to happen if those people didn't engage to fight against the barbaric forces of Pakistan in absence of BB? The absolute credit score of our liberation of Bangladesh claimed by the current administration is quite deceptive to the generations to come and radicalization of our history. The denial of the contribution of others is egregious — not the real history of the liberation of Bangladesh.

In 1971, the population of Bangladesh was only seventy-five million, and currently our population is more than 158 million, which is more than double. Besides, during the liberation of Bangladesh, those who were less than ten to twelve years old didn't have a proper sense of politics. They have experienced the war only.

The current administration is planning to re-write the history of Bangladesh just to cover up the failure of BB after the glorious liberation of Bangladesh. They are also trying to deny the contributors of the liberation of Bangladesh who were the genuine figures for our victorious success. They know that the popularity of BB declined very sharply and he remained controversial to the majority of the people. They are wickedly trying to inject the parody of our history to the current generation. They already managed to mislead the current generation and are trying to continue the same. It is very crucial for us to protect the true history of our nation, not the parody or fiction.

If we go back in human history, we can see that lot of the leaders in different ages have had lot of success and failure. But the true history preserved those records. The current administration is trying to deny the truth and blackmailing our true history for the egregious causes. They do not want to mention any failure or the cause of the downfall of BB that history can't deny.

They may try to establish the myth but the true history can't. The true history preserves the records of success and failure of the leaders of different ages, place and circumstances. The current administration doesn't want to admit the dismal failure of the leadership of BB after he took over the power of newborn Bangladesh and the causes of his ultimate end. But the true history can't ignore the facts.

On the contrary, they do not want to admit the real contribution of others, those who sacrificed a lot for our success. The recent acrimonious comment made by one of their leaders, Sajeda Chowdhury, including some other men and women cabinet members about martyr Ziaur Rahman are condemnable. The statement she made about our unmatchable hero of our liberation war and the declarer of independence of Bangladesh is quite disgraceful. She couldn't have been the member of the parliament of Bangladesh today; BB wouldn't come back alive amidst us if those heroes didn't fight for our country Bangladesh in 1971.

Obviously, because of the abusive behavior, sometimes we pay the serious deadly price. If that occurs, we jump on the conclusion and start to blame others. But we never blame our own actions and deny its consequence. We never take into account whether our greediness, abuse of power and selfishness contributed to our horrible consequence.

We all know that the prevention is better than the cure. But we don't take any preventive measure before something happens that we can't afford. We do not hesitate to flaunt the rule of law. The recent horrible rampage of BDR forces against their officers is another example in our history.

Importance of Legitimacy: In our real life, we have to confront legitimacy and illegitimacy, fairness and unfairness, justice and injustice, etc. To reject the illegitimacy, unfairness and injustice, you need lots of guts and audacity. But it's not so easy in our society. We hardly can control our temptation of gaining anything with the easiest, cheapest and meanest ways. We are constantly defeated by our ill temptations and arrogance. Justice and injustice, fairness and unfairness, discrimination and exploitation, greediness and selfishness are not matters at all.

We take for granted those mean practices as our culture. As a consequence, sometimes we pay very excruciating prices too. On the contrary, the real ideal personalities of high moral and ethical values become the enemies of those egregious groups and take the ultimate toll too. That's what happened to martyr President Ziaur Rahman and many other great leaders in the history of human beings.

I believe it is one of the important parts of my solemn duties to raise my voice against any irregularities and illegitimacy rather than to remain silent timidly. We can't be diminished by fear. The fear keeps killing us constantly. Our death is a must, but it should be for the solemn and rightful causes and should be with honor and dignity. Both of our iconic leaders lost their lives, but they left two different images in our history.

We need to be courageous enough to stand against those defectors to protect the rest. While I started to write about myself, I couldn't avoid the ongoing horrible and corrupt political and judicial crises those are pushing us towards the devastating direction, not only us but also our nation.

In fact, the current situation is quite risky for me to write about those issues. Should I be afraid of raising my voice? Certainly, I shouldn't. The systematic corruption and violence have been dominating our country Bangladesh since our independence.

I personally fought a lot against the corruption for the moral and ethical reasons and eventually left my country Bangladesh as I couldn't go further beyond. I could easily have chosen other ways for selfish reasons. But I couldn't. The strength of my moral and ethical uprightness prevented me from being a part of them. My personal fighting against corruption was not only the riskiest business but also too little to compare with a glass of distilled water in the salty ocean. As a patriotic citizen of Bangladesh, I'll not remain silent at all and the rest of us should follow the same to protect the interest of our country and our nation.

Our leaders always pledge under oath to protect the sovereignty and integrity of our country prior to taking the leadership. But they shamelessly breach their commitment for their selfish reasons. Under those circumstances, hiding in the dark hole and not speaking out for the cause of our country and our nation is not the act of patriots. The real patriotism is to challenge those problems with courage and wisdom.

It's Important to Honor their Causes: It's not enough to place some wreaths in the monuments of the martyr freedom fighters in some very special occasions to tribute them. But it is very important to honor the cause of their sacrifice too. The cause of their sacrifice was to change the course of our country towards the bright future of our nation where there will be no injustice, exploitation, discrimination, corruptions, etc. Are we honoring their causes or we are betraying? Who was responsible for those crises since our independence?

Unfortunately, the blood of the historic culprit of Mir Zafar is still flowing to some treacherous leaders. Can we let them continue the same and expect different results or we need to stand up against those betrayers? We need to restrain them and hold them accountable without any prejudice.

I also believe that a tiny little limelight is radiant from the distant darkness. The darkness has nothing to lose. It's already dead, very disgracefully and hidden invisibly from the nearest reach. Remember, the greatness remain great when we act greatly with courage. The great men and women in human history are still known as the beckon of mankind. On the contrary, the mighty sadists and betrayers lost miserably and left examples of atrocity and sadism with a disgraceful end. Historically, they are known as the curse of the entirety of mankind.

We need to move towards the modern civilized world order. Let the civilization be flourished and the incivility be perished. We need to stop political bickering for selfish causes. The defiance of justice and fairness, indiscrimination, moral and ethical values are too costly to afford. If we fail to change ourselves, we can't get away from paying the devastating prices we have been experiencing since our independence. If anything happens due to those causes, we shouldn't amplify our voice to secure their legacy for the consequences of their own. Rather, we need to take lessons to change the behavior of our own. We need to embrace the truth, not the myth.

We need the real transformation and transparency of our system in this digitalized era. We need to reject the hidden regressive and abusive practices that caused so much damage and destruction to our nation. We need to reset our clock to move forward, matching with the progressive world order. We need to uproot the foundation of corruption and destruction.

I have devoted my writings not only to criticize the behavior of our corrupt politicians and bureaucrats but also our own in general. I have also stressed the importance of the abolition of abominable practices for good and forever. The real change is possible only with wisdom — not by the arms and weapons. The power of compassion and wisdom are much more superior to arms and weapons.

Introduction

Even though I'm neither a historian nor one of the genius types, my personal experience is well enough to express my sincere opinion on our political, economical, bureaucratic, judicial, social, and cultural infections and defections. Indeed, I miss my country, our people, and most importantly, I believe as one of the sensible citizens of Bangladesh, I must raise my voice when something has caused the immense disturbance and damage to our country.

A Brief History of Our Liberation War: My first writing was "The Political Drama of Bangladesh" in June 2006. I was an early teenager when our country was liberated from the Pakistani brutal rulers. Like many of you, I have many unforgettable memories of 1971. I have shared some of my memories with the readers. I wanted to be concise but it became considerably longer than I expected. Our Liberation War was inevitable and it could happen long before 1971.

In fact, this sentiment grew seriously in 1952 soon after the liberation of Pakistan in 1947. We didn't have a very good relation with the West almost from the very beginning of the independence of Pakistan on August 14, 1947. They not only mistreated us but also discriminated us systematically with no respect! They widened the disparity between the East and the West in all respects. They even wanted to take away one of our most important rights: to speak in our mother tongue, "Bangla," and tried to impose their language Urdu as our national language. Naturally, it was unacceptable to us.

We were the majority at that time and it was legitimately unacceptable for us, and we didn't want to let that happen. Then Mohammad Ali Jinnah was fully responsible for such an irrational and unjustified issue that he wanted to enforce his corrupt mission. But they failed to exert their mission against our language movement, which turned to a serious disintegration and eventually, the separation or independence.

The Language Movement: In 1952, our student leaders stood against their mission and strongly demanded that Bangla, our mother tongue, should be our national language, not the minorities' language Urdu. Later, on February 21, 1952, the Western leaders carried out a brutal attack on a students' demonstration and killed Salam, Barkat, Rafiq, Jabbar, and wounded a number of other students and people using their brutal forces. Since that day, our student leaders and politicians understood that we couldn't go along with those barbaric leaders of the West and we were able to be separated from those evils.

The Glory of Our Language: Today, February 21st is recognized as the International Mother Language Day and has taken a very glorious place in the United Nations (UN). No other nations had to sacrifice their lives just to speak their own language. Eventually, our mission to be separated from the West became the reality because of our heroism in 1971 under the leadership of Bangabandhu Sheikh Mujibur Rahman (BB).

Our Liberation War: Our liberation was not an easy one. We had to fight against those savage forces for about nine months, which is historically the shortest period of time in the world for the liberation of any nation. We lost about three million innocent lives (as recorded in our history), including men, women, children, and intellectuals. The actual number of lives we lost during the liberation war was yet to be ascertained.

Variable Repots: *Bangladesh authorities claim three million, while the Hamoodur Rahman Commission of Pakistan absurdly put the figure as low as twenty-six thousand civilian casualties.*

*The international media and reference group have also published variable figures from two hundred thousand to three million as a whole. It is believed in certain quarters that the figure of three million has its origin in comments made by General Yahya Khan to the journalist Robert Payne on February 22, 1971. The war monger Yahya Khan made the comment, "***Kill three million of them and the rest will eat out of our hands."** (This report has been taken from archives).

The butcher and his other co-butcher generals planned to murder the Bengali intellectual, cultural, and political elites.

The Genocide: The discovery of mass graves in all major cities was the clear evidence of ruthless atrocity carried out in the East by the West. They also planned to murder Hindus and drive them to India. Whatever the number might have been, the crime against humanity was quite evident. The political evil Zulfikar Ali Bhutto and the military butchers became blood-thirsty and cowardly attacked the innocents on the East. The statement of butcher Yahya Khan was enough to convict him in international court as a mass murderer. But that didn't happen. The supporters of Yahya Khan should be recognized as guilty of the same crime. The rest of the seventy-five million of the East got a catastrophic threat by the evils of the West.

As a result, millions in the East were displaced and took shelter in India. If this is not genocide, what then is genocide? The international politics started to take place even amongst the super powers. The whole world overwhelmingly supported the cause of the liberation of Bangladesh and condemned the atrocity of the West against the civilians of the East. The contribution of India and then USSR to the East was quite remarkable and must not be forgotten.

However, the butchers were not meted out by the international court due to the conflicts of interest amongst super powers. Rather, they were vindicated from justice. The barbaric Pakistani forces arrested BB on March 25, 1971, and cowardly started genocide and persecution on women soon after his famous speech. The crime against humanity shouldn't have been ignored by any sensible world leaders. In that speech, BB directed our people about our future agenda with a clear message for our preparation to fight against the Pakistani forces by any means if there was no political solution.

The Glorious Victory: There was no political solution, and our liberation became inevitable in the absence of BB. Our unique unification, strong determination, and our heroism helped us to achieve our victory only in nine months. Our heroes taught them an unforgettable lesson. We introduced ourselves as one of the heroic nations in the world. On December 16th, 1971, they surrendered to us and the name of Bangladesh took place in the map of the world as a land of the heroes. Our liberation, our country, and our nation are the most solemn and honor for us.

Our Solemn Responsibilities: It is our obligation to protect the interest of our country and its sovereignty and integrity. With all due respect to our freedom fighters and all other contributors, we need to move forward to honor the cause of their sacrifice. They gave us the freedom at the cost of their precious lives and we need to protect the sovereignty and integrity and tribute their sacrifice at any cost. If we fail to do so, we will be accountable for their sacrifice.

The Serious Setback: Unfortunately, our corrupt politicians and bureaucrats have been doing everything for their personal interest since our independence at the cost of our national crisis. They engaged themselves in profit-sharing business soon after our liberation with the establishment of paramount corruption. Their administrative ways and means was to establish corruption against the dedication of millions of innocents. This was the real cause of the downfall of those giant leaders and immense misery of the war-suffered people.

The current disclosures of the extortion of money and wealth, and many other corruptions, are beyond imagination. The corruption rate had been climbing in geometrical progression. Hundreds of millions of taka or dollars are no longer a fairytale to them with exploitation of the rest. How much money did they have before? Where and how did they get such an incredible amount of money? How much money did they need to lead a desirable way of living? How did they forget that the rest of the people are also Bangladeshi who had tremendous contributions during our liberation war? How did they become so greedy and selfish? How did their conscience become so dysfunctional? Why shouldn't they pay the price? Did they forget that greediness leads to sin and sins leads to death?

Importance of Justice: It will be a serious mistake, if we do not hold them accountable for the crimes they have already committed regardless of any party, party members, or leaders. We need to bring them to justice without any prejudice and disputable manner. We can't allow them to commit any crimes with the excuse of their inherited images. Our nation can't afford those criminals anymore. The legitimization of corruption is not the solution or way of paying off their greatness, if any.

The greatest damage was caused by the deceivers **Dr. Fakhruddin Ahmed and Gen. Moeen U. Ahmed** in the history of modern era. It is the time to stop them for good and forever. We need to reform all political parties with honest and capable leaders — not with those inept and immoral ones.

Democracy doesn't allow any political absolutism. The anti-corruption slogan was used by the deceptive CG just to re-establish the corruption on a wider scale both in army and civilian authorities in a distorting manner. They are proven disastrous and destructive elements of our country and our nation, and they should be brought to justice immediately before further damage is likely to take place that we can't afford.

The Cause of My Writings: From the above standpoints, I started to write time to time since June 2006 and tried to express my reactions in different circumstances. I understand that many of you may not agree with me. But I believe, as a patriotic citizen of my country, it is my solemn obligation to raise my voice, and it is not too much at all for any citizen, if and when they courageously stand for the rightful causes. My effort is simply to remember those freedom fighters with honor and tribute them for the cause of their sacrifice for the generations to come. Our success and failure will depend on how we act now.

Why I'm in the USA

As I'm the only the son of my father, I never had any desire to settle in any other country of the world. I had been happily living in my own country Bangladesh since I was born. My life has a unique attachment with my motherland Bangladesh. In the short span of my lifetime, I have experienced many unforgettable memories, which are sometimes very pleasant and sometimes very disturbing. Those are the parts of my life. But when I imagine the beauty of my country and our people, and the way we introduced ourselves in 1971 with the rest of the world, I forget all negative feelings. I shared with others all the happiness and sufferings whatsoever.

I experienced our liberation war in 1971 when I was an early teenager. Those horrible experiences ended up with the liberation of our glorious Bangladesh. The barbaric Pakistani forces couldn't terrify our people committing genocide in our land. Rather, they were known as one of the disgraceful nations in the world. Our courageous roles during our liberation war surprised all other nations and we earned the immense support of the rest of the world.

My Motherland Bangladesh

We're your children living in your heart and soul
You're so magnificent and so bountiful!
We're proud to be your children with lots of your bounty
You're designed by The Almighty so magnificently!

You're carrying out the rivers, mountains, and sea-sights
The sun and moon are lightening you over the days and nights
You're dressed with evergreen plants and colorful flowers
You're so magnificent and charming to the rest of the world.

The coastal mangroves beautified you with amazing sights
You look so awesome in the winter-morning sunshine
The green grasses get covered with the drops of distilled dews
The morning sunshine turns those like a diamond queues.

You cried a lot losing millions of your children in 1971
Your tears filled the ocean with the blood of those martyrs
You didn't want to lose any of your children in vain
They protected the rest of us to stop your further pain.

Your children are brave enough to protect your cause
We'll not remain silent and committed to response
You can't prevent us calling from behind
We'll not listen to you, if we do need to fight!

We're committed to respond to any aggressors
We'll defeat those evils no matter what it costs
We're ready to sacrifice our lives for your cause
We're not afraid to stand against any aggressors!

Our challenges could be unthinkable
We can't remain silent without any answers
Aggressors will be defeated as it was in 1971
You're known as my motherland **Bangladesh** *in the whole world!*

Mohammed D. Hussain

Heroic Fight: Our people fought against one of the most sophisticated arms and forces with incredible valor just to protect our legitimate rights from the evil discrimination. Our freedom fighters along with the people of all walks of life fought together to make such a victorious history. As one of the smallest countries having one of the most densely populations in the world should not be underestimated by any nation. Unfortunately, our corrupt politicians and bureaucrats caused us the extreme vulnerabilities for our nation.

Disorientation of the Leaders, Soon After our Independence: Soon after our glorious liberation, our selfish politicians started to abuse their power with total disrespect to the cause of the sacrifice of millions of precious lives. Of course, some of them paid a very painful price for their distrustful and selfish behavior as a consequence. They paid the deadly price not because they loved and respected our people and our country, but they did as a consequence of their selfishness, greediness of power, and for illegitimate gains. But the magnitude of the consequence was quite devastating.

What did little Russel and other family members of BB do wrong that they had to lose their lives? The killers did lose their very fundamental judgments to carry out such a horrible assassination. Who was responsible for the cause of their lives? I condemn those killers who didn't hesitate to kill that defenseless and sinless child and those who did should face the justice. Sadly enough, some of our real dedicators also became the victims of intrigues by some of those evils and lost their lives too!

The New Definition of Sacrifice! Currently, those corrupts are politicizing corruption as their sacrifice. I think they're trying to give us a new definition of sacrifice with the denial of our true history. I hardly found few of our leaders and bureaucrats that I could trust. No one can force earning the popularity and trust of the people; that is spontaneous recognition given by the people for the character and wisdom of our leaders. But our corrupt politicians have a tendency to become popular by force even though they do not have any creditability for the cause of our country by their own.

What they Know and What they Don't: They can hijack the bank, treasury, and election with evil power. But to earn the popularity and trust of the people, they can't. They can carry out any horrible violence but they can't move forward for the peace, progress, and prosperity of our nation. They know how to scare and intimidate the people but to be attractive by virtue of their behavior and actions, they don't. They know how to set up the corrupt mechanisms but to serve the country with patriotism, they don't. They know how to wound and kill our people. But to love and protect the people, they don't. The evils are always happy with sadism and get frustrated when they fail to do so. They worship the injustice but the justice is unacceptable and immoral for them. They need to know how to choose the right therapy to cure those evil diseases.

Why People are Leaving our Country: The incivility and barbaric behavior by horrendous actions for the selfish causes against the innocents are not acceptable to any civilized society. Our people, our soil, our culture, and the natural beauty of our country have irresistible attraction to enjoy our lives with immense pleasure. Regardless, our innocent peace-loving people are always at risk and fearful of living in such a beautiful country. Many of them already lost their lives and others are still in the list of the evils. As a result, the genuine potential ones are leaving our own country and contributing the other nations with great success.

I painfully had to leave my country due to the excessive corrupt system established by so-called intellectuals, politicians, and bureaucrats. They are the causes of the misery of all ordinary people of our country. They are so powerful that no one can do anything against them. They are well organized and well protected both nationally and internationally. They are the obstructions of peace, progress, and prosperity of our country.

Brain Drain: I'm not a very resourceful or intellectual person, but many highly talented people are. They are leaving our country simply because of the insecurity, deadly forms of violence, and extremely abusive corrupt system. They have produced the evil gangs everywhere. The word justice no longer exists. Their opportunities have shrunk to naught. In other words, this is called brain drain. Those people could contribute a lot to our country as they are doing on foreign land with great success. The honest and law-abiding ones can't compromise with those corrupt ones and become their enemies. The peace-loving people can't live without any risk of their lives, wealth, and their future generations.

Some of the so-called corrupt intellectuals are the key elements of all those abusive practices. Others became their enemies. The corrupt politicians use them to serve their purposes. Some of the so-called legal experts and bureaucrats are already part of those corrupt regimes. The current Law Minister, Barrister Shafiq Ahmed, is a clear example. He has released and withdrawn all serious cases of bigger criminals and multiple murderers of his own party.

On the contrary, he is abusing his undue power against the opponents. He is trying hard to bring new allegations against the opponents with fabrication and falsifications of new charges and torturing them inhumanely. He is formulating new charges against his opponents and torturing them in the name of remanding. He is also making the list that is against this illegitimate administration and trying to eliminate them or torture those honest voices. His mission is how to re-establish old, disgraceful, failed evil regimes that we experienced soon after our liberation.

I would Like to Prosecute them in the International Court: Knowing all about this, I have chosen the hardest, riskiest, and bravest choice with courage to challenge this administration. I would like to hold them accountable for all those devastations that occurred immediately after taking their illegitimate administration. Since there is no justice in our land, I would like to prosecute the whole administration in the international court, if there is any provision on behalf of our country and the peace-loving people of Bangladesh. Let me quote the following:

"Courage is the first of human qualities because it is the quality that guarantees the others." - Aristotle

Tragically, our country has turned back to the realm of regressive tense culture. Our valued culture and civilization are being destroyed by those corrupt politicians and bureaucrats. I tried my best to maintain my living style with high moral and ethical values in my country. But I became their enemy. In many cases, I had to pay an enormous price for my uprightness.

The Role of the Super Powers and the United Nations (UN) Around the World: The peace, progress, prosperity, and stability of the world depend on the roles played by the super powers to other countries. The peaceful living and misery of the millions of people in the world depend on how the super power countries play their roles to the leaders of the rest of the world. If the super powers support the few wrongful leaders of those countries, the fate of the millions of peace-loving general people leads to devastation and chaos. As a result, we can see lot of horrible incidents take place and cause the obstacles of peace, progress, and prosperity of those countries.

Many of the leaders of the developed and underdeveloped countries are corrupt and totalitarians. They are the causes of the problem of the overall population of those countries. Finding no other ways, the peace-loving people try to leave their own country and look for a safer life somewhere else. Sometimes they violate the rule of law as an alternative just to get protected as the last resort. As a result, some developed countries experience the influx of immigrants both legally and illegally.

Some of the stronger countries try to play their undue roles to other sovereign smaller and weaker neighbors and cause the problems of regional peace, progress, prosperity, and stability. Currently, Bangladesh is exactly having that kind of problem and the people of Bangladesh are in real concern about the sovereignty and integrity of the country.

The Current Controversial Regime: The current regime of Awami League (AL) is playing a very damaging role in our country. They are spreading the political toxic acid to re-establish the regressive tense culture against the democracy. They are trying to identify who is against them and in some cases they are eliminating them too. Their past administration was the regime of evil culture and didn't have any chance to come back to power with free, fair, and credible election. Therefore, they decided to start horrible, deadly violence and destruction during the administrations of the extremely popular party BNP.

Their Past Administration: During their administration, the peace-loving people couldn't lead their normal lives. Their sponsored gangs, multiple murderers, donation collectors, and kidnapers claimed lot of innocent lives. The revitalization of corruption was the way of their administration. They dismally failed to regain the popularity and trust of the people. Because of their deadly violence, the constitutional Caretaker Government couldn't hold the election on time and eventually imposed the emergency. Thus they opened up the wheel of fortune to get back to power by evil means with the hidden connection of the treacherous, unconstitutional CG.

If the superpowers would play the corrective role to those leaders, they couldn't act like the mafia in the name of legitimate administration. The people of our densely populated country Bangladesh could live peacefully with stability.

I couldn't choose the easy way of living in Bangladesh like those corrupts. I was known as an honest man of very strict principle. But that cost me a lot. Sometimes my close companions were not happy with me at all. They were not comfortable enough with me mostly because of the conflict of interest. I had to swim against the evil powerful current with fullest fortitude and never tried to take advantage of any easy ride for moral and ethical reasons. Having lifelong struggles against the corrupt political and bureaucratic culture, I became exhausted and tried to look for a new shore to get relief from those adversaries and thus ended up here in the United States of America.

Who am I: I have written a lot about my country, people, politicians, bureaucrats, and the glory of our nation, but who am I? You may have the curiosity to know about me. But as an ordinary citizen of Bangladesh, I'm not any prodigious or high-profiled one you may assume. But everyone's life is special and unique. No matter what kinds of spoons we're born with — gold or silver — our fate could change everything. Some of us never experience any thorns but roses. Some of us experience both thorns and roses. Unfortunately, others experience only thorny bushes with no roses.

Most of those unhappy lives are the result of the miscalculation and misjudgment of their own actions. As a result, when we experience the consequence of our wrongful actions, either we blame others or we use the term of fate. What does fate have to do when we face the consequence of our wrongful actions?

Where the Fate Changes: Every child is born as quite innocent. But in most cases their fate is changed due to the raising process by their parents. They could've been raised with the quality of life or could be worst of the worst depending on their upbringing process by their parents. But everyone's life is very important. Every child has the birthright to get utmost loving care of his or her parents and enjoy the beauty of nature as bestowed by the Almighty Creator.

The parents and the foster parents are fully responsible for how they raise their children. In fact, the family value leads us the way of our future. If the parents themselves are corrupt, naturally the children become infected with the germs of corruption. As a result, in course of time, they become the same and become problematic for others. If that occurs, sometimes they pay a very painful price in their life.

All human beings should be respected. Everyone's biography is different than one another. Some of our biographies could contribute a lot to others' lives and vice versa — whether it is pleasant or unpleasant.

In my brief autobiography, some of the contents I didn't want to write because they are not very pleasant. But those disturbing ones could be part of a lesson for many other lives, and could be protected from their abusive behaviors. Some of the contents that have taken place in my autobiography are embarrassing — not only for others, but also for me. This is not fiction, and I couldn't ignore the facts that I have experienced in my life. But I've written those contents to understand the unthinkable realities that one might face even as born as an innocent baby and remain to be so in this beautiful world.

I would like to insert the part of my autobiography so that you may understand me and the reasons for my reactions. Let's get started.

Greetings! I'm quite unknown to most of you. I left behind a lot of unforgettable memories from my childhood and boyhood and detached from you for quite a long time. Some of you may remember me by my name Delwar.

I reached from newborn baby to manhood in my beautiful country Bangladesh. Perhaps some of you may flash back your memories and can easily recognize who I am. But I'm deeply saddened to miss you all for so many years. I overcame many difficult situations from my childhood, which are extremely rare to many. My autobiography could be like second to none.

I came through incredible vulnerabilities even before I began to understand myself. I was the only son of my father, late Alhaj Ramizuddin Sarker, Houshdi, Daudkandi, Comilla, Bangladesh. I was born on September 18, 1957, and was so lonely for very unusual circumstances. As a result, I had a silent struggle throughout my childhood onward. My future was quite obscured with dark clouds. But I tried to flash the light to find my ways to move forward. Sometimes, I continued my journey without any specific direction and made many U-turns, such as and when I got struck against the wall at that early age.

My Education: My primary education started from home. My father had a very big dream for me and he tried to educate me with special care. I was pretty advanced as a beginner. I was the youngest in my classroom. I was the youngest and very quiet with great potential as viewed by my teachers and others. But sometimes I used to surprise my classmates, including my teachers, with my funny childish behavior.

In those days, in our culture, the teachers used to punish the students very harshly. But as I was the youngest in my classroom and the son of a very respectable person, I was very sympathetic to them. Sometimes, those tough teachers used to change their usual behavior when I myself was one of the troubled ones for any indiscipline causes.

My Funny Childish Behavior: I would like to mention a very funny story from when I was in second grade. I was a good student from the beginning. But there was another student who was the best. His name was Nabaddip and he was the best in math. He was so good that he never made any mistakes and scored full marks on all exams. Once we all had trouble with a lesson given by a very tough teacher and none of us learnt that lesson except him. The teacher got mad and asked him to twist each of our ears five times each as hard as possible. He also asked us, had he favored any of us to return the same to him as hard as possible to make sure he really did so.

He started to do so, and everyone was crying. Finally, he was approaching to me. I knew that he was going to do the same to me. I decided to do the same to him in return. I was fully prepared to do so. As soon as he was about to start with me, I returned him the same, even harder than he did with others. He was crying and the teacher asked me what happened. In reply, I said he favored me with an easy twist of my ears.

The teacher was laughing at instead of getting mad told me, "Is that right? Your ears are red, how come he was favoring you?" I replied that didn't hurt me. That was the funny story for the day amongst all other teachers and students. All of my classmates were very much happy while I did that to him.

At the end he told me, "You didn't even let me twist your ears. You started to twist my ears even before I did to you!"

I said, "That's what I did. Why did you twist their ears that hard?"

Soon after I finished my primary education, I decided to get admission to Daudkandi High School. But some of the religious leaders proposed my father to educate me in Madrasha (the Islamic school) as a son of a very religious person. He proposed me to do so as he was blessed having me after his past irreparable tragedies.

Tragically, my father lost both of his sons, one after the other, long before I was born. Both were very handsome and incredibly talented.

Disagreement with my Father: My father proposed me for religious education. But I respectfully didn't agree with my father (May Allah forgive me!). I used to pray five times a day with my father in the mosque, and I respectfully tried to practice my religion and all other valuable advices since early childhood. I had a strong desire to be an educationist. I told my father, why should I go to Madrasha to learn about only religion? I could easily practice my religion and know more about the theology along with my general education.

Family Values: Later, he agreed with me and didn't insist me against my will. He always gave me good advice to do the best, especially about the honesty, modesty, wisdom, and compassion, self-reliance, self-respect, respect to others, and very high moral and ethical values and dignity as the way of our family.

The details of my life history are written in my autobiography **"Incredible But True,"** but I would like to insert a tiny part of my autobiography in this section.

Uncompromising with Corruption: In 1985, I reacted very differently with one of the high officials of the Office of the Controller of Imports and Exports in Bangladesh. I was not a government employee. I was working with an international organization, Worldview International Foundation (WIF). Sometimes, we had to deal with the government offices to re-import some of our equipment to and from Bangkok, Thailand. We had to deal with that office pretty often. I was almost new to deal with those corrupt officials and personally, I didn't like their notorious tactics of bribes to get something done. My predecessors used to compromise with those bribes.

As a new one, I tried not to get involved myself with those corrupt practices. I followed all the procedures but bribes. They tried to get a bribe from me by holding my file without any action. But I decided not to bribe them because I knew that the bribe givers and takers are equally guilty. I tried to talk directly to the concerned authority but I was prevented by his secretary/clerk. At one point, I told him to return my file. He replied that he couldn't, which caused me to become pretty upset.

Later, I managed to get directly to that officer disregarding the official norms and greeted him with full respect. The officer was not happy with my surprise presence. At that time, I changed the pattern of my attitude, which I never did, and he was scared. My purpose was not to threaten him.

I introduced myself and asked him if he knew anything about my file. I saw about fifteen files were lying on his side-desk without any action. He was looking for my file and found mine. I asked him why he held my file without any action for so long. He understood my attitude and got nervous.

He apologized to me and told me that he would never ever do this again with me. He also assured me about my future needs, if any. He did that instantly offering me a cup of tea. But I left when I got it done. Since then my single telephone call was enough to get things done almost instantly.

I couldn't take pride for this; rather, I repented when I saw him. He was much older than me. I learnt from my childhood to always be respectful to others and be modest to the people. In fact, I do. I never initiate any misbehavior with the older or even younger ones. I had a very good reputation in my known circles. To some, I was known as a role model. I used to leave my seat for elderly people and for females when I saw them standing in the bus or any social gatherings. But I can't respect those people who do not maintain the decency or respect themselves. Everyone wants to be respected or well treated. But the depravity leads to an embarrassing return.

In those circumstances, my modest behavior doesn't fit very well and I react differently. My question is, was it my fault? I didn't want to do that, but I did, and I got better service thereafter. Is this the way we should behave? Certainly not, and we shouldn't. But he led me to do so, which was not an acceptable behavior to consider me as a nice person. But still I don't know what the right alternative was in that circumstance! Wasn't it at least better than not to compromise with dirty bribes?

We Know How to Blame Others But we Don't Care about the Causes: We always blame the wrongdoers but we hardly look for the causes. Every effect must have some causes. Our history left many instances of horrible ends. But we never talk about those causes. We jump on the conclusion only and go after the wrongdoers. Of course we should. But can we ignore the causes? If we do, can we escape from those potential problems altogether? Why do some of our influential people abuse their authority and expect nothing would cost them as a consequence? This is their miscalculation and they should pay the price for, rather than blame others. This doesn't mean that I encourage disregarding the rule of law, if and when needed. But I strongly demand to establish the real justice where there will be no prejudice or misinterpretation of the rule of law.

How the Corruption and Violence Get Legitimacy: In those circumstances, some of us lose our patience and carry out something that is not appropriate at all, and never, ever intended to do so. People do not want to take the justice in their own hands. But justice is not there. If anybody complains and does something against their interest, that is unlawful; he or she is mocked by those corrupts saying oh! So and so complained too much, rather than supporting the legitimacy and fairness. This kind of mentality legitimizes the corruption and violence in our society and becomes the norm and culture of the nation at large.

Disrespectful to So-called Intellectuals: In 1984, I was introduced to Dr. Sirajul Islam, Director of Bangladesh Institute of Distance Education (BIDE), and was also the principal of the Teachers Training College (education department). I was interviewed for a job in an international Organization, Worldview International Foundation (WIF), in Bangladesh. He used to host a program on Bangladesh Television (BTV) every Friday on long-distance education.

Fortunately, I was selected out of many by Mr. Sverre Christophersen, Director of WIF. The salary was negotiable. Dr. Islam was one of the members of the selection board. My salary expectation was the highest amongst others. Dr. Islam jokingly told me my salary expectation was much higher than others and of his own. In reply, I smiled and said, "That's why I'm here." But later on, I found out how corrupt he was! Normally, the salary in NGOs, especially in any international organization, is much higher than the government officials.

It was an amazing place to work. Mr. Sverre Christophersen was a very friendly person from Norway. We had a fun-filled working environment. WIF was affiliated with the Ministry of Education. Mr. Kazi Jalaluddin Ahmed was the secretary of the ministry of education. We had close contact with Dr. Islam who was in touch with us on behalf of the Ministry of Education.

In the beginning, I profoundly respected him. But later, I found him to be a disgraceful black ship. He used to take as bribe Tk. 3,000.00 in cash per month, which was more than his salary in 1984 with rapid increments of Tk. 6,000.00 to Tk. 10,000.00 per month (all in cash) plus lots of money with different excuses.

As I didn't like any corrupts, I didn't like him at all. Gradually, he tried to keep control of the authority of WIF with corrupt exercises. The NGOs in Bangladesh have to deal with bureaucratic irregularities and have to compromise with them with their corrupt practices. Mr. Christophersen didn't like his behavior and left WIF Bangladesh and got transferred to Colombo, Sri Lanka.

Subsequently, there was another director, Charles M. Rycroft, from the UK. He was another younger friendly person of a very dynamic character. He was so young that we worked with him like our friend. I enjoyed working with him a lot.

Unforgettable Tragedy: I can't but mention another young man, late Iftikhar A. Beg, whom I can't forget. He was a young, smart and a decent person of a very pleasant manner. In fact, he was the youngest one amongst us. His desk was just across from me. We used to chat with each other about his daily experience of outdoor shooting, etc. He got killed in a road accident while he was going out for official shootings. The news of his death shocked us all because he was such a wonderful person. I found many things in common with him, and he always smiled. In addition, he never got upset for any unpleasant causes.

As I was working with the director of WIF, everything was happening under my knowledge. Within a very short time, Charles M. Rycroft, the new director, was not very comfortable in dealing with Dr. Islam because of his undue exercise over WIF. Finally, he managed to get a better job with UNICEF Bangladesh and left WIF.

Later, Dr. Islam successfully misled the secretary general of WIF to hire a local director to reduce the expenses. It was not his business because that was funded by the Norwegian funding agency, Stromme Memorial Foundation, IFAD, etc. He proposed the secretary general to hire a local cheap director so that he could keep control over WIF better.

The Secretary General Arne Fjortoft didn't like that idea. But he agreed to keep him happy. Later, Dr. Islam got an opportunity to hire a director of his own choice. Despite very highly educated and experienced candidates, he called someone whom he knew personally and didn't call those competitive candidates. Mr. Arne Fjortoft, Secretary General, couldn't apply his own choice against the will of Dr. Islam.

With his undue influence, he hired a local director who could be his loyalist. He hired Anish K. Barua, a mean-spirited person who was working with BRAC as a manager of the media section. We got responses from very highly educated and experienced candidates in response to our advertisement. But Dr. Islam didn't let us call them for an interview because some of them were overly qualified and pretty influential than Dr. Islam himself. His other loyalist, Nazrul Islam, a cameraman, became the deputy director whose educational qualification was about S.S.C. or H.S.C. the most, with no quality at all.

He was not only the most loyal to Dr. Sirajul Islam but also the biggest mischievous person and didn't have any connection with his own family. Both of them and Dr. Islam were the perfect blend of compatible corrupt ingredients. Others didn't like his undue exercises at all but remained quiet to protect their job. The Accounts Manager, A.Q.M. Munir, didn't like them at all. But he remained silent. I was the only one who couldn't accept their mischievous activities and superiority. All those black ships conspired against me and tried to oust me with a package of concocted allegations against me.

Qualitatively, Anish Barua was not good for anything as the previous directors. WIF used to make lots of educational and motivational films along with the documentary films for national and international organizations. Mr. Christophersen and Charles Rycroft made several documentary films for Grameen Bank, ICDDRB, ILO, UNICEF, WHO, UNDP, etc. But Anish Barua was quite happy with less than one-fifth of the salary of those expatriates. That salary was very much lucrative for him based on his quality. He did nothing but draws the salaries and enjoyed all other undue facilities sharing with Dr. Islam. He was appointed by Dr. Islam to work as his loyalist.

Finally, I had an argument with Anish Barua regarding his mean and corrupt practices as he wanted to involve me with him. He tried to associate me with those who were morally unacceptable to me. I strenuously rejected their approaches. He and his associate Nazrul shamelessly complained against me with false and fabricated allegations to Dr. Islam, their master with his tearful eyes. Dr. Islam studied my personality and was not comfortable with me for a number of reasons. Dr. Islam notoriously tried to compromise both of us, but I strongly rejected his interference.

I learned a lot about Dr. Islam. To me he is a total disgrace. Besides, Dr. Islam was not my boss. I always respect the intellectuals but in his case, my respect to him was below naught. He was involved with many other NGOs and possibly took that sort of advantage from all of them too. In those days, he made an incredible amount of money and thus changed his disgraceful fortune. I didn't want to degrade myself and left WIF.

Dr. Islam didn't know that I was a relative of someone who was the cause of his success. Knowing about me, he called me privately in his office and tried his best to resolve the matter. But I already made my decision and didn't like to reverse it.

They impudently denounced my rightful causes with shameful conspiracy. Unfortunately, there are many in our society. It is very hard to fight against them. They are the biggest problem in our society and are damaging the image of our country. They are well protected by the corrupt bureaucrats. But I had a very good reputation as a trusted fellow as well even to those depraved ones. M.A. Mannan was one of our project directors of Nutritional Blindness Prevention Program (WIF-NBPP) and knew everything; we were not happy with this group at all.

My Unchallengeable Performance: I left lot of remarkable examples and many of you may be aware of those who had any opportunity to deal with me directly and know me personally. I also believe that Mr. Christophersen, Charles Rycroft, and certainly the secretary general of WIF, Arne Fjortoft, can't deny anything as I stated above. I'm not against WIF. WIF owed me lot of money of gratuity (provident fund) but I didn't like to deal with that depraved group anymore.

I do not know about the current situation of WIF and I'm not interested at all to go further beyond. But the director like Anish Barua and Nazrul are quite a ridiculous joke and Dr. Sirajul Islam is one of the bureaucratic crooks. I think for the greater interest of our country, the government should investigate these kinds of organizations and their activities with high beam.

The Evils are Everywhere: Later, I managed to get a job in a diplomatic mission in Bangladesh in a better environment. I was very much happy to work there. But unfortunately, I had to work with another problematic person. He was a non-Bengali, an Urdu speaker (Bihari) and spoke very funny Bangla working there for about seventeen years. But I couldn't speak Urdu at all. He didn't like this issue.

He was very abhorrent to the Bangalis. He was so hypocritical that it was very difficult to understand what was false or what was true. He talked very nicely and behaved very friendly. But he was an introverted person and acted different than what he really is. I trusted him very much with full respect and tried to learn a lot about my duties and responsibilities.

During our routine works, we used to chat with each other very frankly. As he was senior to me and was working there so long as I always tried to learn a lot from him and didn't want to do anything unfriendly. But I didn't believe that he was working against my interest. He tried to block my salary structure as revised and wanted to make me too much different from him. He was jealous about my raise as a new employee.

It became clear to all our national staff that he unfairly tried to degrade my salary scale. It came to my knowledge that he did the same to others and they left. He also conspired against his own boss who was also a Bangali and eventually he left too. He is a Bihari living in Bangladesh but he is awful to the Bangalis. I didn't want to confront him. I had a private discussion with one of the highest officials in that mission and made him aware of his practice. But he managed to misguide him with my job description and responsibilities in a very contradictory manner. I couldn't believe that living in the soil of Bangladesh, he is so anti-Bangalis.

Later, he wanted to talk to me and tried to give the false impression that he was trying hard to revise my salary scale. There was nothing to try. It was the existing grade to revise the salary scale as was his own and the rest of the national employees. I was not an exception! But he already did the damage without my knowledge. They are so ungrateful to the Bangladeshis that they forgot the mercy of our nation in 1971. Finally, I left too and headed to the great country of United States of America. The rest is in my autobiography "**Incredible But True.**"

My Political Views: I have never been a politician or an activist of any political party, and still I'm not. But I always supported the party who did better for the country. Sadly enough, instead of progressive direction, our leaders founded the corruption almost everywhere. After so many years, I was delighted to see some signs of the political change that was likely to be taken by the unconstitutional CG. But this was another betrayal to our nation.

Hypocritical Behavior of the Chief Advisor: The Chief Advisor, Dr. Fakhruddin Ahmed, and the Chief of Army Staff Gen. Moeen U. Ahmed of the emergency Caretaker Government (CG) took some popular agendas as a false pretence to uproot corruption and restrain the political hostility. But it was a false alarm and they became deviated and widened the corruption on a larger scale both in the army and civil administrations. They divided the most popular party BNP prior to election and arrested their leaders discriminately even though their crimes and corruption were far lesser than those other violent major parties.

They tortured them inhumanely with the violation of the sanctity of justice and human rights. On the other hand, they treacherously established their relationship with one of the most violent party AL for selfish reasons.

They didn't carry out the justice of extreme forms of deadly violent leaders that our nation has ever experienced; rather, they released them. They've magnified and overly exposed the corruption of BNP through media to the people to mislead the voters and to cover up the deadly violence and corruption of their darling parties prior to **1/11/06.**

They inhumanely tortured the sons of martyr Ziaur Rahman, including other leaders of BNP and arrested Begum Khaleda Zia, who did relatively better than those other major corrupt political parties combined. They were the procreators of corruption historically.

BNP was repeatedly elected by the people and made significant progress in our security, education, and economy. They are still overwhelmingly popular. But they were not free from corruption either. However, their corruption was climbing up in arithmetical progression, not the geometrical progression like CG themselves. The corruption in our country was originated and strengthened from the inception of our independence.

Of course, they should be accountable for their wrongdoings if they are found guilty. But they should have been listed after the originators of corruption. The chief advisor and the chief of army staff are deeply associated with AL, JP, and some other fragmented destructive groups so-called 'Mohajot.'

They very hypocritically became connected to those destructive parties and got themselves involved with them for mischievous gains. Now they are hidden in the dark hole. The current circumstance was created by them to re-establish the regressive evil empire. As a consequence, the misery of the people will have no bounds. The protection of the sovereignty of our country is the biggest concern as it already is under their current unconstitutional illegitimate administration.

The Biggest Deceiver: The biggest deceiver is Gen. Moeen U. Ahmed. He not only betrayed outgoing PM Khaleda Zia but also the nation. He had a strong illusion to be the president of Bangladesh and acted cowardly with the outgoing CG president Dr. Iazuddin Ahmed. He pointed the gun toward him and snatched the power away to become president with the association of another corrupt, Dr. Fakhruddin Ahmed. But he didn't have the guts to protect our borders. Both of them are the resurrection of historic culprit Mir Zafar.

Who is Gen. Moeen? : Our defense forces are to protect our country from foreign aggression including the security of our borders, not to point the gun to the unarmed civil administration. But he did. He violated the rule of law and his preamble while he joined as an army officer. He failed to protect our borders of our country from foreign aggression within our land through our borders and maintain the integrity in the army.

He tried to follow the same path of tyrant dictator Gen. Ershad who betrayed martyr president Ziaur Rahman. With the exception of very few, any military leaders who act like this are all cowards. By definition, he is one of them too.

These cowards should not be forgiven. We need to demand immediate justice to stop the military interference in civil matters in the civilized world order. They should follow the orders of civil administration. Taking power from the civil government by pointing guns and being illusive to become president should be stopped for good and forever to protect the democratic process of our country. They should have been confined in the cantonment and should work under the direction of the defense department as the policy made by the civil administration.

Look at the most powerful countries in the world: the USA, the UK, Russia or even India. Did any general attempt to snatch power from the civil administration just because of political instability? Show a single instance. You can't. That's why they are superpowers and will remain so.

Minus-Two Formula: They tried to rid off our existing two leaders and intended to take over the power from the civil administration. But they were not successful because of international pressure. Finally, they got hooked up with one of the most violent parties AL who were acting as the traitors. This is also the clear act of cowards.

In fact, they wanted to eliminate the martyr Zia's family. The inhuman torture on his sons is the clear example. They are murderers. The people of Bangladesh should claim their justice in the open public court. The RAB forces are eliminating the multiple murderers in the name of crossfire. Why don't they use the same rule for these massive murderers?

The people of Bangladesh should demand the justice of all those associates of unconstitutional CG as well. They acted like historical culprit Mir Zafar and betrayed our nation. We don't need to use the name of Mir Zafar anymore to set an example of treachery. From now on, we should use the names of both Fakhruddin and Moeen Uddin instead of Mir Zafar! The reason, Mir Zafar betrayed Siraj-Ud-Daula centuries ago but they betrayed our nation in the modern civilized era!

It Was Glorious: Not a Cheap Shot!

As one of the ordinary citizens of Bangladesh, I couldn't remain silent when I saw something awful about our national history. I'm neither a writer nor a historian. To the best extent of my personal experience, I've expressed my views time to time about the politics of Bangladesh that I couldn't agree with some of the radicals and muckrakers. I have experienced the abject failure and also the glorious era of our nation in 1971 even though I wasn't mature enough to understand the nitty-gritty of the political matters and our history. But I don't want to be misled by the deceptive history. I'm proud to be a Bangladeshi no matter where I live.

Unfortunately, since our independence, we have been going through awful experiences due to the behaviors of our corrupt politicians, bureaucrats, and intellectuals. Our leaders misled us a lot. Our history left both glorious and miserable examples. Some monolithic distorted fanatics are trying to mislead our current and future generations with controversial history denying the truth. They want to gain the unfair credit scores with total disrespect to the real contributors during our liberation war in 1971.

The biggest controversial issues are; **who is the founder of our nation?** And **who declared the independence of Bangladesh?**

Indeed, these are very important issues and shouldn't be controversial at all in our true history. However, we do have serious controversies due to the behaviors of our iconic leaders of the past. They might have had different political and moral differences, but they shouldn't have acted by any means that caused the adverse impact on our national interest and image. But we did have experience of those elements that divided us from the inception of our liberation. They became controversial by themselves.

We neither can deny nor change our history. The true history of any nation is the real identity of the nationality. The true history also helps us to prevent illusions of mischievous gains. We can't accept any myths or fairytale as our national history.

We lost millions of lives of all walks of life — students, children, men, women, intellectuals, etc. — during our liberation war. Most importantly, many of our freedom fighters including innocent civilians sacrificed their lives just for the cause of our nation. We need to tribute them not only by remembering them by placing some wreaths on their monument on some special occasions but also for the cause of their sacrifice. Nevertheless, we must not ignore some of the extraordinary contributors and should recognize them with great honor.

Misleading our Current and Future Generations: Sadly enough, some of our so-called politicians and intellectuals got corrupted and politically motivated with myths or self-aggrandizement. They are trying to make up our history the way they want. They totally deny the declaration of the independence of Bangladesh by martyr President Ziaur Rahman then Major Ziaur Rahman in 1971.

I couldn't remain silent in such a crucial point and I decided to dedicate my writings with full recognition that martyr **President Ziaur Rahman was the declarer of the independence of Bangladesh and our freedom fighters followed his call who have sacrificed their lives with highest spirit of the liberation of Bangladesh in 1971 to carry forward the unfinished mission of Banga Bandhu (BB) while he was in jail by the Pakistani brutal dictators.** His declaration of independence of Bangladesh was the defining moment of our **Liberation War, and was glorious — not a cheap shot at all!**

Some of the fanatics of different ideologies are trying to deny his contribution altogether; and some of them agree with his Declaration of Independence with no significance, saying that was on behalf of BB. It was necessary to carry forward his mission at that critical moment. Martyr Zia did exactly the same for our success. It doesn't matter whether he declared the independence by himself or on behalf of BB.

How Important His Declaration Was: It is undeniable that in absence of BB, his courageous declaration of independence reinvigorated the spirit and aspiration of the people to fight against the Pakistanis as against despair. It also expedited the glorious victory of our Liberation War. If he wouldn't have played that heroic role at that moment, the liberation of Bangladesh would have been in dream only. Those who deny his contribution are not only undermining his success but also vilifying our freedom fighters.

I believe the rest of us should follow only the true history to determine the quality of the leaderships of the past. We shouldn't be distorted by any deceptive monolithic propaganda. We shouldn't be the capitulators to those violent and distorted leaders. We should reject the phony historians and muckrakers. If we don't, this will discourage the rest to do something great for our nation.

It's time to wake up to protect our country from both internal and external evil influences. Our corrupt politicians are working as an agent of the outsiders and causing internal disaster. They are also misdirecting the current and future generations with the false and fabricated history. Now they have undertaken the agenda to re-write our national history the way they like.

What Should Be Our Responsibility? We must be courageous enough to protect our true history and the sovereignty of our country and our nation. We ought to be vigilant enough to identify both national and international conspirators to protect our country. We can't betray our freedom fighters of 1971. If we do, it will not only be betrayal to our freedom fighters but also be disrespectfully unpurified the sanctity of our nation. In order to protect our nation, we don't need to fight with weapons but with wisdom.

Unfortunately, our violent leaders have chosen the act of evils and engaged themselves with deadly violence and horrible destruction. Their dupes became fully active to carry out any kinds of violence as we have seen prior to the genuine election-2006 that was not held because of the illegitimate current administration.

Well, I may not be perfect with everything, but I do believe that we shouldn't be distorted by both internal and external destructionists. We need to restrain and reject them just to protect the sovereignty and integrity of our country. Our nation is in serious crisis due to some cheap, selfish, and destructive politicians and bureaucrats. We need to challenge those elements and hold them accountable with great courage before the worst happens, as is already happening under the current illegitimate administration of PM Sheikh Hasina.

What We Need to Do: The old evil political syndromes have already caused the devastating impact on the vital interest of our nation and now they are back to their business even with further devastating plans. We need to end the political hostility amongst the politicians with the old issues and need to move forward for the greater cause of our country.

The horrible history as we have been experiencing since our independence were the consequence of their political miscalculations and breaches of the trust and commitment to the people by those leaders. The current generation has nothing to do with the old issues but taking lessons from the past. We also need to move forward in an orderly manner bearing in mind those consequences. We need to alleviate our moral and ethical values and move forward with high spirit to achieve our goal.

The Justice of the Assassinators of BB: The justice of the assassinators of BB was necessary long ago, soon after his assassination. But it was not possible because of his controversial leadership. People were shocked and stunned to silence after his assassination with different reactions, but didn't demand justice very strongly because of his colossal political miscalculations and unpopularity. The wrath of the people was growing intensely for his abusive political behavior.

He didn't Believe in Consequence: He thought that he was the political absolutist. Nothing could prevent him from exerting his will. He turned back to the imperialistic notion of the medieval era at the end of the twentieth century. Because of his colossal miscalculations, he paid such an unprecedented price and lost all-available family members, including himself.

People were shocked but took that horrible assassination as a consequence of awful corruption and his political absolutism. But unquestionably, it was one of the cruelest assassinations in the history of Bangladesh and that shouldn't have had happened. It could have been prevented easily only with his corrective administration with the preservation of the trust of the people. If that was the case, he would have been one of the great leaders of the world. His legacy would remain uncontroversial.

The current administration of Sheikh Hasina with her corrupt associates is trying to mislead our people with falsification of the dismal failure of the past of her own and her ancestor. She is fully engaged in spreading the political toxic acid in our democratic process in the modern era. She is attempting to do the same as her father. But she shouldn't forget that as a giant politician, her father was not successful at all, and ended up with no popularity after the liberation of Bangladesh.

They are also trying to steal the credibility of their opponent as against their own irreparable failures and failed administrations. They may have different motives and political philosophies but they can't divide our nation with misleading history.

What Was Her Best Alternative? Her best alternative was if she could identify the cause of the failure of her father and taken some corrective measures to regain the trust of the people. But she did exactly the opposite. That's why she couldn't achieve anything with any popularity. Her worst choice was to continue the deadly violence as an opponent, and revitalization of corruption and horrible gang production during her administration.

Under the above circumstances, we as the sensible citizens of our nation should hold them accountable to protect the interest of our country. We need to smash the fangs of evil traitors and reset the clock to move toward the progressive direction in the modern globalized world, rather than strengthen the old systematic cycle of corruption, deadly violence, acting as traitors, etc. We must not forget the consequence of imperialistic notions of past leaders. Any attempt to play back the same style of politics could lead to devastating consequences.

Despite their success and failure, I would like to pay my tribute to those leaders for their dedication and contribution based on the difference of their political and moral philosophies in different circumstances. Let me start with BB followed by martyr President Ziaur Rahman.

Farewell! Banga Bandhu Sheikh Mujibur Rahman (BB)!

He was one of the most respectful leaders from my childhood. I heard his name and his symbol "boat" at the early stage of my life. I was also addicted to his symbolic coat (Mujib coat). Without understanding anything about politics at that early age, I chanted many slogans with the seniors. His picture, his thunder voice, and his courageous leadership attracted and inspired all of us. We chanted the slogan to free him out from the jail of tyrant Western leaders. It was absolutely necessary at that time of the political crisis of Pakistan between the East and the West. His starting was likely to be glorious. He sacrificed a lot and spent his precious time in jail only for the cause of the Easterners.

He did get immense support from the people of the East. People trusted him profoundly and titled him as **Bangabandhu (BB)** (friend of Bengalis), the friend we trusted the most. People of the East didn't care about their life to follow his calls. They did put him on the highest peak of the political mountain. The immense support of the people of the East was the main source of his courageous move. Thus he became the iconic leader of the East.

In 1952, February 21st, our students and general people Salam, Barkat, Jabbar and Rafiq sacrificed their lives for the cause of our mother tongue "Bangla." Their sacrifice was glorious and most honorable for our nation.

In fact, the seed of our independence was sown from that moment. His politics probably started from that point of time as a disciple of Hussain Shaheed Sarwardi and he dedicated a lot that our nation can't forget. He continued the political movement and spent most of his time in prison by the barbaric Western rulers. His political movement was believed to be genuine to the people and they supported him, risking their lives too. Many other leaders, including students, spent their precious time in jail as well. The most controversial figure, Khndakar Mustaq Ahmed, was also one of them.

Politically, he achieved a lot until 1971. In 1970, he won the election with a landslide victory from AL. He became the iconic majority leader of Pakistan. But the mean-spirited Western leaders didn't respect the constitution of Pakistan and didn't hand over the power to him. They believed that he wanted to separate Pakistan and could take retaliation of the past discrimination of the West. But he didn't want the separation. He wanted to be the prime minister of undivided Pakistan.

He had legitimate right to take over the power as a majority leader. But the uncivilized Pakistani leaders disregarded the rule of law and the constitution of Pakistan. The political criminal Zulfiker Ali Bhutto and tyrant dictator Gen. Yahya Khan were fully responsible to lead toward the separation of Pakistan.

The people of the East got frustrated of their behavior and were ready to move forward, even if it was necessary for the separation or independence. People expected that BB would declare the Independence of Bangladesh on March 07, 1971.

He made a couple of very important speeches on March 7th and March 25th in 1971 at the time of decisive political decision. The people of Bangladesh expected a precise declaration of independence instead of the tone of any compromise with that rogue nation of the West.

However, he intended to be the prime minister of Pakistan. He gave an ultimatum to the West with some legitimate conditions. But the barbaric Pakistani leaders arrested him and started genocide in the east. His life was under threat too.

We prayed for his life to the Almighty Allah at least five times a day and for our subsequent success. The people of Bangladesh got involved in the Liberation War by themselves with some of the courageous military leaders like Major Ziaur Rahman and many others. The Liberation War became inevitable.

Our people got involved in fighting against the most sophisticated arms and forces of Pakistan almost with nothing just for our liberation and to get him freed from the Pakistanis safely. They magnificently won the war only in nine months and we got both **liberation of Bangladesh** and **him.**

During that war, he had been in jail and seventy-five million people of the East were in the war-field. We lost millions of precious lives of all walks of life: men, women, and children, young, old, students, teachers, and intellectuals were amongst them.

However, the people of newly liberated Bangladesh overly exhilarated having him back from the Pakistanis safely. We all had the highest hopes and aspirations with profound trust that he, as a leader, would lead us toward progressive direction with profound respect to our martyr freedom fighters. People no longer used his original name Sheikh Mujibur Rahman — we called him **Bangabandhu** (BB).

The Cause of the Sacrifice: The expectation of our people was very high not to change their fortune overnight. But they expected a very progressive future where there will be no injustice, discrimination, exploitation, corruption, cronyism, nepotism, and so on. In fact, those were the causes; our freedom fighters sacrificed their precious lives and fought against the West. The devotion of the rest of the people of the East was the history of heroism of our nation.

Sadly enough, people almost instantly had been experiencing quite the opposite. He started to lose the trust and popularity of the people very dramatically. As an iconic political leader, it was quite unaffordable. The real leaders can't ignore the responsibility, trust, and accountability. To most, he became very suspicious and was no longer BB. He became Sheikh Mujibur Rahman. I myself lost my hopes and aspirations like the vast majority of the people of the newborn Bangladesh and couldn't hold his banner anymore.

The Biggest Dilemma: As a consequence, some of his close companions became rebellions and started to form new political parties and weakened the strength of his party, Awami League (AL). He became too controversial and eventually tried to act as a political absolutist as an alternative. He also created some extreme group of friends and foes in different circumstances. He failed to realize what could be the consequence of his political absolutism. Instead of realizing the cause of their sacrifice, he started to play a dangerous hardball against them using his Rakhi Bahini (his private defense forces) and Red Forces (Lalbahini).

The strategy of the political absolutism with the formation of BAKSAL and Mujib-ism (Mujibbad) was totally unacceptable to the people except some interest groups who became his friends. But that hardball hit him back so gravely. He could have been like Nelson Mandela, but he ended up with lot of awful controversies. He dramatically lost the popularity and trust of the people and was knocked down from the highest peak of the political mountain.

Finally, we lost him in such a horrible way that the whole nation was stunned to silence with different reactions. I didn't like his administrative style. But as a human being, I didn't want to see his ultimate end with his family members in such a horrible way that once I honored him the most as my leader. Farewell, BB, farewell!

Farewell! Martyr President Ziaur Rahman!

He was not known to me at all. He became known by name to the people of the East during our Liberation War as Major Zia. He was a Pakistani army officer until he courageously revolted against the Pakistani military leaders' right after the arrest of BB, the moment our Liberation War broke out in his absence. Some of the timid officers were worried about the court martial law, if it was not success, and were reluctant to revolt against the military leaders of Pakistan. As an officer of the Pakistani army, it was an extremely courageous and risky move to revolt against the Pakistani Military Leaders. But he did with great courage with some other heroes!

Indeed, the history can't deny this defining part of his heroic role. He declared the independence of Bangladesh just to finish the unfinished chapter of BB and continued to lead the liberation war until our glorious victory.

As an early teenager, my excitement of our liberation war was beyond control. To pick up the arms against the Pakistanis were only a few days away. All of us had only one single question: why didn't BB declare the independence of Bangladesh? But after Major Zia's declaration of the independence of Bangladesh from Shadhin Bangla Bethar Kendra (the secret location of broadcasting centre of Bangladesh Freedom Fighters), people cheered a lot and engaged them in the Liberation War with the highest spirit of our liberation.

The Declaration of Independence of Bangladesh by Major Ziaur Rahman

"This is Shadhin Bangla Betar Kendra. I, Major Ziaur Rahman on behalf of Bangabandhu Sheikh Mujibur Rahman, hereby declare that the independent People's Republic of Bangladesh has been established. I have taken command as the temporary Head of the Republic. I call upon all Bangalis to rise against the attack by the West

Pakistani Army. We shall fight to the last to free our Motherland. By the grace of Allah, Victory is ours".

It was extremely important in that defining moment. But I didn't see who he was! Indeed, it was the defining moment of our Liberation War.

Almost at the same time, our political leaders in absence of BB formed the temporary government of Shadhin Bangla from the secret location known as Mujib Nagar. Our Freedom Fighters started to organize under the leadership of Col. M.A.G. Osmani (Retired). There was no media except the radio. Sadhin Bangla Bethar Kendra was the most popular station aired by very talented figures to inspire the people of all levels to move toward our glorious victory.

The whole world started to condemn the Pakistani barbaric forces and their leaders that carried out genocide and killed so many innocents of all walks of life in the East. Our liberation was very costly. The fresh blood of the East was streaming toward the ocean. We lost many of our precious lives. Our heroic freedom fighters like him continued fighting against those barbaric forces.

Eventually, only in nine months, on December 16, 1971, the Pakistani barbaric forces surrendered to us very disgracefully. The magnificent victory of Bangladesh freedom fighters was exhilarating all over the world. The name of the Bangladesh had taken place in the map of the world with our pride. We were known as one of the proudest nations in the world!

Sadly enough, right after the liberation of Bangladesh, we had to face a lot of troubles both domestically and internationally. Our political leaders became controversial because of excessive corruption and philosophical differences about the future of our newborn Bangladesh. Besides, some miscreants didn't return their arms soon after our liberation war was over. They were engaged in nefarious activities: robberies, murders, and other lawlessness also took place almost openly.

The real freedom fighters returned their arms very honorably. The innocent people were scared to sleep at night. The law and order became useless. It was a very tough time for almost all of us during the period of immediate post-liberation.

The political leaders got divided. The hostility amongst army and civilian leaders took horrible shape. As a result, assassination after assassination, coup after coup took place beyond the imagination of the general people. People were wondering what was coming up next. Because of the coups and assassinations, people had to spend their lives with total uncertainty. People were experiencing the frequent changes of the leaderships both in military and in civilians.

Advent of Khondakar Mustaq Ahmed: He became very controversial soon after the assassination of Sheikh Mujibur Rahman. It was believed that he was behind the assassination of Sheikh Mujibur Rahman. Since it was very difficult time of famine and paramount corruption, countless people were dying for want of food; BB lost the popularity and trust of the people.

As a result, people didn't blame Khondakar Mustaq Ahmed very seriously. He successfully managed to control the famine with some positive steps to end the famine. People didn't die anymore for want of food soon after he took over the power. To some extent, he gained the popularity of the people during the short period of his presidency soon after the assassination of BB. He also formed his political party "Bangladesh Democratic Party". But he remained questionable figure for the assassination of BB.

Finally, Gen. Ziaur Rahman took control over all those horrible circumstances. Despite all of his courageous contribution, I didn't like him when he took over the power from the civilian leader, the controversial figure Khondakar Mustaq Ahmed. But circumstantially, it was necessary. Any democratic society rejects the military interference in the democratic environment. But in that situation, it was appropriate.

His Political Philosophy: Initially, martyr Zia didn't have enough general support and people were worried about his potential dictatorship. We preferred the civil administration. But by virtue of his noble mission, he managed to earn the reputation and gradually changed the course of the politics of our country. His progressive visions and philosophy, and honest leadership, changed the attitude of the people of Bangladesh. Instead of dictatorship he initiated the democratic process and decided to form his party Bangladesh Nationalist Party (BNP). He became a magnetic politician amongst the people. Under his leadership, Bangladesh was moving toward the progressive direction. He did very successfully and raised the image of our country to the rest of the world.

I was fortunate enough to shake his hand only once in his lifetime and the PLO leader Yaser Arafat just a few days before his assassination on May 30, 1981. The news of his assassination shocked not only me but also the whole nation. His enemies not only assassinated him but also gradually took control over the power treacherously.

The tyrant dictator H.M. Earshad wickedly prosecuted many other high-ranking talented army officers including Maj. Gen. Manzoor with the deepest conspiracy in the name of justice of the assassinators. Those were his potential rivals and were loyal to President Ziaur Rahman! Eventually, he snatched the power, pointing the gun from the elected President Justice Abdus Sattar.

The resurrection of the centuries-old historic treachery of Mir Zafar took place for the first time in Bangladesh! The historic culprit was gone centuries ago but his evil-blood is flowing to certain circles.

He also divided the armed forces between the real freedom fighters and the non-participants in the liberation war who were confined in Pakistan, including himself. He had a silent jealousy to President Ziaur Rahman.

Finally, he managed to execute his plan with that horrible plan. Thus he managed to obtain power and started his dictatorship that continued for approximately nine years. Nobody realized that martyr Zia did take place to that extent in the minds and hearts not only of the people of Bangladesh but also many other nationals so honorably!

Lost Opportunity of Justice: There was a golden opportunity to carry out his justice. But it was not possible because of the current distrustful PM Sheikh Hasina and inactive judicial system. She is the one who shook his hand with the violation of the commitment of political integrity between BNP and AL and ran in an election while he was out of jail with phony justice. Both BNP and AL committed not to allow him to run in the election with him. BNP didn't but AL did very mean-spiritedly. Thus, she managed to obtain power for the first time after the assassination of her father BB and set the record of distortions.

Zia's Biggest Achievement: There was an unprecedented mourning nationwide for several days spontaneously after his horrible assassination. People of all ages flooded to his coffin just to pay their final respect to him, which didn't happen in BB's case! His biggest achievement was he didn't lose the popularity and trust of the people and he ended up with the glory and glory! He was almost from nowhere in the political field, but he became everywhere! He will remain immortal in the history of Bangladesh! His dedication was the best of all! His legacy is quite unmatchable!

The difference he made is just because of the quality of his leadership, and as a man of superior personality. He is a glorious example in our history! Our nation should follow the quality of his wisdom. He is no longer with us! But his glory is undeniable in the history of our nation! The end-best is the best. But his best was both at the beginning and ending! Farewell, martyr President Ziaur Rahman, farewell! We miss you with great honor!

Serious Objection to the Eviction Order of the House of the Former PM

Recently, the controversial PM of the current administration Sheikh Hasina issued an order of eviction notice to the former Prime Minister, Begum Khaleda Zia, to vacate her house of the cantonment. I believe this is absolutely against the will of the vast majority of the people of Bangladesh. It is clear how jealous the opponents of BNP are, those who deny the honorable services and unmatchable contributions of martyr President Ziaur Rahman that our nation can never forget! Martyr Zia had an unmatchable contribution than any other leaders of our history!

The people of Bangladesh mourned spontaneously for him unprecedentedly longer than any other assassinated leaders of the past. He was an exceptional statesman not only as a soldier but also as the successful president of Bangladesh. Above all, he was one of the rare personalities in the history of Bangladesh.

Why His House Shouldn't Be Taken Away: Martyr Zia didn't leave any presidential palace for his heirs. He left empty-handed and served his country and his nation with no illusion. He served his country as a heroic soldier and as a president with the highest spirit of hopes and aspirations of our people unlike any other leaders.

He made the difference by virtue of the quality of leadership and as a man of superior personality. To compare him with any other leaders of our history will be quite inappropriate. There were some other leaders but they couldn't get to power. Therefore, the people of Bangladesh had high emotion to honor him with that house for his family. The eviction order of the house is nothing but the egregious step taken by the current administration just for their jealousy and animosity.

The vast majority of the people didn't and don't care about that house. They didn't vote her to take as an agenda to force her to evict the house of former PM. They tribute martyr Zia for his remarkable contribution to our nation. The opponents can hijack the election, bank, and treasury by the evil power but can't hijack the trust and popularity of the people. If there were no heroes like Zia, there was no liberation of Bangladesh in 1971. The denial of his heroism is the denial of our own history.

Indeed, this is one of the most disgraceful behaviors of the current administration and they should refrain from this sort of mean-spirited politics. The people of Bangladesh do not care about that house but they do care about the peaceful and progressive future of our country. If they still continue the process of eviction of the house, they will be disgraced very badly with the disclosure of many of the odious behaviors and failure of the past of their own. In fact, we don't have to disclose. It is already known historically.

Within a very short period of time of ninety days of their administration, they started to throw mud to their opponent leader, who is still very popular and very successfully administered her terms despite their constant deadly violence. She left significant improvement in education, prosperity, and security of our country. She also made significant progress both economically and environmentally. During her administration, the current PM Sheikh Hasina as an opponent did nothing but engage herself with constant deadly violence and destruction. She is the innovator of politics of horror.

How the Weeds Get Stronger: The current administration also magnified the corruption of BNP to mislead the people forgetting their own, especially to the younger generations. They never admit their own abject failures of their administration. They are the ones who laid down the foundation of corruption historically. Now they are delivering the sermon of corruption.

They attempted to take **Ghonobhaban,** our nation's symbolic property, against the will of the people. Now they want to revoke the recognition of the people of Bangladesh as honored to the martyr Zia's family in 1981, in honor of his outstanding contribution to our nation. He dedicated his life with noble mission and served our nation with distinction. This is not the house! This is the symbol of honor to martyr Zia!

Martyr Zia didn't take that house by abusing his power. It was the unanimous support of the people of Bangladesh to honor him with that house to his family who left behind his family with no resources prior to his assassination in 1981. You may snatch away that house with wild egregious behavior but you can't snatch the honor away of martyr Zia. Rather, you will be known as one of the meanest personalities in our history as you already are!

Her Horrible Regime: People of Bangladesh shouldn't forget so soon what her previous administration was like. People got killed for no reason, the gangs and donation collectors got free license with the support of her administration. There was no justice. People were considered lucky if they could return home safely. People couldn't build their houses in their own land without a hefty donation to her sponsored gangs. Lots of innocents lost their lives by her procreated gangs. These are very few examples out of many. She was famous for the innovatory deadly violence with the poles and oars, which her father didn't do in his lifetime against the barbaric Pakistanis prior to our liberation.

She is impudently claiming that her last administration was a golden era in the history of Bangladesh! If so, why couldn't she get re-elected term after term? Over and over, her shameless rhetoric was rejected by the sensible people of Bangladesh. The continuation of the same rhetoric is nothing but a laughable joke.

The people of Bangladesh do not want to see any jealousy and atrocity like the past. They want to see the progressive direction to move forward. Any action against each other like a dog-fight is quite detrimental for our country and our nation.

Within a very short period of her administration, people are already experiencing the horrible gang activities. Her protected gangs in foreign soil are returning to create the same regressive situation. I believe the current administration should look in the rearview mirror of their own with their correct vision to identify their own corruption and horrible scenarios of the past. They need to identify the causes of their past failure. They need to change their attitude and behavior, which are unacceptable to the people.

My Simple Advice: Look at the most powerful country on the planet, the USA, and their election and the way of their administration. Our election was held almost at the same time. Learn some lessons from them. Frequent visits to the developed countries are quite useless and wastage unless you learn anything from them. They are not clamoring too loud about the mistakes of the past administration. They are trying hard to overcome those serious problems both domestically and internationally. If you know nothing, learn from others.

Most importantly, you need to protect our national interest instead of pleasing others at the cost of the sufferings of our own. The protection of our border security and our sovereignty must not be compromised with the policies of corridor, transit, and trade agreement with our risky neighbor.

The honeymoon with our neighbor for the mean-spirited political gains at the cost of the sufferings of our nation will be disastrous for us as it was in the past. We need to be cautious enough based on the past behaviors of our neighbor. We shouldn't forget that quite often our border forces BDR and many other innocent along the border areas are being killed by BSF with the violation of UN charter.

The Horrible Crisis of BDR: The recent horrible rampage of BDR on the officers is another mysterious issue for Bangladesh too. We need to figure out who is against our defense forces and so on. Why and how were so many high-ranking talented officers of the army killed on February 25, 2009, soon after she took over the power from the previous administration? We have many questions to ask and we demand the answers from the current administration.

The direct blaming of the opponents to get away from the fact is quite unacceptable and inconvincible to the sensible people of Bangladesh. The quick justice of those BDRs is the clear sign of covering up the real story. We strongly demand justice, but we need to find out the real cause and clues and the responsible ones after thorough investigation of the causes of that rampage.

The Dire Consequence of Quick and Unfair Justice: The radical justice could cause many innocent people to be convicted, which could lead to the potential death penalty. Many of them might not have been the part of that rampage but became part of the systematic rules of the forces. Most of them might have opposed to carrying out such a horrible rampage. The whimsical justice without finding the facts, figures, and unavoidable circumstance could cause the death penalty of many innocent people.

As a result, many of their family members including their innocent children will suffer and could grow with violent nature, if there is any unfair justice. No politics should get involved to carry out their justice. But it is very important to find out the facts and figures and identify the real killers before carrying out the quick justice. We need to standardize the rule of law to exercise the duties of our forces. Our defense and armed forces are still following the backdated formula of the colonial era.

The current administration will be fully responsible for any unfair or wrongful trial of those forces. In the future, if anything is found wrong, the current justice system will be fully responsible and they must pay the same price. They shouldn't be forgiven by any means. If there is any conspiracy behind this rampage, they should be prosecuted under the same rule of law. We need to follow the justice system of the developed countries of the world. Justice means justice, not the conspiratorial practice.

Dhal mey kuch Kala hey! (Something is fishy!) What kind of joy Bangla is this?

Soon after the BDR rampage, I was watching an interesting program of NTV. I couldn't watch the whole program. But I watched a couple of segments of that program. It was a program of the parliamentary session.

Firstly, I had a chance to watch while former PM Begum Khaleda Zia was making her statement pretty eloquently about the success of the last two terms of her administration. She highlighted the issues of education, security, economy, and reduction of corruption, etc.

During her statement, the opponents tried their best to impede her in a very disorderly manner. In one point, she asked the Speaker for orderly atmosphere of the parliament. But the Speaker ruled out, saying that they were listening with a mockery smile!

I believe this was his incompetency to act as a Speaker. It was disappointing to watch. He lost his neutrality and became questionable, if he was fair at all, to work as a Speaker. In fact, he was not.

The opposition leader Begum Khaleda Zia continued her statement until the parliament was postponed for Magrib Prayer (the evening prayer). I missed thereafter.

Secondly, I had another chance to watch another part of the same session. It was the turn of our current illegitimate PM Sheikh Hasina. I missed her first and last parts too. I was listening to her statement very curiously.

In her statement, she not only denied every success of her opponent but also tried to steal the success of former PM Begum Khaleda Zia and started to claim whatever the success they had was because of her own past administration. She claimed as usual that her term was a golden era in the history of Bangladesh.

Again, if it was true, why was she not re-elected by the people? Why again and again was her rhetoric false claim rejected by the people? Does it require the re-clarification that her administration was the worst of the worst?

She also blamed her opponent with the very sensitive issue of the recent BDR crisis and pointed to her opponent, Begum Khaleda Zia, and blamed her indirectly that she was involved or well informed with that horrible conspiracy. She also asked her who were they who used the mask while they carried out that rampage on those BDR officers and killed them.

She concluded with her irrational comment in her favorite language, "**Dhal mey Kuch Kala hey!" (Something is fishy).** Is this our language that we fought for in 1952? This comment clearly indicates who she is working for and the root of her origin. Truth comes out itself and is consistent enough with the BDR crisis. This is the genetic syndrome of her political root.

Martyr Zia was the protector of Bangladesh and had never been a capitulator to Indira Ghandhi. But BB was. This kind of mockery comment is absolutely provocative. The Speaker was enjoying her offensive statement with a pleasant smile with zesty taste. Her derogatory remarks lowered herself to the bottom of her own status. Who is having the closest tie with those who kill our border security forces very often along with other innocent people in our border areas? I don't know her language. But let me try.

In response to her comment, may I respond to her saying, "Your **Dhal tho bilkul kala hey!" (You yourself are absolutely fishy!)** The horrible PM! My simple advice to you is this: instead of running after somebody, you better run yourself. Your history is muddier and more dangerous than your opponent and it is threatening our national security and the sovereignty of our country.

You opened up your living room for them prior to the election. Now you have opened up the corridor, transit and trading doors of our country to your master neighbor!

You and your loyalists used the term that your opponent likes the muddy water for fishing. But you've already caused the disaster even in the clean water. Don't try to make the people of Bangladesh so foolish. They are watching you from the distant part of the globe from our country. You don't have to digitalize Bangladesh. Bangladesh is already digitalized to watch your actions.

The people of Bangladesh are much smarter than you believe yourself. If you don't know how to dance, don't blame the stage. Blame yourself. We don't want to see your pugnacious behavior anymore. It is quite dangerous for our peaceful country Bangladesh and too abhorrent, and we are already tired of your behavior. Most importantly, do not betray our nation. Please! Please! Please!

Protection for the Destructionists; not for the Protectionist! Recently, you have managed to pass a bill for the security of your own and for your upcoming generations with the support of your mean-spirited loyalists. I'm not against your protection. This is vitally important for all human beings.

May I courteously ask you a question? Do you think you are above our people, our country, and our nation? If yes, then it's okay. But if not, do you deserve any special protection at all at the cost of the disaster of our country and the rest of the people? You are known as the biggest destructionist of our country. Instead of your own protection, you better think about the protection of our country and our nation first before yourself.

Who Should Get the Protection: Only the protectors should get the protection, not the destructionists. Who are the protectionists? The simple answer is the people of our country and your opponents who liberated our country, not the betrayers.

The Truth is Coming to Light: Recently, one of your senior associates Abdul Jalil disclosed the truth of the election fraud that you came to power with a conspiracy. It is too late. But eventually, the truth came to light from your own loyalist. I believe whatever I have written about you and your ancestor is not only true — it is the real history.

I like to deal with the real history, not with the parody or fiction as I've mentioned in the beginning of my writings. I think you have already crossed the regressive, corrupt regime of your father. You are dealing against the sovereignty and integrity of our country. I think the people of Bangladesh should not forgive you and they should hold you accountable for the treachery against our country. Within a short period of your administration of ninety days, you caused the biggest destruction in the history of Bangladesh.

Under your corrupt capitulatory influence, those betrayers, Dr. Fakhruddin Ahmed, General Moeen U. Ahmed, and many others have taken shelter outside the country.

I personally didn't like Abdul Jalil because of the nature of his life-long arrogance, provocative and violent behavior, especially prior to the election-2006. But I admire him for telling the truth. Now you and your party leaders are against him saying he is mentally unbalanced. Yes, you are right, if anybody tells the truth they are known as crazy or mentally unbalanced. Isn't it so? Don't blame me; there are many other crazy and mentally unbalanced people in Bangladesh and around the world who do not agree with you at all.

You better get diagnosed yourself and go under treatment of your own before you make any remarks against those rational people. Now you are scaring the rest, putting him in jail. One of your junior law ministers openly stated that they're being tracked down who were against you and your administration.

To say something or write anything against you is not unlawful at all, it is the democratic process and freedom of speech. And, most importantly, this is the guts and audacity to tell the truth. This is far more superior to your deadly violence as you did prior to the election-2006. You will definitely be failed, if you try to do something against the truth.

This is Just the Beginning: You shouldn't be surprised if you see many more crazy people come out from your party to tell the truth. This is just the beginning. One of your junior home ministers, Taz, already left from your Cabinet for the same reason.

The former dictator, your phony brother, the biggest corrupt ever, also known as Marcos of Bangladesh, General H.M. Ershad, impudently said that he is not in favor of justice of the chief advisor and his advisory groups. He said in the parliament that if there was no unconstitutional CG you couldn't obtain power. See, I'm not the only one telling the truth. Your loyalists also started to tell the truth. Many more of your own party has the same opinion but they remain in pause.

Abdul Jalil is a Tax Evader!: Is this a big deal to put him in jail as a tax evader? Is he the only one or are many more of your own Cabinet members and bureaucrats in the same situation or even bigger crooks?

I believe, if you go behind many other tax evaders, you will automatically become the minority leader and your corrupt political ambition will come to end automatically. Most importantly, if the proper investigation is carried out neutrally, you must be one of them too — not only as a tax evader, but also many other overdue serious charges of corruption and deadly violence.

However, if you get permanent protection, what about your opponent who was quite opposite to you? You obtained power to change the signboards of all important national institutions to rename on your late father to protect his legacy. I think there will be the scarcity of signboard industry in Bangladesh if you continue to do so. Don't worry, your masters are ready to supply you the aids you need and that's why you have opened up the corridor, transit, open-border for speedy shipment.

The Legacy of Martyr Zia Is too Glorious: You are also trying hard to deny the legacy of the genuine contributor martyr President Ziaur Rahman. I would like to remind you that the disgraceful legacy doesn't last long and the genuine ones go way beyond. You may try hard to obscure the real light with an evil cloud but eventually the cloud will die down by itself against the power of light. Martyr Zia's legacy is too glorious and too radiant to obscure.

I strongly suggest you to protect your opponent too, the protectionist of our country and our nation the way you want to be protected. It is overdue to put you on trail for the damage you have already done for our country, and our nation is suffering dismally.

Currently, you are trying to control your opponent with false and fabricated allegations of corruption, grenade attack, and many other falsifications and fabrications just to suppress the most popular party BNP. You and your illegitimate administration are conspiring against BNP to dwindle their party with the help of the outsiders and a misled group of insiders. Your masters and loyalists are amplifying the propaganda that the opponents are planning to kill you, that's why you need extraordinary protection. Do not forget that your late father did the same but couldn't protect himself. Bangladesh is not your paternal property; it is the property of 158 million people.

Your latest strategy is to establish the connectivity of martyr Ziaur Rahman as an assassinator of BB. If he was really an assassinator, he won't be able to lead the country so successfully with extreme popularity until the last moment of his life. Rather, your father lost the trust and popularity of the people. If he would have the same image like martyr Zia, people would remember him spontaneously and unanimously with great honor as martyr Ziaur Rahman! You don't need to change the signboards to protect his legacy. Don't try to radicalize the history. Let the history be intact and move forward to do the best.

Why You Became a Destructionist: You are very much aware that you lost the popularity and trust of the people. Therefore, you have chosen to be a destructionist and engaged yourself in all kinds of deadly violence prior to the emergency and even acted as a traitor of our country. You were deeply involved with the outsiders to help you out in order to get power to serve their purpose. You caused the most horrible BDR crisis that our nation has ever experienced. You shouldn't ask for your own protection before our country and our nation. The destructionist shouldn't get any protection.

It is my utmost request to you that no matter how you managed to obtain power, please serve and save 158 million people; protect the sovereignty of our country and our national interest first before anything else. Anything else is nothing but the acts of traitors. You better read for yourself what you are doing.

I personally rejected you prior to the election-2008 as my leader for the greater interest of our country and our nation! You are so awful! You may get sold but don't sell my country! If you wish to carry out Indian passport, you better go on their soil, not on the soil of Bangladesh.

I don't know if you are capable of understanding from the part of the speech of the founding father, George Washington, of the United States of America. He cautioned the high-level politicians and policymakers in his farewell address to the Union. But I would like to quote here, if you can learn something from the following excerption:

"A passionate attachment of one nation for another produces variety of evils, because it leads to concessions to the favorite nation of privileges denied to others; which is apt doubly to injure the nation making the concession, both by unnecessarily parting with what ought to have been retained, and by exciting jealousy, ill-will and disposition to retaliate, in the parties from whom equal privileges are withheld. It gives to ambitious, corrupted, or deluded citizens (who devote themselves to the favorite nation). Real patriots who may resist the intrigues of the favorite are liable to become suspected and odious, while its tools and dupes usurp the applause and confidence of the people to surrender their interest."

CHAPTER I

This chapter contains some of my previous writings with the expression of my reactions to the extreme form of violence carried by the opponents of the outgoing administration of the Bangladesh Nationalist Party (BNP) in 2006:

1. The Political Drama of Bangladesh
2. The Political Volcano of Bangladesh
3. The Political Purification of Bangladesh
4. The Comprehensive Rebuttal of The Political Purification of Bangladesh
5. If I Could Agree With the Former Prime Minister, Sheikh Hasina
6. The Consequence of the Unfair Deals
7. Black Badge Against the Justice!
8. Be A Progressive, Not A Regressive
9. The Caretaker Government (CG), Politicians, and People
10. Unveiling the Mask of the CG
11. Who Sowed the Seeds of Corruption
12. Blackmail of our History!
13. What About May 30th?
14. The Unforgettable Memories of 1971

CHAPTER II

15. Is This Not The Election of Disfranchisement?
16. Our Liberation, Banga Bandhu (BB), and Joy Bangla
17. Circumstantial Issues #1-2010

The Political Drama of Bangladesh

June, 2006

Due to the current political turmoil, I'm extremely concerned about the future of our country. An ordinary citizen of Bangladesh, my heart and soul have a strong attachment to this land, no matter where I live. I'm neither a politician nor an activist of any political party. This is the expression of my reaction only. I'm equally sensitive, as is everybody else, to the common cause of the country. I believe it is the obligation of the citizens to exercise their rights and duties in a civilized manner. Any irrational, selfish, and reckless action could cause a very serious consequence for the nation.

We should not forget our own history and should not ignore the consequences that we have already seen in the past. If we do, the consequences will not ignore us. To exercise our rights and duties as citizens, we have to have very strong moral and ethical standard of principles, rather than greedy and selfish ones. Unfortunately, that's exactly the cause of the problems we have been experiencing since our independence.

We all want the democratic way of living. But we have very wrong concept of democracy. We think democracy allows us to do anything we want. There shouldn't be any restrictions, even if they are harmful or damaging to our country and the nation at large.

The current opposition parties are using exactly the same formula and doing everything we see in the media. Some of their behaviors are not acceptable as representatives of the people. This kind of leadership is not only a tragedy for the country, but also damaging the image of our nation outside our country.

We are living in a very critical era. We have to have a very clear vision to move forward with a well-thought out plan.

Bangladesh is one of the most densely populated countries in the world. Our population is many times higher than many developed countries. About 158 million people live in about 55,598 square miles. This would amaze any reasonable person of any nation.

Bangladesh is already like an overloaded ship in the middle of a deep ocean. Any irresponsible or reckless captain should not navigate this ship. The leader of Bangladesh is not only the leader of the country but is also responsible for the fate of these 158 million people. If any irresponsible leader happens to be in charge, the situation of the country could be devastating, just like the ill-fated ship "The Titanic."

In 1971, we introduced ourselves as one of the heroic nations of the world. The year 1971 is very significant for many reasons. This is the year of the ultimate sacrifice, devotion, pain and sufferings, and the immense excitement of the joy of the victory of our liberation war. In only in nine months, we liberated our country from the brutal dictators of Pakistan. No nation has such a history in the world.

This liberation cost us 3 million (as recorded in our history) innocent lives from all walks of life. Many more, including women and children were killed during our liberation war. Our unique unification and strong determination made it possible to achieve our victory. Our heroes taught an unforgettable lesson to those brutal Pakistani forces. Eventually, they surrendered to us and inherited a very shameful, dark history for themselves for their generations to come. Our freedom fighters sacrificed so much for a very solemn reason – the bright future of our nation.

In spite of the monumental success in politics, until 1971 Banga Bhandhu Sheikh Mijibur Rahman (BB) was very controversial after he took charge of the newborn Bangladesh. He dramatically lost the popularity and trust of the people. His close companions laid down the foundation of corruption, nepotism, favoritism, and cronyism with total disregard to the aspirations of the people such that the nation could not afford any more. His political creditability diminished quickly. He failed to demonstrate that he was capable to lead the nation. Instead, he was an imperialist or a political absolutist, and thus, wanted to hold the power forever and pass it on to his next generation. When all this occurred, there was no room for fairness and justice in his administration. His loyalists believed that he was very generous and kind to the people.

I can't agree with them because, in my view to favor some particular group of people at the costs of the suffering of the rest is not generosity – it is quite immoral and unethical. A real leader should be both compassionate and tough enough to protect the common interests of the country – with no favoritism. BB tried to distort the people with the formation of Bangladesh Krishak (Farmer) Sramik (Labor) Awami League (BAKSAL) and his own ism with his fallacious doctrines was also known as Mujibbad.

At the same time, BB started using scare tactics, the very unpopular Red and Rakhi Bahini (his own private forces), beyond imagination. There was a serious discontent amongst his group. Instead of realizing the sentiment of the people, he chooses to be tougher to them using the Rakhi Bahini. His close companions started to form new parties. His once strong party, the Awami League (AL) became weaker. Even though he was my most respectful leader, at that time, I personally rejected this party for this reason.

His Administrative Failure: The public didn't want to change their fortunes overnight but expected a progressive future. But for the interests of a certain group of his own people, BB's group institutionalized his administration with corruption. Even his son was a very controversial figure at that time. He didn't have any control over those people. That was his significant administrative crisis. People were also doubtful about his moral and ethical questions. The justice system couldn't play its independent role because of their excessive influence. As expected, when the judicial system is compromised, the crime and corruption rate increased and vice versa.

BB's mismanagement caused the famine in 1974. A certain group of his political insiders controlled the necessities of life: food, medicines, clothes, even fertilizers. Those people changed their fortune, as if hitting a lottery jackpot every week at the cost of millions of lives that were hard hit. The crisis of those necessities was created by black-marketing by the license holders of BB's group only. Everything was available at 10 to 12 times higher than the actual price. People had to live with corruption as a part of their culture.

The Ruthless Assassination: During that terrible moment, many horrible actions took place: assassination after assassination, coup after coup, and so on. The people were so fearful and wondered what was coming next. Indeed, it was a very difficult period for many other reasons. Some of the miscreants didn't return their arms when the liberation war was over. They engaged themselves with robbery, murder, and many other nefarious activities. BB failed to protect himself. Since that was his critical time, for many other reasons, a rebel group of army officers assassinated him, along with most of his family members. Their frustration and wrath revolted in the ruthless assassination of his family. The nation was stunned to silence with mixed reactions by the tragedy of that magnitude. The majority of the people wanted BB to step down from the power. But he didn't want to relinquish his power even though he became extremely unpopular.

Human reaction is so unpredictable and incalculable that it can cause serious damage even for a minor reason. But the corruption, nepotism, and abuse of power are not minor issues. These are far more serious than one could compromise with any easy acceptance.

Needless to say, perhaps that was the reason for such a tragic end. That was a very excruciating price to pay for any power greedy politician. From these terrible actions, we should learn that by abusing power, we may flaunt the rule of law but that the consequences do not forgive anybody. It is a matter of time, place, and circumstance only.

The Most Controversial Figure: Khondakar Mustaq Ahmed was another controversial figure, who was very shrewd but abusive of power. After the assassination of BB, it was very much known that he was behind it, further proved by the assassination of four more high-ranking leaders in jail: Syed Nazrul Islam, Tazuddin Ahmed, Mansur Ali, and Kamruzzaman.

The late Tazuddin Ahmed was prime minister during the liberation war, also known as the Architect of Historic 6-points. All of them made enormous contributions during the liberation war. At that time, justice did not serve as usual. In spite of that, he managed to save millions of lives from that famine. Soon after he took over power, people didn't have to die from starvation anymore. Ahmed made all necessities available in the open market with affordable prices. The criminal license holders went out of business with their grim faces. Circumstantially, it was a huge success for his short period of time.

Advent of Gen. Ziaur Rahman: Then Gen. Ziaur Rahman removed Ahmed from power and put him in jail. That was the blessing period of Bangladesh. This time, justice was about to be served. But people had lots of doubts about the future of the country. I personally, like many others, didn't like to see military rulers take over power. But soon after, he demonstrated that he had a vision and he identified the real problems and solutions. Most importantly, Gen. Rahman was a true believer and tried his best. He very carefully formed his political party, the BNP (Bangladesh Nationalist Party), which was very acceptable to the people. His contribution during the liberation war glorified him greatly.

Unfortunately, lots of his opponents are denying his creditability with the issue of the declaration of the independence of Bangladesh. BB declared the clear direction of independence but not decisively in his famous speeches on March 7th and 25th, 1971 and was arrested. The same night, Pakistani barbaric forces started the genocide, killing many innocent people, including children, students, women, and intellectuals.

Declaration of Independence: in the critical absence of BB, Major Zia not only declared the independence of Bangladesh but also fought in the war-field until full accomplishment. The controversy remains whether he himself declared the independence or he declared it on behalf of BB. It doesn't matter how he did, but that he did. The true historical record is the only answer, not the denial of his declaration.

After the BB's arrest, people were in despair. Major Zia revolted against the Pakistani military leaders with extraordinary courage and declared Bangladesh independent. He gave a new hope and reinvigorated the spirit of the people. And it required tremendous strength for all Bangladeshis to fight against the brutal forces. This was the turning point of real independence. Circumstantially, it was vitally important at that time. I believe that it was **glorious: not a cheap shot.**

It is disgraceful that those who do not want to admit the truth contradict themselves. It was disrespectful when those people denied the truth and engaged themselves with propaganda. It was the mission of all Bangladeshis to fight for liberation and to bring back BB. Eventually, that's what happened. BB should have been appreciative to those people for taking the country forward in his absence. Instead, he targeted those people and was disoriented.

Assassination of Martyr Ziaur Rahman: Then, on May 30, 1981, another terrible assassination took place. Some of the mean spirited, selfish group of army officers assassinated the best leader Bangladesh ever had – Gen. Ziaur Rahman. He was the extraordinary president with the correct vision of peace, progress, and prosperity for the country. His popularity was so extensive that no one else has reached at that level in the history of Bangladesh. The spontaneous reaction of the people after his assassination was clear evidence how beloved and popular leader he was!

Advent of Khaleda Zia: It is undeniable that because of his image, Begum Khaleda Zia continued to materialize his unfinished mission. I do not want to mention Gen. H. M. Ershad, the killer of democracy. He not only conspired to assassinate President Ziaur Rahman but also forcibly took power from the elected president Justice Abdus Sattar. He didn't contribute to the liberation war. He killed so many high-ranking army officers that had a questionable role in the assassination plot of the President Ziaur Rahman. His conspiracy was deeper than people could imagine. He was a tyrant dictator.

His total administration was full of corruption and hypocrisy, very similar to Khondakar Mustaq Ahmed. But for the ineffective judicial system and the loopholes of laws, justice was not meted out to him. His justice is overdue.

In view of the current political drama, I believe no matter how hard the opposition parties' demagogues try to go to power; they all play a very destructive role for the country. They believe in destruction and the obstruction of justice, peace, progress, and prosperity. They shut down the government and public activities. They boycotted themselves from their duties and responsibilities.

They walked out from the parliament for a so-called long march, short march, or whatever. The leaders in the front line who engaged in destruction in the name of demonstration are not leaders at all. They want to politicize their crimes of destruction. They are the elements of severe destruction of our nation. For the greater interest of our country, they should be prosecuted and put on trial. But doing so, it wouldn't be undemocratic, unconstitutional, and unlawful at all. Rather, this would be real justice. This would be the only way to protect the country from those mobsters.

The recent open statement made by one of their so-called leaders to disregard the Supreme Court's order and to continue the violence until the downfall of the current administration is the clear violation of rule of law. Their illegal demand of the resignation of the PM is totally unconstitutional. They are fully responsible for all those deaths and injuries by their misled murderers and gangs. It was not the choice of this administration to use force to restrain them but there was no alternative way to control the situation. No civilized nation would do it differently. Rather, they would take tougher actions against those responsible so-called leaders.

If an ordinary group of people with no affiliation with any political party did the same, they would have been prosecuted. Why is this not the case here? No one should be above or beneath the law. They should be fully accountable for all destruction in the country. I'm so surprised to see that none of their high profiled lawyers, including Dr. Kamal Hussain and their legal advisers, made any statement to stop these unlawful activities of violence and destructions. Rather, they were participants in those destructive demonstrations.

The opposition parties also instigated the minorities with the baseless issues and so on. They never looked for the interests of the country. They wanted to gain everything at the cost of the sufferings of our nation. They should understand the importance of the unity and integrity.

The minorities in Bangladesh are in paradise compared to many other countries in the world, including our neighboring countries. The relationship with the minorities in our country has been very harmonious for several centuries. The minorities are an integral part of our society. They are teachers, doctors, engineers, carpenters, goldsmiths, blacksmiths, and in many other noble services. Without them, our daily lives would be missing a part.

Bangladeshi people never initiated any chaos with any religion; rather they maintain a very peaceful relationship as an integral part of our daily lives. Some propagandists, with the support of opposition parties, are trying to make something out of nothing. This is really very unfortunate. They should look back to the history of our nation with the correct vision and they should stay on the course of peaceful co-existence as always. This is wrong message to send to the rest of the world and damages the image of our nation.

Problems of Extremism: Unfortunately, Bangladesh is facing a new kind of threat of 'extremism'. If this can't be eradicated before further expansion, the misery of the people will have no bounds. When the present administration successfully managed to capture the top leader and many others related to the extremists group, the opposition leader was mocked about saying "It's a drama part-I and part-II" rather than congratulating and praising the capture so successfully. This extremism is no longer a national but an international issue.

When the current administration was praised for such a remarkable success internationally, the opposition leaders were so jealous that they made this kind of comment without using any commonsense. This is a clear indication that they do not believe in any positive outcome. Negativity, pessimism, arrogance, and constant violence are their ways to scare the people and to destabilize the country.

It is not difficult to understand who really they are! The true leaders always cooperate for every positive step taken by their opponents even if they have irreconcilable differences in many issues. That's what leadership is all about. That's how the policy should be made. The cheap rhetoric does not lift them up; rather it puts them down to a great extent.

Characteristics of Real Leadership: When leaders want to convince the people, they must have some basic qualities. They have to be patriot, honest, compassionate, shrewd, and decent in their attitude and behavior, making statements very rationally. They have to have a clear vision, and have to take responsibilities with accountability, respecting each other, even when they are opponents, and be steadfast for the right cause. Missing any of those could have a serious negative impact. I hereby leave it up to the politicians to qualify themselves to gain my support no matter who you are!

The opposition leaders are already lacking all of those elements and have disqualified themselves. They have been already proven the most distrusted ones. The recent comment made by the opposition leader about the health crisis of the president of Bangladesh was so shameful and disgraceful that I wonder if any normal person could agree with her, and again the question is how low she can go.

They forget that they had been in the power. The people tested and rejected them through elections. They didn't carry out any acceptable reforms during their time and this is what they are demanding now from the current administration. It is hard to understand their so-called reforms. Their reforms mean deform everything until or unless they are satisfied. None of their demands are considered to be for peaceful purposes.

The Scenarios of Their Administration: During horrible PM Sheikh Hasina's administration, there was no security of the people. The gangs and god-fathers were overly procreated. The crime rate took a horrible shape. All those nefarious activities were daily phenomena. People were killed for no reason. People were considered lucky if they could return home safely.

During her administration, the investors had to pay terrible price because of her protected gangs. Some investors lost everything, including their own lives. People couldn't even build their houses in their own land. That was a serious setback for the economy and for the creation of job opportunities.

Her Justice System: The justice didn't work for the innocent victims; rather, it protected the ruthless murderers. Many of those leading murderers are still under protection in foreign soil. People were scared to go out while they were always fearful at home too. The law enforcing agencies were within her control. What did she do at that time? She was busy with the retaliatory actions of the past. Absolute security for her, but forgetting the rest of the people.

She disregarded all the laws and orders passed by the previous administrations. She put back the trade mark of her late father on everything. The unprecedented way of abusing the power, the wasteful way of spending the national revenue to meet her selfish desire, of attempting to take over **Ganabhavan** while the real freedom fighters were not rehabilitated, and living in temporary slums. Is this not total disrespect to our heroes?

The Media: The media was her personal propaganda toolbox, fully engaged with the programs of her late father and her own desirable ones. All programs were as if we were in the 1971 war again. These kinds of leaders are national disgrace. If I support this kind of leadership, I would be the guilty for its consequences. I hope people will choose their leaders very carefully.

Modern technology is way beyond the imagination even from a decade ago. Why don't the politicians take the advantage of technology for their campaign rather than shutting down everything with constant violence? Why are they so shy to present better political agendas whatever they have? In fact, they don't have any agendas. Their only agenda is constant violence using the misguided groups of young gangs to get involved in destructions.

The current violence is almost everywhere, including burning the garment industries. They are the ones who taught them to achieve everything with such a violent manner. They should be held accountable for all those destructions. Why don't they limit the public gatherings and avoid the obstructions of the normal course of their activities? Why don't they move with sophistication rather than backdate unruly means? Did they ever calculate how much damage they have caused for the country? If they didn't, how do they expect to gain the support of the people and why should the people support them? They need to redress themselves.

They may erratically argue that they have the democratic right to do anything they want. In their view, democracy means the freedom of destruction, obstruction of peace and progress, violation of rule of law, creation of a miserable situation with constant violence – not the freedom of speech and press in a civil and constructive manner. They don't want real democracy. They believe in atrocity, hostility, and in hypocrisy.

In fact, they want the regression of the past. They want everything at cheaper and more terrible means. They know that the majority of the people do not trust them anymore from their past experience. So they need only certain groups of people who are easily misguided to create any panic or scary situation: burning both government and public properties, shutting down all public activities, throwing bricks or anything to the law enforcing agencies.

When the politicians organize these kinds of violence in the name of surrounding the Secretariat or other important places, this is another clear sickness in the name of politics. If this is the kind of politicians we choose for our leadership, what will the fate of the country be?

All their demonstrations are fully unconstitutional, illegal, and undemocratic. It is absolutely unacceptable. They are the root cause of all that violence and destruction. No civilized nation would allow this. It's very easy to misguide and mislead the people with false rosy and sunny assurances. But the nation will pay the ultimate price.

This nation has the legitimate right to restrain those destructive elements by any means. Now the question is why don't they do that? Because, they don't care for our country! Their children are not studying in this country. They have their secondary foundation on foreign soil. They have already looted our country to make their safe haven in foreign lands, and this is the cost of our national tragedy.

As a matter of fact, they consider this land as their optional one. They have nothing to lose but to gain everything at the cost of the suffering of all walks of life. How did they forget that during their administration, on all counts the situation was far worse than it is today! Their future also remains in serious question.

Now they even do not want to dialogue with the current administration. Rather, they are exchanging so-called letters. This is another laughing part of their drama. This is nothing but the signal of constant major violence.

They are demanding the unconstitutional and undemocratic issue of exclusion of a party or party members to engage in dialogue with those already elected by the people. What kind of democracy is this? They think everything has to be their way or no way. They think they are the only ones who will decide who should be included or excluded. They should know that inclusion is the only way to move forward and exclusion is nothing but falling apart.

I think it is high time for them to question themselves if they really want a peaceful solution and to try to find out the ways to resolve the problems. Ignition of violence is nothing but the problems and sufferings of all people. The violence in the streets, schools, colleges, and universities is not solving the political problems. These are the institutions to build up future generations only. All political parties should stop encouraging the students to become their activists and become involved in violence. Only a few students are the problem for selfish reasons but the rest of them are the potentials of the future of our nation.

Now let's see the difference between the current and their administration. Of course, the current administration is not perfect in many cases but they are moving forward on a priority basis. In spite of constant obstructions by the opposition parties, the current administration is moving toward the right direction and making a significant difference almost in every field – like security, economy, and education.

They have taken the most important issue – security – very seriously. They have tracked down many ruthless murderers using the Rapid Action Battalions (RAB) forces. Some multiple murderers were gunned down in crossfire. This sounds very harsh. But what is the alternative? In any civilized nation, if the criminals challenge the law enforcing agencies, they would do the same. Besides, all those were multiple murderers. Some of them didn't know how many innocent lives they took. All those were protected by their administration. The elimination of those ruthless murderers saved many more innocent from certain death. The protection of those in the name of human rights is nothing but the protection of ugly vicious hyenas against beautiful innocent antelopes.

I profoundly respect human rights. But the human right is for the human only. In real sense, no human is human without any humanity. Those who have any humanity can't kill the innocents in such a horrible way and allow the victims' families to live in indescribable misery for the rest of their lives.

The tougher actions against those thugs have significantly improved security. People started to breathe fresh air from their suffocation. They are no longer threatened for donations or kidnapped as previously. Everybody has started to back to their normal lives. They feel much more secure and safer than in the past.

In my opinion, this is the right direction to secure the people. And this should be continued until the last one is ended. This will send a strong message to the grown up ones. Security itself is the sign of peace, progress, and prosperity. It may be difficult for the opposition leaders to see the real picture with their blurry vision. We don't need that kind of crippled politicians.

On the other hand, the opposition parties are worried about this improvement. Because, this is the obstruction for them to achieve their wishful desires!

The opposition parties are blaming the current administration for the price hike of necessities. This is one of the major problems for all walks of life, especially for the lower income group. But the root cause of this problem is a very complicated one. Normally, when the supply is not enough to meet the demand, the price goes up. But in this case, multiple causes are related to this crisis.

Historically, the government bureaucrats, with the combination of corrupt law enforcing agencies, politicians, and donation collectors are the real cause of this crisis. Sadly, nothing could be done without bribes at any level. If the bribes and donations take place from production to distribution with every movement of commodities, the cost automatically adds up until it reaches the consumers.

In addition, the retailers take additional advantages to make extra profits too. The constant violence by the politicians is fully responsible for shutting down the transportation and production in the name of so-called demonstration. How do they deny that they are not contributing to this crisis? How do they forget that during their time, prices of the necessities were even more unaffordable? They need to treat their dysfunctional memory.

To make the real change, I believe, with the extensive investigation, if all corrupt bureaucrats, law enforcing agencies, politicians, and donation collectors are identified and brought them to justice with no exception, the situation will definitely come under control. They are the elements of this crisis. Their ill-gotten wealth has to cease. This will be the key role for protection and distribution. Without any protection, the distribution will be nothing but throwing everything into the quicksand. Blaming each other will never solve this problem.

I seriously condemn the police brutality in Bangladesh. The recent attacks on journalists are totally unacceptable. I strongly demand the responsible police officers to bring them to justice and to hold them accountable with the maximum extent of law.

The current administration will also be responsible if any of their own members are corrupt. Nobody should have a free pass for corruption. If they want to maintain the difference, they have to set the example by going after their own members too. If not, they will have to pay the painful price as well.

On the other hand, we should educate ourselves to choose the right leaders for our leadership. We need to change the concept of self-centered and a selfish purpose to choose our leaders. We have to look for the national interest, not the personal or regional interest. We don't need any corrupt disgraceful face value. We need to change the political atmosphere to welcome the honest and decent people into our political process, even if they are not as known as much as those corrupt ones.

In order to do that, we don't need to confront those mobsters. The only simple way to reject those who are corrupt is not to vote for them anymore. Our votes are powerful enough to change the course of our nation.

We need to establish the independent justice system that can't be dictated by any outside influence. We need to introduce the 'firing and hiring' process. All corrupt officials have to be replaced immediately with tougher action. Lots of the officials are not eligible to hold those positions in the first place. The capable people are in the shadows because of the notorious influence of the corrupt politicians and bureaucrats.

This is not possible if we can't change our mentality. We have to be patriots with responsibility. We have to be contributors, not solicitors. We have to be positive, not negative. We have to be optimistic, not pessimistic. We have to be protectors, not defectors. We have to move forward, not backward. We have to love our nation with all necessary contributions. If we can do that, our nation will shine by itself and that will be the best way to tribute to those freedom fighters who sacrificed their lives and to the devotees of all Bangladeshis in 1971. If we fail to do so that will be the betrayal to those freedom fighters and contributors.

As we know, one of the great presidents of the United States of America, John F. Kennedy said, *"Ask not what your country can do for you. Ask what you can do for your country."* These few words said everything about the characteristics of a good citizen. But our leaders are saying by their actions, *"Ask not what we did, what we are doing and what we will do. Ask how much more suffering you will be able to endured."*

The historic assassinations of two major leaders left two different images. The current two major parties have inherited their political philosophy from those two leaders. We all know who did what and who they were really! Now it is our choice whom we should support and whom we shouldn't, if we do not have any other choice. The peace and misery will depend on our choice only.

Virtuously, we as a nation believe in self-reliance and self-respect. The highest quality of the human being is to live in dignity. Our culture is so rich that we can make the difference everywhere. Many of our highly talented people are contributing remarkably both nationally and internationally in different fields. In many cases, they are able to maintain the distinction, even in adverse situations. Our people are very ambitious and perseverant. They are doing very well compared to many fortunate nationals. We can be proud of them. They are the potential for our nation and not a burden at all. We need to protect the rest from the evil influence and open up the opportunities for brighter prospects with progressive agendas. However, we have to be very concerned about the growth of our population too. Our population already crossed the capacity of our country long before our independence.

In conclusion, I urge the politicians, please try not to be the selfish ones and to try to do something that the nation can remember you with great honor, not disgrace. Please refrain from all kinds of violence in the name of politics and serve the country the way the nation can proud of you. Also, come forward full of greatness and make the difference.

As citizens, it is crucial for us to choose leaders who can rescue the nation from the current turmoil. When the ship is being navigated safely, the opposition parties are trying to push that ship toward the ice to make something happen, like the ill-fated ship, "The Titanic."

It is up to us to change the direction, not the corrupt politicians. It is our obligation to choose the right captain. It is our responsibility to stay on the course of peace, progress, and prosperity, and to reject those elements of severe destruction in our nation. We also need to hold them accountable for the destruction they are causing every single day.

The Political Volcano of Bangladesh

November, 2006

When our country had one of its proudest moments by winning the Nobel Prize for Peace; when the name of our country was taken by the whole world with great honor; when the country was celebrating the biggest religious holidays with profound joy and best wishes for all; when the sun was shining matching the smiles of millions; when the people left for the remote area of the country to celebrate one of the most significant holidays with their loved ones; when people were embracing each other to forget and forgive their past wrong doings and were wishing for the very best future; and when the children had a chance to get together after a long time missing each other – right at that time, some mean spirited evil politicians carried out such a brutal attack on others that the entire world could not ignore. The ruthless murderers killed 26 people and wounded hundreds more.

Some of their distasteful activists went with oars and poles to exchange the Eid greetings to their leader and their innocent children, and disrespected not only the holy Eid but also degraded them to evil. These kinds of parents are passing the germs of hostility to the next generation in the name of politics. If they are too addicted to politics, why don't they carry their party-symbol boat? I think their boat has sunk and the oar and pole are their last resort. This kind of sickness tells everything about them. Their brutal attack turned their party into a league of the denial of civilization. This kind of behavior crossed the barbarism of barbaric forces of Pakistan in 1971.

This is so unfortunate for us that whenever we watch the news of our country, we hardly hear anything good. The corrupt politicians are the cause of the 158 million people's problems. The peace-loving people are suffering so much that they don't have any breathing room to continue their lives. They are so selfish that they don't care about the country and the rest of the people.

Over the last few weeks, I had little chance to watch the news and other programs of NTV that I really like. But some of the news coverage that I did see was so upsetting.

On a news report, I watched some of the opposition leaders engaging themselves in a physical confrontation with the security forces as they tried to surround the office of the PM. Some of them were wounded, including many misled groups of individuals. I don't have any regret for them. I'm always against police brutality. But at that time, those leaders were fully responsible and earned whatever they deserved. I watched their actions and I couldn't recognize them to be the leaders of any political party. Their rational and moral sickness disqualified themselves altogether.

In a democratic society, I would like to see the engagement of multiple parties for the common interest of the country. But none of them has a minimum standard of quality to lead the people in the right direction. All of them were so outrageous that they wanted to gain everything at the costs of the serious destruction of national resources and the obstruction of the normal activities of the public by shutting down the government and private businesses.

In an another news report before that, I did see that some of the prominent leaders of the opposition parties had made some serious igniting statements and repeatedly uttered that the entire country would be blazed if there was no reforms. This kind of statement was enough to have them locked up in jail. It was so offensive and destructive that it could lead to instigate the violators to become engaged in serious destructions. In fact, that's what exactly happened.

A few days later, I watched other news coverage where some angry people burnt vehicles and properties because of the acute problems with the gas and electricity. I absolutely agree with their cause but I certainly couldn't agree with their destructive activities. All this is happening because of the corrupt bureaucrats and destructive politicians.

I don't care who takes control in the upcoming election. But I do care about the right kind of leaders who could work better for the country.

Unfortunately, those kinds of leaders are missing in almost all parties. Most of them are inept and corrupt.

The opposition parties have been demanding reforms throughout their entire terms, without any constructive plans and programs that people could support. They are so desperate for reforms that they think that so-called reforms themselves would help them for a miracle change to win the election. The reality is, to gain the popularity and trust is far more important than the so-called reforms or deforms.

They can't trust the interim government as the constitutional basis. They want to deform the constitution and make their wishful amendments until or unless they are certain about their victory without any popularity. Instead of presenting any popular agenda, they have chosen an easy way to win the election. Everybody is aware of their plan. History itself is the testimony of their past behavior. These are the same group of people who are so desperate to take power and are doing everything we see in their actions and words.

In the concluding session of the parliament, they acknowledged themselves that 80 percent of times, they had been absent in the parliament because they couldn't go along with the outgoing administration. If so, what did they do rest of 20 percent of their times? Isn't it true the rest of the 20 percent, they planned to walkout for long or short march, countrywide demonstration, destruction of government and private properties, shut down everything, seriously obstruct production and normal activities. The rest of the 80 percent of their times, they executed all those destructive activities. This was their only performance during the last term as the opponents.

If everything is taken into an account, what was their performance in their last term as opponents and what was the result? If we take it as zero, it would be wrong because they did nothing but destroy. Their performance was way below naught. If that was the case, wasn't it a total waste of the budget that we spent for them? Aren't they fully responsible? Is this not our responsibility to hold them accountable? Wasn't it their moral obligation not to enjoy any salaries and benefits, including facilities? Despite doing all that destruction, is this not a shame for them to ask for the votes to the people? The public voted last time for to do anything but destroy.

They gave us enough violence, destruction, and non-cooperation with the outgoing administration with each issue from day one. I believe if they analyze their performance, they should be ashamed for their past performances. They should look for the exit door from this kind of destructive politics.

I don't know about their winning strategy. It looks like they are trying hard to get the foreign votes rather than the national votes. They are trying hard to get foreign support, having frequent meetings with the diplomats with negative campaigns of the outgoing administration.

We know that a good family never discloses their domestic problems to others and tries to resolve it by themselves. But the opposition parties, especially the AL, are doing exactly the opposite. What a shame! For the greater interest of our nation, we should reject them altogether to protect our national interest. These kinds of leaders are so cheap that they could be bought and sold very easily. They are not trusted at all. They don't even honor the views of those diplomats and intellectuals who are engaged to resolve the problems. Now they are so aggressive against the interim government. The interim government is acting absolutely on the basis of our constitution.

They failed to use the most controversial one, the former dictator Gen. H.M. Ershad. They wanted to use him as their trump card. Both parties equally made him relevant while he was totally irrelevant. They gave him the opportunity to bargain his position. He took the biggest opportunity to demand his desirable goal, instead of facing his fair justice. They freed him from all serious charges and he widened his notorious moves again. He was the killer of democracy and he is our national disgrace. His corruptions and shameful scandals were way beyond the modern history of our nation. He is a nasty joke. His misdirected Bidhisha, lost her direction with the phony affair with him. His former first dictator controversial woman is trying to regain her previous position after longtime isolation, but just for political gains only.

When both parties managed to put him in jail, why did they release him without proper justice? Instead of real justice, they made him an important figure in the political platform. Knowing all about him, a significant number of people are supporting him and trying to make him more important than other parties are. I think if the justice system worked properly, he should have been in jail at least for the rest of his life for the crimes he committed. The mystery of the justice system is losing its importance and remains questionable to most people.

I believe that if we support him, we will degrade ourselves as a nation. We shouldn't forget his darkest regime in the history of Bangladesh. Some of his so-called supporters irrationally argue that during his time, he beautified our capital city Dhaka. This is nothing but a narrow view. This is like making a fancy gate in the front, leaving behind a big dark hole.

When the country was suffering with his tyrant dictatorship and he became the Marcos of Bangladesh with extreme corruption, people couldn't express their views. They had no rational basis to support him and they even let him to play his political role in Bangladesh. He was very good at false acting. Sometimes he used to go to the mosque and to other so-called priests and act like a nice guy. He used to visit the poor and make fake emotional speeches to fool the people. He committed so much impeachable crime but no one could say anything against him.

The interim government has the authority to take any kind of action against any destructive movement by any politicians and political parties. It is their solemn responsibility to exercise their duties and responsibilities based on the constitution of our country. Any kind of violation by any party should be taken seriously for the greater interest of our country. This country has lost a lot and can't afford anymore. I, on behalf of the peace loving people of Bangladesh, condemn all kinds of destructive activities and strongly demand justice with the maximum extent of our laws. We don't want our laws confined in the leather binding volume. We want their proper application.

Before I conclude, I would like to figure it out where should we go now?

Let's see the difference between two current leading leaders.

Both of them are common in many ways with sharp distinction. They are both women. They are special on their own. They inherited their political philosophy from their ancestors: one of them from her late father and the other from her late husband. Both of those leaders were assassinated. One of them paid too high a price for some of his political miscalculations. The other one paid the ultimate price from some evil conspirators. Both of them left two different images.

The current two leaders are persistent enough to move forward with their inherited vision. One of them failed to diagnose the causes of the successes and failures of her late father and his tragic end, and the other one is trying to move forward with her late husband's dream. The corrupt and arrogant ones overwhelmingly misguided one of them, and the other one had to compromise with many corrupt ones as well with no choice.

The total political environment is not immune from the stronghold of the corrupt leaders. One of them looks pretty cautious and the other one is naturally uncomplimentary. One of them inclined to dialogue or to negotiate, the other one simply declined almost everything but her awful demand.

Both of them had a chance to obtain power and we experienced ourselves their administrative styles. One of their times, the entire country was full of gangs, donation collectors, and ruthless murderers. There was no security of life and we had to compromise with those horrible gangs. The other one tried to change that and took some strong measures against those killers and gangs and made a significant progress.

The other one was not happy at all and became too critical. She wanted to re-establish her gangs and her cronies and engaged in terrible destructive activities throughout her entire term. The current violence is also their continual process. Their behavioral difference is also noticeable. On top of that, they look different too. This is the reflection of their personality as well.

Our Demand

Our demand is for peace, progress, and prosperity
These should be only our utmost priority.

The peace loving Bangladeshis want only peace and justice
These are replaced by with the total injustice.

The corrupt politicians and bureaucrats are so greedy
They lost their total morality and dignity.

They are so horror and terror in their words and action
They are the biggest enemies of our nation.

Their decision in the upcoming election is only destruction
That's why they are acting so wild with no justification.

The whole world watched their recent horrible violence
How do the people of Bangladesh can remain silent?

Our responsibility is to bring them to justice with no violence
Let the justice decide their fate with their guidelines.

The peace loving Bangladeshis can't act like them
Use our strong laws to restrain them to end.

Their crimes are so horrible and so terrible
No one could think about that it is forgivable.

Our mission will be only for the peace
The enemies themselves will be broken in pieces.

They are the ruthless murderers as we have seen
We don't have any other choice but to lock them up in.

Our demand is to punish them all with the fullest extent of law
The leaders should be listed on top of all.

With all those differences and their latest hostile violence, you do not have to be a rocket scientist to decide whom should you vote for and whom you shouldn't. It is your responsibility to make the right choice. Otherwise, you will have to pay a serious price in a future that you haven't experienced before.

May God bless Bangladesh and protect its people and its sovereignty from those evil destructionists!

The Political Purification of Bangladesh

During the last BNP administration, we also experienced the activities of other political parties. During that period, we have seen how badly they hated each other and saw them acting with the utmost non-cooperation. We saw them as if enemies of each other instead of opponents. They have abused the democracy and the constitution of Bangladesh. As a result, our country and the innocent people have suffered.

After the independence of Bangladesh, we experienced the ruling flavors of both major parties and military dictatorships. The current political players of those parties are of the same ingredients blended with a few added chemicals. They shamelessly rebuked each other and did everything the worst of the worst that Bangladesh has ever experienced. They are very good at distorting the people.

The corruption, destruction, nepotism, and abuse of power were not uncommon to them. The only difference was the scale of violence, destruction, and constant obstruction of the peaceful living conditions of the people. The life of any human being did not matter to them at all. Their hostile behaviors claimed many lives with their symbolic weapons, poles, oars, and other sharp weapons in the name of politics, in an unprecedented way.

If we really want to eliminate those savage practices, we need to create a sound political environment. We have to stand against them and bring them to justice for the undeniable crimes they have committed. We can't allow those savage practices any more in the 21st century. We need to move forward with clear vision. It will be a big challenge for us. But someone has to come forward to start this noble mission.

The current political circumstance is the high time to do so. Since the political parties failed to protect our constitution, their outcries cannot be counted.

They forced the interim government into an emergency and this is the opportunity for a new political direction. We are already tired of their destructive politics. We need a new direction. I applaud the steps taken by the caretaker government (CG). They have arrested the corrupt politicians, fired corrupted bureaucrats, apprehended the gangs, and recovered the unauthorized government properties occupied illegally by the corrupt groups. These are certainly positive steps to moving forward.

Since the election process has already collapsed due to the hostile politicians, it doesn't matter how long it takes to hold the election. But we need a free, fair, and credible election. In order to do that, voter ID and National ID cards are extremely important. This will prevent false and proxy votes. Since the previous irregularities are so extensive, it can't be fixed overnight. Let them take as long as they need so that the elected government won't have to deal with those problems anymore.

We need to reestablish the justice system. It must be independent and shouldn't be influenced by any political party or by corrupt bureaucrats.

I totally disagree with those unhappy politicians about the current actions taken by the CG. To them, it looks like the constant destruction and violence are the democratic rights of those destructive politicians. The provocative statements and horrific violence of the past were not unnoticed by us. The violence with the poles, oars, and other sharp weapons and the threat of civil war should not be ignored nor forgiven. They killed nearly 100 people and wounded hundreds more in a single day. The justice of those responsible criminals should be taken seriously by the CG as well.

If we could successfully fix those problems, I believe many decent people would come forward to participate in our political process. We can't compromise with the corrupt and destructive politicians. Rather we have to hold them accountable case by case for their past behavior. That's how the nation will move in the new direction.

Under the above circumstances, in response to the open letter of

Dr. Muhammad Yunus, I, with great honor support and welcome him and many others alike to participate in the upcoming election to rescue the country and our nation at large.

We, as the citizens of Bangladesh, should take a different position to change the course our country. We need to educate ourselves to make the right choice in the upcoming election. If we fail to do so, only the God knows what the fate of our country would be.

May Allah bless Bangladesh and its people from those destructionists! – Amen.

The Comprehensive Rebuttal of the Political Purification of Bangladesh

In response to the open letter of Dr. Muhammad Yunus, I openly responded in support of his political participation during the emergency period. Indeed, I gave the reasons why I did that and why the country needed his political participation at this critical moment. I received much feedback with their reactions and views. Some of them are supportive, some of them are critical, and many others are concerned about his political risk as an honorable person like him. I equally respect them all except the one who was so critical with stark madness and dirtiness.

Some of them expressed their challenging views of the legitimacy of his political participation during the emergency period. Some of them mentioned his banking system with the high rate of interest, etc. I may not agree with them the way they've criticized him, but I value their concerns as well. I believe in rational and ethical opinions — not the daftness.

I certainly can't agree with those who believe that the monkeys and parrots can read their fortunes. I can't agree with those who believe in misdirecting peers; woman or child or any others alike. Millions of people are misdirected by so-called peers like Aat Roshi or others. Many of the so-called corrupt politicians, including former tyrant dictator H. M. Ershad, are followers of that misdirecting peer! You might not have forgotten that in 1981, some of his followers collected the urine of camels for their wishful purposes! These awful people will vote to change the outcome of the election too.

I know it is very nerve-racking to those people because they are already radicalized. Many of them are benefitted both politically and financially by misleading the general people. They already got brainwashed by those leading figures with fallacious and radical ideologies. There is no religious significance to follow them for the divine causes.

Some of the wicked followers get together and start business for political and financial gains. They target only those innocent and take advantage of the simplicity of those who easily get motivated by their tricks. They are very organized. Most of them do not exercise their reasoning to be part of them. That's how they are so successful to misguide the ordinary people. Eventually, some of them get ridiculed themselves with added superstitions and spread the mythical germs to the rest.

Those people overemphasize their faith in paradoxical actions, not The Almighty Creator. I'm neither a theological nor an Islamic scholar or very knowledgeable about the spiritual matter. But my commonsense rejects the practices of those so-called peers. I believe the quest of knowledge about the purpose of divine and self-purification may lead us to get closer to The Almighty, our Creator — not the superstitions.

The corrupt politicians and some misdirecting groups carry out the banner of religion with different myths and use their own ideological formula to mislead the people. This is a very dangerous sign for all mankind. All kinds of extremism we see are the result of those groups only.

Besides, they don't need a massive number of people to serve their purpose. They need to use very few violent groups to scare the rest. What is the use of those vast rational voters, those who can't even cast their votes? Who disfranchised them? What is the impact of those irrational voters? Is it very difficult to congregate those people to manifest them for destructive purposes? What was our political scenario before the emergency period? What more do we need to see? What kind of attack was that on the dark day of October 28, 2006, in the history of Bangladesh? Who organized that hyena's attack on others and under whose direction? What kind of human beings are they who carried out such an attack in broad daylight and danced on the bodies they killed on that day?

Instead of demanding the justice of those horrible evil leaders, people support their leadership! Their so-called leader made an argument that "if our people get killed by the opponents, what our people should do?" Is this not a hyena's like provocation? I really don't know what kind of world we are living in. What does the general public want? What was their past experience? Who can they trust? Do they have any leader that they really like or do they have to go without any choice? Do they need any change? If they do, what kind of change do they want? Do they have any clear answers to all those questions or will all those remain questions with no answers?

The criticism is good with constructive views to make the right choice. But any misleading irrational criticism could cause the adverse effect to our people. The current situation is so different than the past; for the greater interest of our country, it became inevitable to make a different choice. In order to make our right choice, we have to be careful whom we can trust and who will be able to lead us better than the past? Our choice will change the course of our country. It could be too good or too bad. But we all hope for the best. We can't blame anyone else for any consequence, if we make any wrongful choice. Any irrational choice will have a serious consequence as we have seen in the past. I totally reject any form of erratic and senseless views.

In light of the above, I have profound support for Dr. Muhammad Yunus and his party "Nagarik Shakti" (Citizens' Power). I believe it will be worthier for Bangladesh if we get more people like him to join him in the upcoming election process. His policies may not be perfect but could be relatively better than the past. I don't mean that everybody has to be a Nobel Prize winner. There are many others in Bangladesh who are noble and know how to contribute — not to take everything away. These are the people we need for real change.

As one of the great presidents of the United States of America, John F. Kennedy said, *"Ask not what your country can do for you. Ask what you can do for your country?"* I want to see that our leaders and all of us should follow this principle. In order to do that, we need to improve our moral and ethical standard. We ought to reject our selfishness, jealousy, anger, and animosity and embrace the fairness with the willingness to serve our country with innovative ideas and well thought of plan.

Unfortunately, those are in the shadows. They can't serve the country for the lack of suitable political environment. As a result, all peace-loving people are in hostage by those selfish and horrible politicians. If we can change that environment, we will see them out of the shadows. Just for the name and fame, Dr. Muhammad Yunus neither needs to be the prime minister nor the president of Bangladesh. He has already achieved something that many others can't even dream of. Specially, the current political players are already tested. But our country and our nation didn't get as much as we expected. Over and over, the general public was misled by them.

I don't want to talk about him too much because he is already known to everyone. The whole world recognized him as a man of peace, progress and prosperity. We as a nation are so proud of him. When he sincerely intended to serve the country with the request of the people then the critics started to raise lots of questions, mostly influenced by those destructive political parties and their activists! Of course, that's the way politics is, and he will have to face those challenges too. But the exaggerations of anything with irrational analysis will lead us to the detrimental direction.

Some of the propagandas are already buzzing around us about his Nobel Prize. Some radical groups are saying that he won the Nobel Prize because the Norwegian telecommunication and technological companies have a major share with Grameen Phone who is the one who awarded him this prize. These radicals are totally misguided by a certain group and even they don't hesitate to criticize him with total insanity. They think the Nobel Prizes are available in the dollar store. Why don't they go there and buy one of their own? These are the people who will cast the votes too and will prevent the genuine intellectual voters and the politicians with an extreme form of violence.

The true leaders have to be compassionate and tough. To judge him with negative views will be nothing but a mistake. His success with his mission can't be ignored with his tough policy. The tough training in the army sometimes seems to be very unendurable but success lies behind it. The successful trainees can see the opportunity of achieving their goals as long as they continue the discipline they learned in their training period. Failure to do so leads to failure and being unsuccessful all along.

To reach the most unfortunate ones to uplift their living condition is a unique and noble mission. His success is undeniable. To criticize his tough policies are re-thinkable. Unproductive talks and wrongful analysis are deplorable. To lend money with no security is unthinkable. To change the life of those neglected ones is admirable. To deny the truth is nothing but horrible. The change of the living condition of millions of the needy is not an accident. The critics should look at their own faces and show us what kinds of noble activities they are involved in and their achievement. If you can show something better than him I will not only support you but also will pay the same honor to you.

Since I openly supported him, one of them used such provocative and freaky, dirty language that I can't mention here because the decency matters to me. He already proved himself who really he is! And he is totally irrelevant to me. I think the readers won't mind if I write something funny about him, which will be part of a lesson for him and others alike.

Before I do that, I would like to respond to a very important issue related to the true history of our country. I absolutely agree with this and it is very crucial. It is so important for our current and future generations. In fact, history should be based on facts. Anything else is nothing but fairytale or fiction. The pick and choose of denying the truth is not the history. It's a parody. This kind of parody will carry out the wrongful messages for generations to come. The true history will help us to know the problems and consequences of the past and the causes of ups and downs of our previous leaders. We shouldn't react based on "what" but also based on "why." We should not forget our own history and shouldn't ignore the consequences that we have already seen in the past. If we do, the consequence will not ignore us.

The false and fabricated history will mislead the future generations and will be obstructive for corrective behavior. I do not believe in any hidden history. Everything has to be crystal clear. The true history shouldn't be based on a convenient and inconvenient basis. I know the truth is very sweet when it is convenient and is too bitter when it is against our interest. Only high moral and ethical people could accept the truth in all situations.

The emergency under the current caretaker government is totally different than the past. The caretaker government is doing their best to conduct a free, fair, and credible election. This is their commitment. In order to control the situation, they are cracking down the corrupt bureaucrats, politicians, and their gangs. It is absolutely necessary and should continue until the genuine politicians and voters are comfortable to participate in the upcoming election.

The participation in the election during this emergency period should not be an obstruction at all. As the current emergency is for a limited time, unlike the past dictatorships, the political participation is quite legitimate. The caretaker government should go beyond the last administrations as well. No previous administrations should have a free pass to get away from their criminal activities of the past and there shouldn't be any off limit. All those big criminals have to be brought to justice.

I just expressed my reaction the way I came across the opinions I received. Now I would like to talk about someone as I mentioned above. The comment he made about Dr. Muhammad Yunus and I that is legally challengeable. I want to take him to the court. Don't be scarred — not the real court. It's his family court.

I've decided to hire a judge from one of his young children, if any, and all of his family members including his brothers and sisters and certainly his parents as well. They will be the jurors. If he is from nowhere, I don't want to know anything about his origin. I know if I hit the dirt real hard it will splash in a broader area and will get worse. The smart way to control the dirt is just put some bleach on it and it will die down by itself. I believe in decency and he believes in indecency. Because that's the way he is. Now I don't want to embarrass him mentioning his full name here. I want to give him a chance to correct himself no matter how degraded a person he is! You know who you are! Don't you?

Well, Mr. (S...), follow the instructions step by step. You are the defendant and I'm the plaintiff. The court is in your own house. I'll not attend there. So you don't have to worry too much. This sounds very funny. Isn't it? Now I will give you a little responsibility. Please go to the dinner table with all of them, enjoy your good food, and create a very pleasant momentum. Take this approach as my generosity to you, as against your provocative behavior.

At the end, you represent yourself and my writing itself will represent me. You know what I mean. Don't you? Let me make it little bit clear to you. You present them the copy of your writing and mine as well. Now you have nothing to do. Just wait for the verdict. Don't forget to look at their facial expressions. Don't be a coward. Be a man with manly spirit. Please do it. I believe if you are from a good family you will be disgraced so badly — if not rejected from your family. I hope you have children. If you do, they will know who you really are! And you, as a disgraceful father, can't raise your head forever. I know that you don't have the guts to do that and you will not.

You also tried to define that Dr. Muhammad Yunus and I are tied up with Jamat Party. Your guess is like a freakish compounder of a lame practitioner. Your brain is fully loaded with the germs of fanaticism, provocation, violence, negativity, pessimism, arrogance, hatred, and full of dirty genes instead of rational and peaceful elements. My simple advice to you is to replace this harmful garbage with the rational elements of peace, progress, prosperity, positivity, optimism, patience, and love. Love yourself, your children, your family, friends, neighbors, your country, and your nation at large. If you can do that you will see the significant difference in your horrible life. I hope that it will heal your serious rational and behavioral sickness. Well, get well. Until then you are quite irrelevant.

Remember, when the light appears the darkness disappears. Keep the lights on and you will see the darkness is gone. Once you are out of the darkness, never get back there and don't get lost again.

I also hope that will happen in your life, and your family will strive hard to make it happen in your horrible life.

I believe the readers will understand the cause of my reaction and the rest of them will also be refraining from this sort of insanity and vilification in the future. This will enhance their rational judgment and will lead to rejection of their horrible leaders. Criticize constructively with decency and never deny the truth. The decency will lift you up to a great extent and indecency will put you down to the lowest scale.

Finally, my sincere thanks to all of you and let's wish for the best and be part of the peace, progress, and prosperity of our country, our nation, and all mankind in the world.

Mohammed D. Hussain

If I Could Agree With the Former Prime Minister

April, 2007

Recently, the British Broadcasting Corporation (BBC) and the Canadian Broadcasting Corporation (CBC) interviewed our former PM of Bangladesh Sheikh Hasina about her current political crisis. I had the opportunity to listen those programs and I could not agree with her response and answers due to the following reasons:

She very confidently stated that all the charges brought against her for the extortion of money and the murders of October 28, 2006 are false and fabricated. This is nothing but conspiracy. I hope she is right and will be able to defend herself from those charges. But those charges are very serious for a PM or a political leader of any country.

I don't want to jump on the conclusion that she committed those crimes but as a citizen of Bangladesh, I'm concerned if those charges are true. If proven true, she will have to face justice no matter who she is, with no exception. No one should be above or beneath the law.

She claimed herself that during her period, Bangladesh had a golden time and her administration deserves that creditability. She also claimed that during her administration, the economy of the country was the best of all other administrations. I wish she was right about it. But I'm not sure if the people of Bangladesh would agree with her. She didn't mention the security of the people and the country during her administration.

I believe that if she was right about whatever she said, she would have been the PM of Bangladesh forever. Why did the people reject her? Why is she facing problems to be re-elected? Why she was leading her party with absolute violence? If I could trust her, I would have been one of her supporters. Of course, I will give the reasons why I can't support her.

First, she was wrong about everything she said. During her administration, there was no security of life or wealth. It was a tense period in the history of Bangladesh.

The economy was crippled for her fiscal irresponsibility. The ruthless murderers were in every nook and corner. The gangs were overly procreated under her protection. People considered themselves lucky if they returned home safely. The donation collectors were protected by the law enforcing agencies. Corruption was higher than any at any other time of our history. The justice system did not work independently. Corruption was the only way of living and the innocent and peace-loving people were their easy victims. All kinds of horrible and terrible activities were common phenomenon. The demand for justice for the innocents was out of question; rather they were threatened to death. That was the style of her administration. Yes, that was the golden period only for the corrupt politicians, bureaucrats, and her cronies and gangs. I think that's what she was talking about.

She also claimed that on October 28, 2006, her people were attacked first and four of her activists were killed. I condemn those killings if there were any, regardless of any party. But why didn't she even demand justice? Instead, in her statement, she said, if her people were attacked what they to do were. Is this not a clear signal to go ahead and kill the opponents? After that unprecedented incident, she and her political companions didn't stop their violence with poles and oars. They continued to threaten that horrific style of demonstrations constantly and the public was in hostage.

Her party-symbol is the "boat" not the poles and oars. Her father didn't use those against Pakistani dictators but the demonstrations were far more effective than this deadly violent tactics. I think she knows that her boat is sunk. The poles and oars were her last resort.

Under the CG, when the situation came under control and those charges were brought against her, she now blames the others. This is the most evil-doing I can ever expect from any politician. This is nothing but total arrogance.

She also mentioned about her father's ultimate sacrifice for the people of Bangladesh. I hope the Bangladeshis didn't forget their history. With all due respect to her father, I would like to say that the general people of Bangladesh didn't assassinate him in such a horrible way. Rather, the people sacrificed their lives to liberate the country and be freed from barbaric Pakistani war criminals. His created rebels assassinated him because of his political and moral miscalculations. In that light, he didn't sacrifice his life for the people.

He dramatically lost his popularity and trust of the people. The majority of the people wanted him to step down from the power. His own companions started to form new parties and so on. But he left no stones unturned to stay in power forever. That was the cause of his tragic end, and everyone of Bangladesh was stunned to silence with mixed reactions after that assassination. The painful aspect was that as a politician, he ascended like a superman but descended like a rollercoaster.

Indeed, if she is wrong about everything, she is not right about anything.

She also said that she was ready to sacrifice her life for the people. I respectfully would like to remind her that you don't have to sacrifice your life. The smart way to gain the power is to earn the popularity and trust of the people first. If you can do that, people might bring you back to power. But the damage you have already caused is quite irreversible. The provocative statement will not help you but will ruin your ambition and your image, just as it already has.

I most respectfully request you to look at the rear view mirror to learn from your own history and to correct yourself and let the people live peacefully under the new able leadership.

The Consequence of Unfair Deals

Whenever something awful happens to anyone, we react very passionately toward the victims. But in our real life, we hardly care about the cause and effect.

Recently, we have seen that ruthless murders killed one of the female Supreme Court's advocates. This is certainly a very disturbing incident and our condolences are to the victim, her family, and to all her well-wishers. It's really shocking for all of us, and we must try hard to control this kind of horrible crime with the utmost application of our laws and justice. These evils can't be eliminated altogether but we can significantly reduce this kind of horrible crime with exemplary punishment with the strict enforcement of our laws.

Conversely, we have to find out the cause of those problems as well. Prevention is better than cure. Most of the crimes are committed because of excessive frustration. Frustration leads to anger, and anger leads us to lose the proper judgment. Losing judgment can cause horrible violence or even murder. Sometimes some of the individuals manifest it and sometimes it is manifested collectively. But it does not require the actions of the mass population. Only a few or a single person are enough to carry out any horrible deeds. We have many examples in our daily lives. This spreads from the individual level to the national level and beyond. This is extremely dangerous for all human beings.

Most unfortunately, the innocent are the easy victims and sufferer more than the real criminals do. Nothing happens out of nothing. Every effect must have a cause. But we hardly deal with the cause. When something happens, we react based on the conclusion. We try to find the criminals and demand justice, which we should. But that does not stamp out re-occurrence of the same. All those are happening from anger. We cannot measure the level of anger until something happens in consequence. When something happens, it is too late to recover.

In our daily lives, we have to interact with multiple businesses. All of us have some sort of profession. Now the question, how respectful we are to our professionalism? Are we really fair enough with our professional behavior? Do we want to take undue advantage from our clients? Do we exploit our clients with unnecessary excuses? These are very relevant questions in Bangladesh.

Many of the lawyers, doctors, government and private officials, and manpower agencies exploit their clients with malpractice. Some of them are directly involved in falsification and fabrication. They demand an excessive amount of money from their clients, and in many cases, they fail to protect their clients or fail to achieve the expected outcomes due to their false commitments. The clients lose their means with their excessive suppression and they don't get their expected outcome. These kinds of practice cause the anger and frustration of these people. They do not get justice. Some of them become extremists. As a result, they do not hesitate to construct a terrible plan to carry out horrible murders and so on without understanding the consequences.

As stated by the apprehended ruthless murderers, it is likely to be clear that the murdered advocate didn't have a fair deal with her clients and scared them into calling the police, if they further raised their issue. As a result, their anger level went beyond their control and led to kill her in such a horrible way.

Of course, this is unacceptable. But she could have avoided that tragedy, if she had been respectful to her profession. We do not know whether their statement is true or false. But one thing is true – she lost her life. Many others of the same profession are doing the same but not necessarily does everybody pay the same price. But who knows who, how and when they may pay their price too. We, as a human being, engage in different professions and we should be respectful to our ethical duties. As we become so greedy, we hardly care about our moral and ethical values and potential consequences, and we become corrupt.

Indeed, there is reward and consequence for everything we do in our lives. Every good work makes our lives better and rewarding, and vice versa. One way or other, we have to pay the price for any malpractice. That price is sometimes very painful, and it is too late to pay it off by alternative means. I hope those who are not respectful to their profession learn some lessons from this horrible murder. I believe we have to be careful whenever we interact with others. We need to be respectful to our professional duties and manner to protect ourselves from any unintended consequences. Honesty is the best policy may sound clichéd but it is proven in real life.

This reminds me of some of my interactions with the private, legal, medical, and government official communities. I have had different experiences dealing with them. Some of them were pleasant and some of them were disappointing. It was not because of the success and failure. It was because of how they dealt with me.

Success and failure are parts of our life. But life goes on. We need to control ourselves in all circumstances. Our moral and ethical judgments themselves can resolve most of our problems. We don't need to go to the court to decide our issues. Our sound conscience and rational exercise are enough to make our life much better – rather than confronting with each other.

Justice should play its role without any prejudice and should be open to all. We must be respectful to the rule of law and must respect ourselves with the best moral and ethical fitness.

The Black Badge Against the Justice!

First, I would like to congratulate the CG of Bangladesh for taking the courageous steps in arresting the corrupt leaders and the former PM, Sheikh Hasina, an untrustworthy and the most violent politician in the history of Bangladesh.

We all know that no one is above or beneath the law. In that principle, it is imperative to bring her to justice for the allegations brought against her. There shouldn't be any scope to politicize the crimes. She was arrested for a series of extortions of an incredible amount of money and many other serious charges are yet to follow. If she is found guilty, then she has to face justice with no exception. We, as citizens of our country, should respect the rule of our law. The obstruction of justice in the name of politics is deplorable for our country and our people. Justice shouldn't be reconciled with the hostile, corrupt, and violent politicians and their supporters.

Everyone has the solemn legal right for self-protection and she should get all those rights under our legal guidelines. But the misleading political outcry by her supporters is not the voice of the rest of the nation. There are about 158 million people in our country. Most of us are peace loving and believe in justice. If there is no justice, there is no peace. We believe in peace and justice, and we reject the ideas of violence and corruptions. We may not go out to the streets but our support for justice remains strong.

We already have a lot of experience from those leaders and they are not unknown to us. Knowing about all their past destructive and criminal behaviors, how can we stand by them and support their release unconditionally? In other words, is this not to establish the injustice as against the justice? Is this not unnecessary violence against the peace?

We believe in democracy, which allows us freedom speech – not the freedom of violence, destruction, and obstruction of the peace and progress of our country. We believe in the transparency of our political activities that have a direct impact on our economy, education, culture, justice, and beyond. If we can improve our political culture, we will see the significant difference in our lives.

We need to strengthen our international relations with the rest of the world through honest diplomacy for the greater mutual interest of our country – not of a certain group of people or political parties. Our domestic problems have to be resolved by our own constitution and laws with their proper application.

It is both a shame and dangerous for us if we depend on others to interfere in our domestic problems. It is like inviting third parties disclose our domestic problems. This could be a serious threat to the security and sovereignty of our country and our nation. In fact, it is. If we believe in ourselves, we can resolve our own problems and that's the way it ought to be.

Why Our Politicians have Failed: First, we have to understand what leadership means. I believe leadership means to take responsibility with the trust and accountability. A true leader has to dedicate his or her services for the cause of the greater interest of the country. He or she has to remain loyal to the country with their words and actions. Good leadership needs a strong sense of principles with the utmost devotion to preserve the unity and integrity of the people for the greater interest of the country. They should respect the rule of law by themselves and apply those laws to the individuals without any prejudice.

Unfortunately, our politicians formulated their corrupt mission and did everything we have seen. Obviously, they have the stronghold to some levels – those who are the sharers of the same practice and enjoy the undue advantages in multiple ways. Of course, it is painful for them when they are being caught one by one. Of course, they have some international hotlines to support them. They also have the means to campaign their propaganda and so on. Now even we can see some of our so-called intellectual communities have also chosen to take the side against the justice. Do we have to compromise with them and let them get away without justice just because they are known as so-called intellectuals?

With all due respect to the teachers association of the University of Dhaka, I would like to ask you where you where when the country was facing absolute violence, destruction, and murder in the name of politics. Did you ever wear any black badge against those nefarious activities? Did you raise your voice against constant violence; walk out from the parliament for a long or short march or whatever with extreme violence? Now you're raising your voice, wearing the so-called black badge against the justice. What does it mean? Is this the voice of the majority of the peace loving people of Bangladesh? Well, I'm not educated enough to teach you but let me quote a few words of one of the great leaders and the first President of the United States, General George Washington. President Washington cautioned in his farewell address to the Union:

"A passionate attachment of one nation for another produces variety of evils, because it leads to concessions to the favorite nation of privileges denied to others; which is apt doubly to injure the nation making the concession, both by unnecessarily parting with what ought to have been retained, and by exciting jealousy, ill-will and disposition to retaliate, in the parties from whom equal privileges are withheld. It gives to ambitious, corrupted, or deluded citizens (who devote themselves to the favorite nation). Real patriots who may resist the intrigues of the favorite are liable to become suspected and odious, while its tools and dupes usurp the applause and confidence of the people to surrender their interest."

This was true hundreds of years ago, it is true now, and it will remain true forever. This is true not only for the leaders of the United States of America, but also for any other country in the world. I think our intellectuals won't make any mistakes and they shouldn't. This is not the act of the real intellectuals. This is the act of the disgraced or astonishingly twisted ideologists.

If we do not learn from our repeated saddest history, we will never learn and we can't change ourselves, no matter what our destiny will be. Our failed politicians already paid a very high price for their political miscalculations and moral and ethical violations in the past and that will continue unless they do not learn from our history.

In light of the above, I, as an ordinary citizen, urge our citizens please to be in favor of justice, not in favor of destructive tactics. Reject the violent and corrupt politicians altogether and hold them accountable. Reject the selfish desires and embrace the wisdom. Reject the hostility and atrocity and embrace the peace and prosperity. Reject the violence and obstruction of justice and demand the justice. You could choose to be anything but choosing the injustice is the clear act of evils.

We need to support the CG to do the right thing for the greater interest of our country. Our national interest is far more important than your personal corrupt ideas and mission. As the highest educational institution of our country, we expect the light that can enlighten the future of our current and next generations. We do not want to see the dark black badge against the justice. This will push us to the dark hole and immense misery of the people and you will be fully accountable for misleading the current situation and our next generations.

You had better pay more attention to improving our educational system rather than destructive politics. My deepest respect will be to those of you who follow the course of justice, peace, progress, and prosperity of our country and reject the evil ideology.

Be a Progressive, Not a Regressive!

Since 1st October 2006, we have been experiencing a revolutionary move to end the political turmoil of Bangladesh. Needless to say, the emergency is the consequence of the unruly political behaviors of all major parties. The nature of the current emergency, with a combination of both civil and military administration, is unprecedented in the history of Bangladesh. In a democratic society, nobody likes any emergency or military rulers. But under the current circumstances, it was welcomed by the people almost unanimously.

The CG didn't have any other choice but to control the deadly political violence and that was the right thing to do. It was imperative to go after those irresponsible leaders who fueled the flames of the deadly violence and who carried out the destruction and the obstruction of peace, progress, and prosperity of our country. They crossed the barbarism of any time of our history in the name of politics.

Despite when the CG was about to reach the process of free and fair election and the politicians were given chance to reorganize them to prepare for election in stipulated time, they were raising the unnecessary issues of the past. Instead of taking responsibility for their atrocious behaviors, they were talking about the justice of the *rajakars (the collaborators of enemies)* and the war criminals of 1971. They are trying to dig out the old issues to avoid the justice of the fresh crimes they have already committed.

They are raising the issues of the so-called rajakars and the war criminals of 1971! How do they forget that they ran the elections with the same group of people and tried their best to be their political allies and failed? This is clearly a double standard. If they are with them, they are good citizens. If they aren't, they're known as the rajakar or war criminals. Since BB, as a follower of his philosophy, forgave them, you should respect whatever he did and move forward.

Most of us did not like to see that happen at that time. But for the greater interest of our new born Bangladesh, BB tried to reduce the tensions, gave hope for all, and forgave them for the greater cause of our nation. Many rajakars were eliminated during and after our liberation war. The rest of them were forgiven by BB himself.

In my opinion, the forgiven ones shouldn't be retried for political reasons. Indeed, we won't tolerate the repetition of the same, if we see anything alike. To raise the same issue for political failure after 36 years may lead to another form of violence and we should not undertake that mistake shortsightedly. The troubled politicians are trying to cover up the fresh atrocious crimes they have committed to get away from the justice. They are misleading the people and trying to lead another form of violence with those old issues.

The revelation of the current corruptions is no longer hidden to the people. Most of the corruption and crimes have come to light. The CG deserves extraordinary credit for their revolutionary actions against those corrupt politicians and bureaucrats for the last 36 years. Their paramount corruptions need to an end. This is not an easy task for the CG to finish overnight. This should be continued until full accomplishment of their agenda.

The clamoring for the justice of the assassinators of BB will reignite the chaos. The people do not want to see anything like October 28, 2006 or worse. The demand for old justice is nothing but a cover up for the fresh crimes. Those sad assassinations took place because of their political miscalculations and those were political coups. Every effect must have some causes. History itself is the testimony for those causes. And yes, why don't they raise the issue of the justice of the assassinators of the best president of Bangladesh, martyr President Ziaur Rahman?

The magnitude of the assassination of BB was beyond imagination, and the entire nation couldn't forget that tragedy. But that tragedy left a serious warning for the future as well. The enemies were created with the abuse of power, injustice, corruptions, disrespect of the rule of law, favoritism, nepotism, cronyism, and the deepest concern of the sovereignty of our newborn Bangladesh. The dream of the political absolutism was also the leading cause of that tragedy. These were totally against the will of the people of the newborn Bangladesh who sacrificed so much during our liberation war. The establishment of corruption was not the cause of the sacrifice of our freedom fighters and the contribution of 75 million people of 1971.

I respectfully disagree with barrister Shafiq Ahmed to file a writ petition against the justice of former PM Sheikh Hasina for the corruption charges brought against her. He said that since those corruptions took place before the emergency; therefore, the CG does not have the authority to carry out the justice. This is quite absurd. Why didn't he say the same for other one, Begum Khaleda Zia and the leaders of the BNP? The emergency came to rescue our nation in an extreme point. When the patient is taken for emergency care, they don't just put the band aid and release. They try to treat properly and try to find other complications as well, if any.

The systematic corruptions of the politicians and bureaucrats reached a state of emergency and there shouldn't be any time frame to treat the crisis. Look! You can't go against the will of 158 million people. Everybody wants peace, progress, and prosperity, except some severe destructionists. I do not know about your position – but don't be a part of the Severe Destructive Elements (SDE). Be a progressive, not a regressive. Do not obstruct the justice. There is no peace without any justice and you had better be a part of it and do not go against the justice, please! Please! Please!

I profoundly support the actions of the CG and will as long as they work for the greater interest of our country and our nation.

Let's Hope for the Best and Reject the Ideas in Vain: Let's move toward the peace, progress, and prosperity of our country. Let's fight against the poverty and corruption. Let's hold accountable those violent and destructive politicians and bring them to justice. Let's strongly demand the justice of those corrupt politicians and bureaucrats.

This needs the courage to change the prevailing condition of our country. We need to change the course of our country with compassion and wisdom. But justice is the precondition to achieving our goal. We can't achieve anything with unproductive words only. We need both actions and words. Our little sacrifice and joint efforts can make a significant difference for the greater interest of our country.

You may not agree with me but you can't deny the fact. You may deny the truth but you can't go too far. You may violate the rule of law but you can't deny the consequence. You may believe in fantasy but you can't get the truth. You may be egoistic for the wrongful causes but you can't achieve your goal. You may abuse your authority but you can't avoid its price. You may not believe in justice but you can't be free from the risk of consequence. You may disregard the history but you can't deny the reality. You may try to change the history but history will not compromise with you. You may lose your morality but you will remain questionable. You may be a wicked one but you can't be a credible one. Once you lose the credibility, then you lose your personality. Once you lose your personality, then you have nothing to lose. Negativity and pessimism lead to the failure. Positivity and optimism lead toward our success.

You may lose the patience to read my writings but they will enrich the sense of your corrective behavior. This may not be interesting to some of you but may contribute to making a sensible choice. Politics is not something that I'm interested in to deal with. But the constant violence with immense destructions and even murders in the name of politics, excessive corruptions, total absence of law and order, total insecurity of the people, barbaric style of hostility, and atrocity forced me to react. My writings are reactionary, based on different circumstances. If you go through my entire writings, you may understand my position, the cause of my writings, and its necessity.

The Caretaker Government (CG), Politicians, and People

The current administration is neither a civil nor a martial law. It could be both or a mixed recipe. The taste is also mixed. Some are happy some are not. Especially for the politicians, it is extremely bitter. The general people also have mixed reactions. This is historically a unique form of government. Any democratic society rejects the ideas of the current system. But why is this? How is this? What ought to be? No matter how unhappy our politicians are, this is the consequence of their extreme unruly behavior.

I may not blame them all; but I can't but blame most of them. All political parties have some defectors, including their leaders. Their arrogance and constant horrible violence forced the CG for the emergency. This emergency was not desired by the people. But has undoubtedly worked as a rescue effort to avert a definite ongoing horrible violence! Our people and our nation could not afford anymore of the ongoing horrible violence with gruesome murders. We should not reopen that barbaric chapter. Over 99 percent of our people have suffered at the hands of less than 1 percent of those SDE in the name of politics.

Under these circumstances, we need to reform all political parties but we can't bargain with corrupt ones. We need to hold them accountable until justice is served. Needless to say that 99 percent of people are more important than less than 1 percent SDE. These criminals are the leading cause of obstruction of peace, progress, and prosperity of our nation. We need to restrain them by any means for the greater interest of our country and our people. It will be a grave mistake if we allow them to resume their usual business before their trial. The real justice is the pre-condition to move forward.

The CG is doing the same. This is their responsibility to hold the election in an orderly manner and to transfer the power to the elected government as soon as possible. This is not an easy task.

We need to be patient and cooperative to carry out this process. Our objective should be for peaceful solution not the resumption of destruction.

Ironically, some of our so-called intellectuals have also become the part of SDE and are contributing to the violence just for their cheap interest. It is so disgraceful. They praise their leaders, even when they are wrong in their actions and words. They ridicule themselves. They are also associated with the violence and misleading the general people. Their behaviors are not unwatched by the people. This kind of sickness is costing our nation a miserable setback.

Now we can see different kinds of problems amongst the politicians and their parties. They can't maintain the integrity of their party and their leaders. Inclusion and exclusion are already taking place. They became divisive and intensified their crisis. Their parties are about to tear up. One of their leaders said that the chaos was created by some unidentified people and so on. They are very good at conveniently making up the stories to mislead the people. They used the same group of people at the time of the violence. Many of them do not have any fixed address and technically, they are their instruments to carry out all those destructive and horrible violence.

Currently, both rival leaders are drinking the water from the same source. They are sharing the same food cooked by the same cook in different dishes, which they never did in normal circumstances. They never thought this could happen in their lives. They were so abusive of power. They worshiped the corruption to change their fortune. The depth of their corruptions and irregularities is unimaginable to the people. They didn't believe in any consequences.

I'm not sure if they are repenting for their deeds. If they do, that will be the right thing to do. They had very good chance to do something better than their ancestors, if they could have amended their mistakes. Instead, they made it worse, and our people and our country suffered so much. It will be their moral obligation to express their regret to the nation for their failure and to hand over power to the capable leaders.

We believe in democracy but I do not want to hear anything about democracy from those politicians who themselves are questionable. As a true citizen, each of us has the right to ask our leaders with courage if they are wrong in any issues and to speak out for the greater cause of our country. I rather remind our politicians to rationalize themselves and to respect the rule of laws. Be a protector not a defector. You may be the leader or whatsoever, but you do not have any right to play any destructive role in our country.

On the other hand, we as the public should educate ourselves to make the right choice rather than be ridiculed ourselves. Our wrongful choice could be devastating for our country and our people more than ever. The current situation helped us to identify the corrupt ones and we must not forget who they really are. Now is the time for change – the change that can lead us to the progressive direction. The peace, progress, and prosperity will depend on our choice only.

Under the above circumstances, I would like to make up a dialogue between our both former PMs about their political lives and their personal relationships. If both of those leaders were given an opportunity to talk together about their current crisis, what would be the dialogue like? I believe, first, that both of them would be embarrassed by themselves. Because, they never got along amicably with any issues both politically and socially. They were like two opposite poles – north and south.

Since the current situation is very critical for both of them and they are almost in the same crisis, they may be inclined to have a talk together. I'm a little bit curious about the probable nature of their discussions. I think they will flash back their political roles and will try to realize why they are here and who was responsible for their current crisis. I guess, despite their huge difference of their opinions, they will start as follows:

Nevertheless, both of them will greet each other and will exchange their best wishes. I would like to abbreviate their names to Madam Sheikh Hasina **(SH)** and Madam Khaleda Zia **(KZ)**.

KZ - Did you ever imagine that both of us would be in this situation?

SH - Are you talking to me?

KZ - Yes, indeed.

SH - Are you not fully responsible for our current crisis?

KZ - I knew you would blame me. What difference did you make so that you were not responsible for our current crisis?

SH - Well, you disregarded our demands all along. Our demands were genuine for the greater interest of our country. You are the one who didn't care about our demands and you used your undue power against us.

KZ - Your demands were unlimited and most of them were practically impossible for any ruling party. Besides, you didn't do anything about those issues when you were in the power. I tried to do my best with other very important issues on a priority basis, such as security, economy, education, and so on.

SH - I was only in power for one term. I had lot of other things to do. I had to protect the legacy of my father. I did everything so successfully that history will remind our people what a golden period it was!

KZ - Quite amazing! Then why you were only for one term, if you were so successful?

SH - I think you are challenging my accomplishment. Aren't you?

KZ - Why should I? It's the people. They didn't agree with you. They were dissatisfied with your administrative style. They were tired and horrified of gangs, murderers, donation collectors, and so on. If you were so right in whatever you said, you would have been in power as long as you wanted to remain in power. Isn't it?

SH - What about you? Your administrations were full of corruptions and irregularities. Isn't it?

KZ - You are trying to blame my administration. The corruption and irregularities are the part of our culture. We inherited this from the beginning of our history. No one was immune from the corruption. You are fully responsible for the constant horrible violence and terrible destruction. When we were your opponents and you were in the power, did we do anything like you did?

SH - This is all about politics. Look! I, as a daughter of the founder of our nation know what is right in what circumstances. My root is from genuine politics and you! You were a housewife of an army officer who was the deputy chief of army staff during my father's administration. You need to know a lot about politics.

KZ - I respect your father as a charismatic leader of our nation. Everybody knows him and his contribution for the nation. But how can you deny the contribution of my husband then Maj. Ziaur Rahman during the liberation war. My husband and many other heroes under the leadership of Col. M.A.G. Osmani carried out the entire liberation war, declared the independence of Bangladesh, and fought in the war-field until our total victory.

Most importantly, everyone made an enormous contribution for our freedom. We lost 3 million lives. Everybody fought heroically against the barbaric Pakistani forces. People not only liberated our country but also brought back your father amidst us from Pakistanis. I think you need to look back to our history with correct vision.

SH - History! My father sacrificed his whole life in jail for the cause of our nation. What did he get? Finally, the same group as your husband's assassinated him. What did he do? He removed Khondakar Mustaq Ahmed, the master planner of that assassination just to take over the power. Can you deny that? No matter how heroic solder he was, he was not a politician. The soldiers should be in the cantonment not in the civil administration. People fought to reject the martial law during the Pakistani regime not to bring back martial law after the liberation.

KZ - There was a civil administration under your father's administration. He was a very charismatic leader but people didn't like his administration. Unfortunately, he dramatically lost the popularity and trust of the people, and pathetically ended up being assassinated. You may ignore the contribution of my husband but people don't. The rest is not unknown to all.

SH - Yes, that was a tense period – but the assassinators were from your husband's group. He acted like the protector of those murderers instead of justice. Didn't he?

KZ - Our discussions are turning to different direction. We can't deal with that past history. We are getting out of our real issues. Only history will evaluate their accomplishment. Both of them were assassinated and they sacrificed their lives for the greater cause of our country and our nation. The people of Bangladesh witnessed their contribution. We need to honor their sacrifice. Now we need to talk about our current crisis.

SH - The current crisis! Just wait and see. The CG is doing too much. Our people should raise their voice with total rejection of the CG. They are violating our constitution and human rights. They are engaged in injustice in the name of justice.

KZ - I agree with you. But how can we overcome this crisis. Both of us are in the jail with serious charges. I'm the bigger victim with my two sons.

SH - See, now you are getting to the point. The real cause is your corruption was bigger than any other administration's was.

KZ - You are personally attacking me. The corruption and abuse of power became our culture from the beginning of our history. Your brother was also controversial during your father's administration. So we can't differentiate each other.

SH - You are attacking me back with the old history. Isn't it?

KZ - The biggest mistake we made was not to take any lessons from our history. History doesn't forgive anybody.

SH - Neither can history stop us nor can we stop the history. Everything has its own course to move forward.

KZ - We have talked a lot but we can't figure out any solution.

SH - We don't have any solution. All those are the consequences of your actions (with regret). Maybe the real solution will be if you retire from the politics and go back to your private life. Let me handle the rest.

KZ - But you are also in the jail with serious charges, including horrible violence and murder.

SH - Look, the real politicians never care about the jail. You need to learn a lot. You have a long way to go to reach in my level.

KZ - Thanks God I didn't reach your level – otherwise, I would have ended up with one term only. The people don't like the politics of horrible violence and destructions. They want peace, progress, and prosperity.

SH - It doesn't matter what the people want. The people will want lot of things and no one can fulfill their demands. The real politicians know how to use the people to serve their purpose. Once it is done, you don't need to worry too much about 158 million people. Just take care of a very limited number of people whom you can use to control the rest.

KZ - You mean gangs and mobsters!

SH - You need to find out the shortcut to deal with any situation. How many people would come out to the streets to burn buses, tires, and be engaged with deadly violence and other destructive activities? But those are the ones who scare the rest and disrupt everything the way we want.

KZ - Oh! No, I don't want to be that kind of politician. I would rather quit politics as soon as I get away from my current crisis with my sons.

SH - Good decision. But it is too late.

KZ - So, what can I do now?

SH - You have to be bold enough to face any challenges.

KZ - I was bold enough to clean up the gangs and mobsters, and to eliminate some of the multiple of murderers. But you are suggesting protecting them to serve our purposes. I really don't get it. We are too opposite like the North and South Poles.

SH - That's why we can't get along.

KZ - But we shouldn't be like this. We have lot of similarities in many ways. Both of us are women, both of our political ancestors were sadly assassinated, both of us got our political image from them, both of us were in the power one after another for quite a long time, and so on. But why we are so opposite both personally and politically?

SH - Look at our ancestors. They were opposite too.

KZ - What about the former dictator and assassinator Ershad and other politicians? Why are they are out of touch? Why are they not facing any trouble for their corruption and other serious crimes of assassinations?

SH - Don't you see who are behind the CG. They are birds of the same feathers.

KZ - It's not fair, justice should be equal for all.

SH - These are in words only. In the real world, it doesn't work. Don't you see who are the most sufferers? Unfortunately, only innocents and honest ones suffer the most. They can never come to play any political role. See, Dr. Muhammad Yunus, the Nobel Peace Prize winner! What happened to him? Our biggest advantage is that we can easily misguide the people and use them the way we want.

KZ - Most of the people do not like the way we behave with each other. What is your opinion about it?

SH - Good realization. Sometimes our behavior is questionable for political reasons only. You are mostly responsible for this negative opinion. People's views and our objectives are two different issues. Our objective is how to go to the power, and we have to deal with it very effectively. Decency is important but it does not work in our political environment. See, most of the decent and capable people are out of politics. We are so successful because we managed to keep them away from the politics.

KZ - Indeed, I have learnt a lot from you. You are so good to maintain your position. I think we are wrong. We are not honoring the cause of the sacrifice of our freedom fighters. I think we have damaged a lot and we should be regretful for our mistakes.

SH - You got enough after the assassination of your husband as a token of his sacrifice. What did I get? I attempted to take over Gonabhaban for my father's sacrifice but I didn't get it. Besides, you were in the power repeatedly but I was only for once. How can I quit from politics so soon?

KZ - I see, still you are dreaming to go to the power.

SH - I'm not a pessimistic like you.

KZ - Well, good luck!

SH - Thank you.

*The above dialogue is not real. This has been designed the way I viewed their political and personal behavior.

Unveiling the Mask of the CG of Bangladesh

Since January 11th, 2007, the CG has had almost the unanimous support of our people. In the beginning, people overwhelmingly supported them. They believed that they were the right group of people who could abolish the evil corruption and constant horrible violence as carried out by the so-called destructive politicians. They also believed that they would open up a new chapter of Bangladesh that our country needed at that tense moment. They are the people who could end up the politics of corruption and the extreme forms of violence and establish the real justice.

The gruesome violence carried out by the hostile politicians panicked and horrified people. They needed someone who could smash those barbaric tactics that caused the interminable misery of the people. People trusted and supported them for their revolutionary steps, likely to be taken by the CG with great courage. The chief advisor and the chief of army staff started to earn the immense support of the people. People were enthusiastic to see the way they started to crackdown on those corrupt leaders from almost all parties. But the people didn't want to see those actions as a mirage. They didn't want to see the blink of change. They wanted to see the real termination of corruption and violence for good and forever.

But the recent behaviors of the CG have became very distrustful to the people. As a result, they've lost the trust of the people very sharply. The CG deviated themselves and have likely taken the side of some of the most violent parties. They purposely divided the major party, the BNP who set the record of huge success in our history. This kind of behavior of the CG is not unwatched by the people. They became questionable for many reasons – like why are they treating the BNP so discriminately as they did much better than any other party in the history of Bangladesh. They were re-elected repeatedly and had a very good chance to win again.

Of course, they were not immune from corruption. But that

corruption was inherited historically. There was no magic therapy to eliminate the cancer of corruption from our culture. Why are the chief advisor and the chief of army staff supporting and making hidden relationships with some of the most corrupt, violent, and destructive political parties? They did so because they love their cousins. They are the birds of same feathers. They are trying to reunite the former tyrant dictator with AL, the worst of the worst administration in the history of Bangladesh. Most likely, they want to be one of the added ingredients of that group as well.

This is the clear sign of betrayal to the people. They want to be another innovative regime of the regressive evil empire. Why is the great family of martyr Ziaur Rahman being treated inhumanely under the custody of the CG? Because they don't want them to remain popular term after term! They have seen that their popularity can't be diminished. They are the obstacles to exert their ill plan. They are very much aware of; if they get free, fair, and credible elections, the BNP will remain unbeaten in the forthcoming election.

The CG must be responsible for their awful behavior and the consequences will not forgive them either. They have violated the constitution and the human rights. But people compromised with that violation because of the extreme circumstances. The reason was that was imperative due to the unprecedented form of violence and the procreation of the horrible gangs and murderers by the opposition parties while BNP was in power.

People unusually welcomed this emergency because of horrible violence carried out by the destructionists and those who denied the civilization. The opposition parties declared the constant violence until their unacceptable demands were accepted. As a result, people badly needed that change. They believed the CG would take strong measures against those who openly declared that the entire country would be blazed if there were no reform. They demanded reform during BNP's administration. Why didn't they do the same while they were in power? They wanted to overthrow the constitutionally elected PM before her term was over.

They also publicly threatened the escalation of civil war. What had to do with the civil war? Whom was the civil war against? Is this not war against the innocent people? They killed so many people in broad daylight in the name of horrible politics. What else needed to be committed to be a real criminal? Are those not enough to prosecute them? What kind of civilized world we are living in? That's why our great poet, Nobel Prize winner, Rabindranath Tagore said with regret, *"You (the Lord) made us Bangalee but didn't as human."* Those who even forgot their party symbol "boat" already sunk and now they prefer to choose "poles and oars" as weapons to terrorize the people.

They know that they can't regain the popularity, so their only option is hostility to scare the people. It reminds me once that we all chanted that slogan for "boat" but we never used the poles and oars. But our slogan was much more effective and meaningful. If this is not the sickness, then what is? Now the CG looks like it fell in love with them and is trying to establish the warm relationship with them. What an affair! Go for it and have a nice time!

Is this the kind of change people expected from them? I've heard about lots of love affairs but none of those were like this. Initially, they understood the demands of the people and pretended to act for the greater cause of the people. They dressed in the gown of real justice and engaged themselves in false acting. They started some popular operations to earn the popularity of the people. But what did we see afterwards? They became deceptive to mislead the people with ill intentions. They arrested many corrupt leaders just to show the people they were engaged in real business as supported by the people. People started to rely on them with the hope of a better future of our country. But they are not trusted ones. They have been proven the false actors. Their real identity was unveiled.

They arrested Begum Khaleda Zia, along with her two sons and tortured them inhumanely. They forgot who they are! They are the sons of martyr Ziaur Rahman who made extraordinary contributions during our liberation war, and subsequently, his great success during his presidency. He dedicated his life for the greater cause of our nation until the last moment of his life. After his horrible assassination, both of his minor sons became orphans and Begum Khaleda Zia became widow very prematurely. The entire nation spontaneously was in mourning for a week, unlike other ones in the past. Then to set up their political goal using his glorious image, the assassinators showed phony compassion to this family. They are the most treacherous group in the history of Bangladesh.

Martyr Zia's family went under the new custody of those criminals who assassinated him. They were the ones who injected the germs of corruptions and misdirected those orphans. They were growing up and being infected by the unhygienic corrupt political environment. Now they are known as one of the biggest corrupts in our country! The real criminals enjoyed the benefit of tyrant dictatorship for so many years and became the Marcos of Bangladesh.

People didn't forget that and shouldn't. Martyr Zia was the most popular one not only as a person, but also as a brave national hero, as a president, and most importantly, as an unmatched leader in the history of Bangladesh. He might not been a politician but his political philosophy was much more superior to many other so-called high profiled politicians of Bangladesh. He was the pride of our nation.

The real difference can be made by character and wisdom not by the corrupt ideology and myths. His dynamic leadership made us proud of to be a Bangladeshi. His success as a soldier and in the politics of production, peace, progress, and prosperity can't be faded by the history of Bangladesh. The CG failed to bring the real cause of our national problem to justice. Rather, they released them all from all serious charges. This is quite a disgraceful part of their so-called accomplishment. They gave the political incentive to those criminals instead they meted them out.

It is crystal clear that the CG lost their credibility because of their false pretence to be the protector of our people. They freed the most violent leader who was not only one of the most corrupt ones but also a horrible murderer. Under her leadership and her direction, some of her ruthless activists carried out such an unprecedented horrible attack that killed so many people in broad daylight that the people of entire world couldn't help but see. That was the darkest day of our nation. They crossed the barbarism of anytime of the history. That single instance was enough to convict her.

Unfortunately, our judicial system lost the purity itself and the justice lost its sanctity. She was never been a trusted one nor will be. People shouldn't make any mistake when they chose their leader. If they do, they will pay the serious price that they've ever seen. She was temporarily released for medical reasons and allowed to go abroad for her ear treatment. But now she is making the political statement to her loyalists and her supporters with her magical strength. This is the clear signs of hypocrisy. She could not attend the court for trial for the serious corruption charges brought against her with the false pretence of serious illness. This was nothing but a shameless joke.

This kind of drama is not only disgraceful but also a waste of every single penny we spent for the fake process of justice – she should not go free! I believe not a single person should be in the jail because none of them has committed bigger crime than she did. All of them should have been freed prior to her release. It is very unfortunate not only for the 158 million people of Bangladesh, but also for our nation.

As an independent watcher, I would like to introduce myself. I'm neither a politician nor an activist of any political parties. But I couldn't remain silent when I saw such an awful discrimination to one party or another. As a citizen of Bangladesh, I must raise my voice against the extreme form of discrimination. I believe all of us should do this too. It is our solemn obligation to raise our voice against this injustice.

Why were both sons of martyr Zia tortured under the custody of CG so cruelly and now they're fighting for their lives? Who is responsible for this? Why they were not properly treated no matter what sort of crimes they might have committed as fabricated either by their opponents/enemies or by the CG themselves. If they really wanted to bring the corrupt ones to justice, why didn't they go back to the history of corruption? Why didn't they go to the root of the corruption? Why did they ignore the bigger criminals and shake hands with them? If they have had the guts to do that they could put many bigger criminals ones in the line before they put martyr Zia's family in.

Finally, they've broken the record of distrust of our history. It will be the biggest mistake of our nation if we do not demand justice for what they're doing now with our nation. I myself feel guilty for supporting them very strongly like rest of the people of Bangladesh. I was one of the strongest supporters of the CG. We did because we trusted them. We believe in decency and democracy – not in hypocrisy.

Their activities are clear to the whole nation. The joint venture of corruption with the army became evident to the people of Bangladesh. They are becoming hooked up with the biggest criminal groups that the nation couldn't overlook. We are all peace-loving people. We don't want any corruption, violence, injustice, hostility, and so on. We want those politicians who have civic sense not those uncivilized nonsense. We trusted them the way they were acting. But their recent behaviors have become the biggest concern for all of us. The people of Bangladesh should not and must not forgive those betrayers. We do not want to see the resurrection of historic betrayer again in 21st century. I would like to remind them again that greediness leads to sin and sin lead to death.

In conclusion**, I strongly demand immediate release of martyr Zia's family and the leaders of BNP unconditionally with no further excuses. I also demand an explanation from the CG as to how those corrupt and horrible leaders were released and why the lesser corrupted ones are still in jail?**

Of course, I can't compromise with any corruption; therefore, all of their ill-gotten wealth has to be confiscated with tougher penalties, if found guilty of any crimes. At the same time, we need to watch those confiscators too. I may be reactionary because I love my country, our peace-loving people, and our nation. I do not want to see our innocent people suffer due to the barbarism of destructive politicians. May Allah bless Bangladesh and protect its people from those evils!

Who Sowed the Seeds of Corruption?

July, 2007

The current CG has taken some admirable steps to control the systematic corruptions of Bangladesh. They have arrested many high profiled corrupt leaders and bureaucrats and are holding them accountable for their wrongdoings for the last so many years. This is certainly a dramatic change for Bangladesh. The people are happy to see this change and look forward for the better future. We, as the citizens of Bangladesh, are also watching who are being caught and who aren't.

The CG should be fair enough to carry out their mission without any prejudice and disputable manner. The history of corruption is not new. Unfortunately, we inherited this evil practice since our independence. So we need to go back to the past regimes as well without any off-limit. To go against any targeted group of corrupt leaders and bureaucrats and ignore the bigger ones will not be enough to convince the people and to earn their trust.

The biggest political criminals are those who committed the crimes of destruction, carried out the brutal attacks on others, and killed so many people using poles, oars, and other sharp weapons in the name of politics. The entire world could not ignore that horrible scenario. This becomes questionable, why are the CG overlooking and not taking those crimes seriously? Those crimes were committed in the broad daylight under the leadership of a leading political party and its leaders. It looks very suspicious when those so-called leaders are not caught and they are allowed to make the misleading statement almost openly, even in the international media. I hope the CG will not make another mistake so that the people lose their trust and intensify their frustrations.

I strongly support forming a new political party or reformatting an old parties, where only high moral, ethical, and capable people participate and will be able to change the course of our country.

I do not want to see those corrupt leaders in those parties. I do not believe in any dynasty of those so-called leaders who are so immoral and destructive for the country. I rather demand the justice for those undeniable crimes they have committed. We liberated our country for a very solemn cause and for the bright future if our nation. It is our obligation to protect its interest at any cost. The cheap emotion to our inept leaders is damaging the image of our country in the modern world. They are the obstacles of peace, progress, and prosperity of our country.

If we go back to our history, we can't deny that the corruption was started right after the independence of Bangladesh and that we saw its consequence as well. Our biggest problem is that we do not want to learn from our own history. Why did Dr. Henry Kissinger make a remark, saying that *Bangladesh is a bottomless basket*? Who was in the power at that time? Why did an incalculable number of people died from starvation and rest of the nation was hit hard from that famine in 1974? Who was responsible? Who didn't get the account of his own blanket? Who changed their fortune at that time at the cost of those lives?

Who laid down the foundation of corruptions at that time? Who wanted to be an imperialist? Who had the desire to be crowned? It was too much and too fast for that unacceptable desire. Why, as a founder of our country, did he lose his popularity and the trust of the people so drastically? Who promised to make the cheerful face of everyone? What kind of cheerful face was that when, because of extreme corruption, people had to die soon after he took over charge of newborn Bangladesh? Of course, some other causes were associated with that famine but the corruption was on top of all.

Yes, I remember that cheerful moment, the Victory Day of Bangladesh, the 16th December, 1971 when the brutal Pakistani forces surrendered to us and inherited a very shameful dark history for themselves for their generations to come.

Whose contribution was the most at that time? Our heroes, under the leadership of Col. M.A.G. Osmani, Maj. Ziaur Rahman and many other heroes, heroically fought with the freedom fighters against those Pakistani barbaric forces and taught them an unforgettable lesson.

The declaration of independence of Bangladesh by Maj. Ziaur Rahman in a very special moment reinvigorated the spirit of the people to fight against those savage forces. But some radicals do not want to admit the truth – why should we agree with their myth? Who freed Banga Bandhu from the Pakistani war criminals? We lost 3 million (exact number yet to be ascertained) of invaluable lives. But we achieved our victory.

Besides, every level of people made an enormous contribution and had a strong determination to achieve our victory, and we did it.

Unfortunately, after the liberation, our corrupt leaders betrayed not only our people but also the freedom fighters. Many of them sacrificed their lives. What else had they to sacrifice to be honored? The corrupt leaders did not respect the cause of their sacrifice – they only shamelessly respected their selfish interest. They were engaged in a profit sharing business of the liberation of Bangladesh. They led the country in a miserable direction with extreme corruption. The administrative mismanagement, with its immoral and unethical behaviors, was fully responsible for the sufferings of those people.

Today, we see that the sons of our former great president the martyr Ziaur Rahman and his widow are the biggest victims of the current operation. Martyr President Ziaur Rahman was a soldier, an honest dynamic leader with correct vision, a pioneer, and an optimist, and most importantly, he was a true believer. Before we forget about his contribution during the liberation war, we should remember his heroism, his philosophy, and his tireless effort to introduce our country as a model for the rest of the world. He rescued the country from the sinking situation.

He believed in self-reliance, self-dependence, and left the examples for us to follow. He was the one who stressed the importance of the politics of production and self-reliance.

Thirty-eight years ago, he understood what was likely to be the future of Bangladesh. When he was talking about the excavation and re-excavation of the rivers and canals to facilitate the irrigation to grow more food, forestation, plantation, and poultry production, those unproductive and naive critics mocked about his addresses. They said he was trying to bring the crocodiles and so on.

Today, 40 years later, we all know how farsighted a leader he was! His optimism can't be summarized with few words. He unified the entire nation for the common goal. He very successfully built up a positive relationship with the rest of the world. Today, he is no longer with us but his contribution, his vision, his ideals, and his dream will remain in our history. His party, the BNP is not the problem. The problem is that some corrupt politicians managed to penetrate in this party for their selfish purpose, which has had not been not uncommon in the political culture of Bangladesh for the last 36 years.

Now let me briefly explain why and how it happened. When the ruthless murderers assassinated President Ziaur Rahman in a deep conspiracy on May 30, 1981, both of his sons became orphans and Begum Zia became a widow. The entire nation was in weeklong mourning for that horrible tragedy. The spontaneous reaction of the entire nation was unprecedented. It was not an easy situation for her to overcome that crisis with those little children. The evil conspirators started to play a very fake emotional game to serve their purpose. They showed strong sympathy to this family and tried to use the image of martyr Ziaur Rahman for political purposes.

Zia's family started to go through a different way of living. They couldn't follow the glorious principle of martyr Ziaur Rahman. They were raised in a corrupt political environment by the new custodians. They fake custodians acted as if they were more well-wishers than anybody else was. They cut the root, started to pour water, and tried to draw national attention. They surrounded this family and injected the germs of corruption. The rest of the story is not unknown to us. Today, his sons are prosecuted as two of the biggest corrupted ones. They are also going through the toughest time under the current CG.

Again, my question is who spread the germs of corruption? Why and how did the epidemic of corruption infect them? At least, they were not involved with bank robberies and other shameful scandals. If their father had have been alive, it wouldn't have happened in their lives. Nobody can deny the impact of the environment. This is the exact cause of their current painful crisis. I know this is very sensitive issue but it reminds us of the history.

I repeat, who sowed the seeds of corruption? Why has the former tyrant dictator Gen. H.M. Ershad remained an important piece of the political puzzle? Knowing all about him, why both parties made him so important, and now again, he has managed to remain untouched. I think it is time for the CG to review the matter precisely. It is our obligation to support the CG in doing everything right for the future of our country. This is the only opportunity to fix our political problems. We may not have another opportunity and we should not wait for it.

If we compare the administrations of former two leaders, we may not give them full credit for their administrative styles, but we can't overlook the significant differences between those two. One of them was only elected once, and the other one was repeatedly elected and most likely would have been for the next term, as well? They were not immune from corruption. Our inherited corruption has been playing a strong role in our political system for the last 36 years.

In spite, there was a significant difference. I'm not defending one party against the other because of my moral reasons. But I can't compromise with any corrupt ones either. I want to see all corrupt leaders have equal justice. It is heartbreaking when I see that the widow and the sons of a hero, the best leader of Bangladesh ever had, are the biggest victims in the current crisis and are going through the toughest time. How did they forget who their father was and why didn't they follow his glorious principles?

On the other hand, the CG is treating the other one so differently. The CG should not behave like the stepmother to one another. The public is not leaving anything unwatched. By the way, what about the former dictator Gen. H. M. Ershad? I don't to know about others;

but in my view, both of them are privileged for special treatment by the CG, even though they are the most corrupt and horrible politicians.

Well, I may not be smart enough to understand about right and wrong, but I can clearly see the difference. I believe history will not forgive anybody if something is not going right. Our history is the clear evidence. I strongly believe the CG will not ignore my concerns and perhaps of the rest of the people of our country. I don't want to see the blink of change only. But I want to see the real change; the change, which will make the real difference we are all waiting for.

Blackmail of our History!

I was surprised to see in the Thikana dated 11th January, 2008 that someone had written in the preliminary school text book of civics that the dictator H.M. Ershad was the initiator of the South Asian Association of Regional Cooperation (SAARC). This myth has taken place in textbooks for current and future generations. If that is the case, I vehemently denounce that claim and strongly demand justice of those who are related to either the writer or the supporters of this falsification. Gen. H.M. Earshad was nothing but a tyrant dictator.

I most respectfully admire those who have already raised their voices, including Prof. Emazuddin Ahmed; Journalist Foez Ahmed, A.B.M. Musa; educationist Moniruzzaman; Col. (Ret.) Wali Ahad; Lt. Gen. (Ret.) Mir Shawkat Ali; the diplomat Shamber Mobin; and all others for their courageous reactions. I also would like be a part of them.

We should not compromise with any falsification that could mislead our future generations and us. If anyone wishes to write any fiction or fairytale, they may do so. But writing in the textbook, our history and in civics lessons with wrong information is absolutely unacceptable and unforgivable. I'm one of the strong supporters of the CG but I can't support anymore if this is true, and if those responsible are not punished to the maximum extent of law. I strongly demand the immediate withdrawal and destruction of those books with exemplary penalty to the writer.

In my previous writings, I have highlighted some actions of martyr Ziaur Rahman during his presidency and I didn't specify the issue of SAARC. Besides, I'm neither a historian nor a politician. It is unthinkable that some interest groups are trying to blackmail our history with total falsifications and fabrications about such an important issue of our history.

Although those honorable writers have written much, I must add my opinion about one of the very best presidents martyr Ziaur Rahman of Bangladesh, in our history. I'm not a fan of military rulers but I must admit the truth.

Martyr Ziaur Rahman was an army officer but his political farsightedness was unique and far more superior to many experienced politicians and leaders. He was a true believer and a real patriot. He proved all of his best qualities during his entire life. All Bangladeshis knew him from our liberation war in 1971 until the last moment of his life, the day of his brutal assassination on May 31, 1981.

I think I should not remind our people who the initiator of SAARC was. He left lots of evidence of when and why he initiated the SAARC soon after he became the president of Bangladesh. Because of his extraordinary intellectual philosophy, he realized that in order to maintain our peace, progress, and prosperity, we needed to build up the bridge for regional cooperation with our neighboring countries. This would also protect from further escalation of any tension of war and occupation by one nation to another. This would also help us to strengthen the positive relationship for a progressive and better future in this region.

The SAARC was his dream and he managed to advance with this mission during his lifetime. He had a lot of correspondences and negotiations with the leaders of those countries. He was very successful in strengthening the relationship of Bangladesh with the rest of the world.

During his presidency, he managed to get the recognition of some countries that didn't go during Banga Bhandhu Sheikh Mujibur Rahman (BB). His opponents always beat their drums hard with their negative campaigning while he was doing all those developments.

Gen. H.M. Earshad was the chief of army staff during BB's administration. How the sensible people of Bangladesh could agree with that and write the phony history that he was the one who initiated the SAARC.

Some of his defective groups of army officers conspired and assassinated BB on May 30, 1981. Their justice hasn't been served yet. Now they are the ones or some other ignorant writers that are writing this phony history. History must be based on facts. To write the history of any country or a nation is an important task.

To write history, you must research the historical facts and figures to find the truth to make sure that nothing is written that is inconsistent with the facts. It's not a fairytale or fiction.

Some of the disgraceful groups of people or defectors are also blaming that martyr Ziaur Rahman was with the opposition group of the liberation war in 1971. How can they deny that he was the promulgator of the independence of Bangladesh? He courageously revolted against the brutal Pakistani military leaders soon after the Pakistani military rulers arrested BB.

BB was the one who wanted to be the PM of undivided Pakistan prior to March 25, 1971. Major Zia, along with other heroes, took a leading part in our liberation war under the leadership of Col. M.A.G. Osmani.

In fact, that was the turning point of real independence. For the greater interest of our country and our nation, please refrain from this sort of propaganda and don't impure our history and mislead our current and future generations.

I certainly was not a supporter of Siraj Sikder – but I can't support any assassination. Who assassinated Siraj Sikder? Who said where is Siraj Sikder today, soon after his assassination? Who started the politics of assassination? I can go on and on but I have already written a lot in my previous writings about the consequences.

I believe, we are in the 21st century and we need to move forward with the sophistication of our politics and policies; rather than unruly and backdated destructive tactics.

Just move in the direction of the peace, progress, and prosperity and reject the ideas of hostility and atrocity. Maintain unity and integrity. Let's fight against corruptions, violence, and poverty, and uproot their origin. Live like a human being and maximize your effort to protect the cause of the sacrifice of our freedom fighters and the other contributors of 1971.

Don't reward the betrayers who didn't have any contribution during or after our liberation war, with false credit. Don't betray those with honorable lives, who made the ultimate sacrifice of their precious lives in the liberation war. Don't betray their blood. We owe the highest tribute to those honorable lives who sacrificed themselves just to present us the glorious Bangladesh.

What about May 30th?

Recently, I was reading some articles in the Thikana, issued on 15th August, 2008 that some of the writers made some historical references about the contribution of BB and very insanely humiliated martyr Ziaur Rahman. With all due respect to BB, I strenuously disagree with them to a great extent. Some of the comments they made about martyr Ziaur Rahman were really outrageous not because they were against those of our national heroes who liberated our country but because they also vilified them with no respect at all.

In their writings, they have mentioned a lot like an eyewitness of the assassination of BB and blamed martyr Ziaur Rahman the most. They accused him as a major partner of the assassinators of BB.

Needless to say that assassination was one of the most horrific ones in the history of Bangladesh. No human being can support this kind of awful assassination. Like most of the Bangladeshis, as an early teenager, I was a strong supporter of BB until our liberation war in 1971. We all prayed for BB, for his safe return amidst us from the barbaric Pakistanis during the liberation war. We chanted the slogan his party symbol "boat" not the poles and oars at lot, for his release from jail in 1968, and prior to his landslide victory in the election in 1970.

In fact, it was not his victory. It was ours. We were all united, trusted him as our leader, and titled him "Banga Bandhu (BB)" (friend of the Bangalis), the friend we trusted the most. We all shared the unnecessary catastrophic war 1971. We lost 3 million (yet to be ascertained) lives as the genocide was carried out by the barbaric Pakistani forces under the direction of war criminals Yahya Khan and Zulfikar Ali Bhutto.

We lost many of our intellectuals and many more precious lives, including men, women, and children. The AL was only party of the people of the East and we were united under the leadership of BB. The other parties like the Muslim League and the Pakistan Democratic Party (PDP) were known as the collaborators of the West (rajakar).

The people of the East understood that we needed to be united to end the interminable discrimination and exploitation by the West politically, economically, and socially. We were treated like second-class citizens. It was a very appropriate momentum for BB to obtain the immense support of the East. As a result, he became the majority leader for both the East and the West. People trusted him not only as a leader but also for the commitment he made to the people.

People didn't care about their lives to follow his direction. But the evil leaders of the West violated the constitution of Pakistan. They didn't want to transfer the power to BB as the majority leader of the undivided Pakistan as the systematic process of the constitution. Instead, they set aside the convention of transferring the power to the majority leader BB. They totally disregarded the rules of law.

Subsequently, after his famous speech on 25th March, 1971, they arrested him and started the genocide in our land. In his speech, he talked about our liberation and freedom but not decisively. He left that option open with certain legitimate conditions. He expected some political solutions and wanted to be the PM of an undivided Pakistan. But his legitimate conditions were not honored by the barbaric Westerners and they arrested him unjustly, almost instantly, and committed genocide on us. This led to the catastrophic war in the East. The people of the East had to take it as an ultimatum of the liberation war.

Who Fought in that Liberation War? The people of the East were not prepared for the war. They expected the political solution. But the evil Western leaders believed that the people of the East didn't have any right to lead Pakistan, even if they were the overwhelming majority. They believed the West should permanently subjugate the people of the East. They underestimated the bravery of the East.

Soon after BB's arrest, no other were options left for the East either to become engaged in the liberation war or to surrender timidly to the West. But this heroic nation rejected the second option, no matter what might have been cost. We fought the war with valor without any choice until our glorious victory. The Westerners learnt the lesson in only nine months.

They shamelessly surrendered to us and begged for their lives on 16th December, 1971. They ruthlessly killed millions of innocent and defenseless people during our liberation war. But we didn't do the same to them without any confrontation. We set an example in the history of mankind and emancipated them, teaching a lesson of what real heroes means. I've already written in my previous writings about the exhilarating success of Bangladesh.

Who Led the Liberation War? Some insensible radicals and muckrakers are trying to deny the real history with no respect to the genuine contributors. They do not hesitate to make any comment execrably. They compared those heroes with the historic traitor Mir Zafar!

The real Mir Zafars are those who betrayed the freedom fighters and our nation – not those who liberated our country Bangladesh, risking their own lives, and making us to be the proud Bangladeshis we are.

Without any doubts and disputes about the contribution of BB politically, who declared the independence of Bangladesh when he was arrested? Who carried out the liberation war to move forward to fulfill the dream of BB and our nation? What would have likely happened if they hadn't fought against those enemies? Who was released in the aftermath of the liberation war with our glorious victory? Who betrayed the lives and blood of those martyrs even before their fresh blood had dried up? Who were engaged with the profit and power sharing business soon after the liberation of Bangladesh? Who tried to establish the regressive monarchism or anarchism in Bangladesh?

Is this the reason they sacrificed their lives in 1971? What was his commitment to the people of the East? Was this the kind of cheerful face he was committed to make? Who tried to be the political absolutist abolishing the democracy? Who established the institution of corruptions, nepotism, cronyism, and abuse of power? Who was trying to compromise with the sovereignty of Bangladesh?

I think the people of Bangladesh know the answers of those questions. I didn't want to use the name of the historic culprit traitor Mir Zafar. But I couldn't remain silent when something was written in the name of our nation's most honorable heroes and leaders who declared the independence of Bangladesh and led the country towards independence with great success. One of them compared Major Zia and other heroes with Mir Zafar! The reference he made with Siraj-ud-Daula and Mir Zafar is other way round.

Yes, the assassination of BB shocked us all, even though we didn't like his administrative style due to his moral and ethical degradation. But we never compared him with Mir Zafar. He has also written about the assassination of martyr Ziaur Rahman and used the term that he was booted by tyrant dictator H.M. Ershad, who didn't make any contribution in our liberation war and was shackled by the Pakistanis.

Ershad was repatriated from Pakistan right after the glorious liberation of Bangladesh. He is the biggest betrayer and managed to carry out the horrible assassination of martyr Ziaur Rahman and many others. Many others were in the same circumstances. He is the one who played the active role of rajakar (the collaborator of our enemies) by assassinating martyr Ziaur Rahman, even after the liberation of Bangladesh. He also killed many high-ranking army officers who fought very courageously and liberated our country Bangladesh.

Didn't he take the power forcibly from the elected president Justice Abdus Sattar? Didn't he kill the students rolling the truck over in their demonstrations? His unlawful regime was one of the darkest times of our history. He was not meted out the way he should have been because of corrupt justice system. The mystery of his justice remains questionable to the vast majority of the people.

The tyrant dictator who successfully conspired to assassinate one of the best leaders in the history of Bangladesh and many other high-ranking army officers is the biggest criminal. Who cooperated with him when he was ousted from the power after his tyrant dictatorship of nine years and eventually not meted out by abusing the justice? Who had close ties with him? Despite knowing all about this, how they praised him and her and disgraced themselves? What is the definition of treachery? What kind of sickness is this? If they knew he was the assassinator of president Zia, why didn't they have the courage to demand the justice of that tyrant dictator?

These propagandists are trying to mislead the future generations with false history. Instead, they praised his treacherous actions. How ungrateful they are to make such an outrageous comment about the real freedom fighters! What is the difference between that criminal and them? I hardly can believe they are from Bangladesh. Is it not clear that they are the real rajakar or traitors? Now they are trying to be the propagandists with false and fabricated stories.

They may talk about other coup that martyr Zia defend himself and our country. But that was circumstantial and quite inevitable. Sometimes real leaders have to be bold enough to prevent worst things from happening at the cost of the elimination of few dangerous groups. They attempted to act against our national interest. Our hard-earned liberation came under danger.

He tried to protect our national interest heroically as he did against the Pakistani barbaric forces. President Abraham Lincoln did the same for the greater interest of his nation. As a human being, I can't support any assassination and those shouldn't have happened. But that coup prevented many worst things from happening. It may not sound right to the propagandists like them but that horrible assassination of BB was the consequence of his political miscalculation, personal bitterness, and enmity to a great extent.

You can't spend more than you earn. If you do, you go broke, leading to bankruptcy. Can they deny that his discriminatory behaviors caused serious discontent amongst his close political associates and some of the high ranking army officers? Didn't they see who formed the new political parties and why? Why his lieutenant leaders became so agitated and couldn't trust him anymore? The people wanted him to step down from the power and demanded his honorable retirement life.

None of us expected his assassination, especially with his young family. One of his extremely angry rebel groups carried out that horrible assassination. Some of them believed that if he was not ousted from power, the sovereignty of our country would not be protected and the sacrifice of 3 million lives would have been in vain. Some of them believed that we liberated our country from Pakistan but were becoming sold to other one.

As a result, they played such a horrible role to assassinate him so ruthlessly. It is undeniable that many of his close associates disagreed with some of his adopted policies, those were considered to be against our national interest. Thus, he created the animosity amongst his lieutenants. The most controversial figure, Khondakar Mustaq Ahmed, was one of them.

One of those writers mistakenly mentioned about the truth of the promotion of Gen. Shafiullah as the chief of army staff with the violation of the rule of seniority. He has mentioned that Major Ziaur Rahman was senior to him as they were enlisted in the armed forces. If so, wasn't it clear discrimination? Besides, many other irregularities took place at that time, most beyond our imagination.

In that critical moment, many other complexities were swirling around that people like us were not aware of. But one thing that was evident was that BB's administration was nothing but the foundation of corruption. As a result, we have seen many coups and assassinations take place as well. The famine in 1974 was mostly because of his poor management. Many of his close companions changed their fortune while that famine hit the whole nation hard.

During our liberation war, we never heard the name of Shafiullah. We heard a lot about Col. M.A.G. Osmani, Major Ziaur Rahman, Major Dalim, Captain Bhuiyan, and many others who really fought in the war-field. Despite how he became the chief of army staff and why was none of them amongst the others?

We had well-established army, navy, air force, BDR (former EPR), police, and so on. We didn't need Rakhi Bahini (his private defense forces). We only needed to reorganize and reshape those forces. They were the ones who fought for our liberation along with the people. BB should have been putting our national interest first instead of his own. His political creditability was diminishing so badly that he lost the popularity and trust of the people with no measure. His son became so controversial that the people lost their trust on him.

The law and order became useless. Instead of enjoying the fruit of freedom, the innocent people were in panic of Rakhi Bahini, his Red Forces, and his mismanagement. People weren't afraid of any other forces as they were of the Rakhi Bahani. His political absolutism and unacceptable style of administration were the fundamental causes of the resentment not only to the rebels but also to his close associates and to the people at large. Serious discontent divided his close partners. He totally failed to resist the temptation of greediness of power even when he was losing his administrative capability.

One of them compared BB with some of the world's greatest leaders of the history of the world: George Washington, the first president of the United States, President Abraham Lincoln, President John F. Kennedy, Martin Luther King (the Civil Right Movement leader), Mahatma Gandhi of India, Nelson Mandela of Africa, and many others.

Interestingly enough, he listed the name of Mohammad Ali Jinnah with those leaders as well. This is enough to identify him as who he really is! All of them were remarkable leaders and the role models for the leaders of any nation. But Mohammad Ali Jinnah was not. He betrayed us from the very inception of the independence of Pakistan in 1947. Other leaders led their nations with full commitment, with great wisdom and integrity, and never acted for the selfish purposes for their regional and personal interest. They did everything for their country and their nation. But Mohammad Ali Jinnah did not. He ignored the East and mean spiritedly, became biased to the West.

The above-listed leaders sacrificed a lot in their lives but didn't expect anything for their own in return. They served their nations with integrity and wisdom. They never lost the popularity and trust of the people. But what about BB! They were not greedy for the power. But what about BB! They were not generous to the point of corruption. But what about BB!

Was He Generous? When our newborn Bangladesh was in the healing process from the liberation war, he was only worried about power. When he was in power, he forgot the causes of the sufferings of the people and gave everything away to his cronies. That's how he was known as generous to them.

They didn't write anything about the causes of BB's downfall. They tried to reintroduce BB to the people with all the positive things he did. But they didn't have the courage to write what caused him to become so unpopular with the people who lifted him up so highly with profound trust.

The people of Bangladesh were not betrayers. The real betrayers are those who betrayed the people and our nation with false commitment. They are examples of betrayers in human history. Real leaders always fought for what was right for their nations, unlike BB, and they left glorious examples for the generations to come for any other nations in the world. BB could have been one of them, if he had possessed those qualities.

Politics is a very risky business. It is so risky that politicians could lose or gain their reputations for any simple reason. But these were not simple reasons. Those were serious issues that people couldn't reconcile them with an easy acceptance. Sometimes, these sorts of behavior cause irreparable damage too, as opposed to the glory.

Politicians can earn the popularity and trust of the people by their words and actions, as long as they are credible to the people. But they can lose their image very sharply when they lose their conscience and become distrustful. It is like a roller coaster. They can ascend and descend. But in politics, it is very hard to ascend and hold. They need to earn the massive support of the people presenting them with their quality of leadership, their agenda, and their vision.

They must be trustworthy. They have to be accountable for their responsibility and their commitment. They have to demonstrate how they will be able to achieve their goals in a very effective manner. They may achieve a lot with false commitment. But they shouldn't be surprised if they face the consequences.

BB achieved a lot but couldn't protect his image soon after he returned from the jails of Pakistan. We, the people of Bangladesh, cheered wildly upon his return. He took charge of the newborn Bangladesh, which was earned at the cost of the lives and blood of 3 million in his absence.

He didn't experience the liberation war nor did his sons, who became very controversial too. The propagandists never ever mention those causes. They are not courageous enough to tell the truth either for their disgraceful self-interest or because of the ignorance. He was arrested just prior to the liberation war breaking out and returned in our liberated country Bangladesh with the highest honor. Who liberated our country? Our liberation had two phases: the politics and the war.

Politically, it was very successful but was futile. But fighting for our liberation was incredibly successful. Who fought in the liberation war and lost so many lives – BB or Major Zia, along with the people? What did the people of Bangladesh expect from BB? What kinds of commitment did he make to the people? If he had tried to do everything as his commitment, he won't have had to face that assassination. He would've been one of the above-listed great leaders. But he lost almost everything he earned in his entire political life just for the greediness of power. He descended like a roller coaster.

Virtuously, those aforesaid leaders didn't have a thunder voice like BB's. But their wisdom, commitment, and actions were extremely remarkable. To compare him with those leaders is quite inappropriate. His devotion can't be denied. But we can't deny that he became deviated from the position where people trusted him. Do not forget that you can hijack the bank and treasury but you can't hijack the trust and popularity.

You can inflate your muscle with evil force but you can't beat the glorious character and wisdom of martyr Ziaur Rahman. You can use your evil force to damage anything you want but you can't get away from the consequences. Once anything happens as a consequence, do not blame others – blame yourself and your actions and take it as a consequential.

Sometimes, some decent people become the victims of intrigue by the evils ones too. Those are really unfortunate and painful for the mankind. But they are universally honorable. And that's exactly what happened to martyr Ziaur Rahman and some of those great leaders.

The people of Bangladesh didn't want the assassination of BB. They wanted his honorable retirement due to his administrative incapability. Instead, he wanted to be crowned when he didn't have any popularity or the trust of the people. He wanted to establish the monarchism for his next generation. His administration was absolutely flawed.

He wanted to privatize his security forces and formed the Rakhi Bahini (private defense forces) for his own protection. He knew that his activities against the will of the people could cause a serious uprising amongst the people against him. But he didn't want to relinquish his power no matter what cost to him. He tried to play a very hard ball against the people. But that hard ball hit him back so gravely.

The above-listed leaders didn't have their personal forces. They dedicated their lives for the greater cause of their nations. That's why their contributions remain examples in human history. When you talk about the glory of someone, you need to talk about the quality of his or her leadership not the rhetoric. To achieve something great is not impossible but to damage something is easier with self-destruction.

But they didn't mention anything about the causes of his failure. Some of them say he was a very generous leader. Generous! Generous to whom! Again, I vehemently disagree with that form of generosity that costs others to serve the purpose of his likable groups only. This is not the generosity. This is mischievous behavior. This is not the greatness. This is immoral, unethical, and irrational.

We have seen the spontaneous reactions of the people after his horrible assassination? I was not a supporter of Siraj Sikder at all. But I couldn't deny him as a human being. If anyone is happy to kill others, how should he or she be respected?

BB was a giant charismatic leader with a thunder voice. But his moral and ethical standards were not up to the mark. He had monumental success in politics until 1971, but he ruined himself very drastically and ended up with such an unprecedented assassination. He earned a lot, but gambled with it all. His created rebel groups that he had caused extreme discontent amongst assassinated him. Indeed, that horrible assassination left a serious message for the rest of the politicians.

The Life of Zia as Soldier, as a President, and as a Person: After the assassination of this great leader, the people of Bangladesh and the rest of the world begun to know who martyr Ziaur Rahman was! The nation was profoundly shocked and mourned for longer than for any other lost leaders. He was not only a soldier and a president but also was one of the great rare men in the history of mankind. His lifestyle was like one of the wisest ones of human civilization. He didn't have any house in Dhanmondi, Gulshan, or Banani (the most posh areas). He didn't have a Swiss Bank account or any other accounts in the world. He was an example of one of that great human being who only served the people and was not greedy for the personal establishment of lavish life.

He dedicated his whole life for the greater cause of our people, our country, and our nation. His lifestyle was one of the very ordinary, even when he was the head of the government. He didn't choose any palatial living conditions. His lifestyle was very simple, the same as a typical Bangladeshis.

As a soldier, he played a very courageous role during our liberation war. His courageous role to revolt against the Pakistani forces and the declaration of the independence of Bangladesh was not a cheap shot. It was the defining moment of our liberation of Bangladesh.

As a president, his able leadership left many successful examples for our nation. He was a leader of progressive vision. He understood what the country needed to be a self-reliant and self-dependent rather than depending on others. He understood that as one of the most densely populated countries in the world, we needed to emphasize production of growing more food, poultry, dairy, fisheries, and other industrial raw materials. He cared about the education, health, peace, progress, and prosperity of our newborn Bangladesh.

He inspired the people to excavate and re-excavate the canals for irrigation and simultaneously to control the flooding that had damaged the grown crops almost every year. The ignorant critics were mocking his politics of production, saying that he was welcoming the crocodiles. He also emphasized forestation against deforestation to maintain the environmental balance of Bangladesh.

In fact, he was the leader of forward thinking not a shortsighted regressive ideologist. He understood the importance of the South Asian Regional Cooperation for Peace and Progress and initiated for SAARC. He successfully managed to get the recognition of Bangladesh from some of the countries that hadn't recognized them during past administrations. He tried his best to strengthen the international relationship with the rest of the world and made a significant progress. Domestically, he tried to unite all of us, irrespective of religion, race, and castes.

As a person, he was very gracious and a man of very high moral character. His relentless effort to change the life of our people was quite remarkable. He was very pious and very inspirational for the common good of our people and our country. He has taken a very special place in the minds and hearts of the people of Bangladesh. He is one of the most deserving personalities that people should remember with great honor and respect.

Unfortunately, after his brutal assassination, his minor sons and his widow Begum Khaleda Zia were deviated by the unhygienic political environment and couldn't keep up his principles. But we can't blame them fully for their current crisis because it was due to the culture of the politics of Bangladesh.

The chief advisor, Dr. Fakhruddin Ahmed and the chief of army staff, Gen. Moyeen Uddin Ahmed of the CG should be held responsible for the unjust torture to this family, and history will not forgive them either. Their biased action is clear to the people of Bangladesh. They have taken the side of one of the most corrupt and hostile political parties of Bangladesh. They have magnified the corruptions of the BNP and his sons, even though they are the ones who left the clear examples of peace, progress, and prosperity of our country. They took serious measures to eliminate those horrible gangs and murderers by using the RAB. The people of Bangladesh started to enjoy the peaceful life.

The opponents of the BNP were sympathetic to those murderers and raised the question of human rights violation. In their view, the innocents were less important than those of their horrible gangs were. The dramatic justice carried by the CG ignored the real corrupts and criminals for their own interest.

The opponents of BNP notoriously mischaracterized their corruptions forgetting their own. I, like many others, was one of the strong supporters of the CG, the way they were cracking down against the corrupt leaders and the bureaucrats. But now I can't trust them anymore because of their hypocritical behavior. It is clear that they distorted the entire nation with their deceptive actions.

We need to move forward with the correct vision and a well-thought-out plan. We may make up history with the evasion of the facts, but history doesn't compromise with myths and fictions. The true history is bitter to those who try to establish their corrupt mission. Their propaganda is louder than the fact. They deeply believe in mythology. They believe in fantasy but expect to get the magical result. They become the horrors to the general people with savagery actions.

The word 'civilization' is painful for them. The incivility, obstinacy, arrogance, corruption, atrocity, myths, and other evil actions are the means of their success. I do not need to write furthermore to deliver the actions of those so-called leaders. The people of Bangladesh and rest of the world are the eyewitnesses of their horrible violence with gruesome murders in the broad day light on 28th October, 2006.

The whole world couldn't ignore their actions. But the CG turned their eyes the other way. They ignored that horrible issue and went against the BNP with fabricated allegations of so-called corruptions. I think history didn't forgive in the past and will not forgive the future.

It is not unusual to get support from some of the international interest groups. But it has already caused us enormous damage to our own country and our nation. In fact, AL or the 14-party didn't work as the opponents of the BNP. They acted like the enemies of each other. The nature of their violence is the clear evidence of what their party means. Now they are trying hard to get foreign support at the cost of our national interest. You can invite someone into your home as a guest, but you can't invite others to disclose your internal facts.

On the other hand, there was no BNP during BB's administration. Why and how did the BNP become so popular in such a short period? It was because of the quality of the leadership. They never invited outsiders to damage our national interest in a way that might cost our internal securities and intelligence.

Unfortunately, this party became corrupted too because of some dissidents. We can't deny the fact that the current BNP and Zia's BNP are not the same. Martyr Zia was not a lifelong politician like BB. But his political philosophy was much more superior to those known politicians. He showed incredible success, both as a soldier and as a politician. Certain groups of people couldn't undermine his creditability. But the reality is very distinct.

True history will measure the quality of his leadership. Sadly enough, some defectors penetrated into this party, which is very normal in the political culture of Bangladesh. All political parties have some weeds. All parties need to clean up those weeds from their parties. The real solution would be to reform their parties with credible and capable leaders with a total rejection of those incapable and reckless ones.

From the above standpoints, the national *mourning day of 15th August is appropriate for his political contribution until 1971; but 30th May should go way beyond.*

Most importantly, we can't go against each other with those old issues and play the miserable roles for the people, our country, and our nation at large. The current generation has nothing to do with the old issues. Those are already history. The current generation can't afford to mangle with the old failures. We need to reset the clock and move forward.

The modern world is totally different from the past. We need to move forward, matching with the rest of the world with a better understanding and with innovative ideas of how to be one of the best nations in the world – not the worst of the worst.

The smart way to move forward is to take the lessons from the past and to correct our behavior. The political bitterness and hatred will not help our people, our country, and our nation. If you really love your country, it is better to be a patriot with a necessary contribution rather than throwing mud to one another with the old issues. We need to follow what President John F. Kennedy said, *"Ask not what your country do for you. Ask what you can do for your country."*

Express your honest opinions to encourage the current generation and the generations to come to make the difference in the lives of our people and our country.

The Unforgettable Memories of 1971

It was the bright morning of Happy Eid Mubarak of 1971. I forgot the exact date, probably sometime in November, just about a month before our Victory Day of 16th December, 1971. We all happily prepared to celebrate the Happy Eid Mubarak, but in that early morning, everything changed.

All of a sudden, we heard the very scary sound of machine gun fire not too far from our village. We have a traditional Happy Eid congressional prayer in our village home. All villagers get together, pray, and exchange Happy Eid greetings with each other every year. The most delightful part was that we meet everyone after not seeing each other for a longtime. When everybody was about to go for prayer, we all understood the real situation.

As a fearless teenager, instead of looking for place to hide, I was curious to go even closer to see the fighting scenario firsthand. We never thought the Pakistani forces would go to that remote area, away from the highways to attack. I, along with other kids, started to move toward where the machine gun fire was coming from. It was extremely dangerous but we hardly cared about that. The sounds like those machine gun fire were coming from next to our village. But from Jamalkandi and Goalmari, Daudkandi, Comilla, about three miles away from our village, Houshdi!

As we were on our way to move forward, we heard a bang slightly over our head, which were the bullets of machine gun fire. We bowed down our heads and continued to move forward. It didn't come in to our minds that one of those bullets could end our lives almost instantly. We were only about a mile away, close enough for the Pakistani barbaric forces to kill us from where they were firing.

We had to walk through the mud and water to get there. At one point, we met one of our freedom fighters, who had taken position to exchange fire with the enemies. We got close to him and sat behind him. The firing continued almost like non-stop. We spent a few hours there and decided to go back home to bring some food and drinks for him.

As it was Eid, we had lots of good food and we got some green coconuts as well. Then we went back there with that food. The fight continued about 10 to 11 hours, from dawn to dusk. The freedom fighters had surrounded the enemies from all directions by the afternoon.

After the fierce fighting, the enemies tried to escape but most of them were killed. The Pakistani forces could not return to their barracks from there and were killed. Some of them tried to flee but lost their ways to return. Some of them were found lying in the standing crops and water hyacinths to live their last moments of their life. The freedom fighters also captured their cargo ship. As the unofficial report came out, we learnt that one of our heroes, along with 12 civilians, was martyred in that fight.

The next morning, we went to see the causalities and destructions of fighting and saw three Pakistani bodies under the bridge of Goalmari where the fighting originated. Many of the bodies had been removed from there while others were probably under the water. The closest villages were Goalmari, JamalKandi, Kalarkandi, Kamarkandi, Sonakanda, Uziara, Mollakandi, Montan, Nasardi, and ours was Houshdi, about three miles away from Goalmari.

That experience is so unforgettable. We missed our Happy Eid prayer but the cause was so tense and so horrible. Indeed, that is historically remarkable. The celebration of our Happy Eid was replaced by the attack of those so called Pakistani barbaric evil forces.

In those circumstances, fighting against those evils was greater than anything else and our freedom fighters accomplished that with great valor and courage. After 38 years, I still vividly remember those days and many other memories of 1971. I believe no one can ever forget those days. Of course, everyone has many unforgettable memories of those days.

The scenario of 26th March, 1971 is really unforgettable too. People from all major cities and towns moved toward the remote villages with their families and children. They didn't use any transport or highways. They walked out and left behind everything just to save their lives. Many of them were totally detached from their villages. Known and unknown did not matter at all. Everyone started to walk, aiming to reach their village homes. People walked day and night to reach their long distant village homes in all different directions.

The villages became crowded than ever. The villagers welcomed them and tried to extend their hospitality from their heart. Many unknowns were also welcomed. Those who hardly used to go to the village also experienced typical village life for those nine months and everyone enjoyed the real hospitality of the villagers. The children of both the urban and country environments were having a lot of fun, even though the reality was the question of life or death.

They became friendlier with each other and spent their fun-filled times in totally different environment. I, as a country boy, enjoyed those days quite exceptionally with games and fishing. The journey was very challenging but the hospitality of the villagers was incredibly welcoming. The pain became comforting. The misery became pleasant. The unknown became known to each other. People adopted both misery and fun together.

Everyone used to spend their times with Shadhin Bangla Bethar Kendra (the radio station of freedom fighters of Bangladesh). The radio was the only media to know all updated information. There was neither television nor any other media. There was no electricity, telephone, or newspapers. We used to listen to the radio stations of Shadhin Bangla Bethar Kendra, Aakashbani Calcutta, New Delhi, BBC, and the Voice of America.

Most of those programs were fully inspirational, with complete updates of the war, patriotic songs, and news analysis with the commentaries of the international viewers. The support for Bangladesh from all over the world was overwhelming. The constant condemnation to Pakistani war mongers from all over the world failed to stop the war until they disgracefully surrendered to us. Our victory was marching towards us very fast.

Finally, on **16th December, 1971** the barbaric Pakistani forces surrendered to our allied forces and got a very shameful dark history for them for their generations to come. The name of **Bangladesh** had taken place in the map of the world as the land of the heroes. The excitement of Bangladeshis knew no bounds. We were exhilarated and chanted the slogan of independent Bangladesh louder than ever.

The Disturbing Period of Bangladesh: Unfortunately, right after the liberation of Bangladesh, it was a very difficult situation for many reasons.

During our liberation war, a lot of arms and ammunitions were in the wrong hands. The real patriotic freedom fighters returned their arms and a notorious group of people kept those arms for ill purposes. The robbery, lootings, and other nefarious activities took place on almost daily basis. People couldn't sleep at night peacefully. There was a horrific situation almost everywhere.

It was very difficult for BB to normalize the prevailing condition of lawlessness. Some of his close companions took advantage of that situation too. They laid down the foundation of corruption, nepotism, cronyism, and violation of the rule of laws. BB failed to control his own people, including his son who was involved with lot of scandals. People started to view him differently than as they had trusted as our leader titling with Bangabandhu (friend of Banglees); the friend we trusted the most.

He failed to maintain the integrity and the aspiration of the people. His close lieutenant leaders became divided and started to form new parties. The unique party, the AL became weaker and he drastically lost the popularity and trust of the people.

Chapter II

This chapter contains the deceptive activities of the unconstitutional chief advisor. Dr. Fakhruddin Ahmed and of the treacherous chief of army staff, Gen. Moeen U. Ahmed, along with their other associates since January 11, 2007, termed as **1/11.**

Is this not the Election of Disfranchisement?

Recently, once again, the Anti-corruption Department of the CG issued a warrant against the leaders of BNP or 4-party, including former PM, Begum Khaleda Zia, along with her two sons for corruption charges. But what about those corrupt and deadly violent leaders of AL or 14-party, including JP, the most distrustful and destructive ones! Why is their corruption and violence being ignored? Who started the deadly violence and corruptions in our history?

Over the period since 1/11, the chief advisor, Dr. Fakhruddin Ahmed and the chief of army staff, Gen. Moyeen U. Ahmed earned the overwhelming support of the general people like us with false pretence. But due to their biased operation and the revolutionary actions taken against corruption, they became the biggest concern of the people. Their popularity shrank to disappointing. We demanded justice against the corrupt of all parties. But why wasn't it unbiased?

The chief election commissioner, Dr. A.T.M. Shamsul Huda technically ejected the popular BNP from the elections with the coalition of some defectors. People may not be smart enough to understand their route but not too foolish to read their blueprints either.

It is quite clear that the whole drama played by the interim unconstitutional CG was nothing but to mislead the people to achieve their selfish mission and to be biased to their alliance 14-party.

In my last writings, I did have different opinions about them. We profoundly trusted them to control the political turmoil that turned into the deadliest political situation in our country. The vast majority of the people welcomed their starting. But as the days are going, the facts are coming to light. Their political x-ray reports become clear to clearer. People found them not to be credible at all.

They thought their propaganda against the 4-party badly damaged the image and popularity of the BNP. They couldn't bring any specific charges against them with any substantial proof. Even though they anticipated in some convincing elements of corruption, their corrupt darling parties culturally developed those from the beginning of our history.

If they really wanted to eliminate the corruptions altogether that would've been the best part of their agenda. But any biased action is the biggest violation of fairness. The current actions are clear to all of us. They are protecting the bigger corrupts on one hand, and going against their disciples of those corrupts on other hand. They are trying to make up something outrageous against the 4-party to misguide the people.

They made some headlines to mislead the people about the corruption of Zia's family and inhumanely tortured the family of martyr Ziaur Rahman only. This is a serious violation of the rule of law. They should be held accountable for their mischievous behavior. But they totally ignored the similar or bigger criminal ones and turned their eyes from those parties, the founders of real corruption and violence.

As an unconstitutional ruling authority, they tried to obliterate the BNP prior to the upcoming election. They thought the popularity of the 4-party had diminished profoundly and there was no chance to win the election. They released the former PM, Begum Khaleda Zia and were surprised to see the popularity of the BNP growing even stronger.

Conversely, they gave a free pass to their darling-parties AL, JP, and others, even though they were the worst of the worst administrators in the history of Bangladesh. The emergency was imposed not to go against the corruptions only. It was imposed because of the horrible deadly violence carried out by the rival parties of the BNP, known as the so-called 14-party, *Mohajot*, or whatever. They are the ones who caused the deadly violence. Instead of holding them accountable, they got animus to the most successful administration that did better than those two combined.

During the emergency period, they disregarded the constitution of Bangladesh and abused the rule of law to resurrect those abhorrent corrupt groups to serve their purpose.

During their dramatic process of election, they accomplished their corrupt agenda on how to re-strengthen the evil empire with the joint venture of the AL, the JP, and themselves. It became the biggest concern of their miscalculation. They failed to divide the BNP with some of the defectors of the party, tortured their genuine leaders, and exaggerated their corruptions through their propaganda media tools. But nothing worked as they expected.

Currently, they are trying to establish new charges and issued the warrant to re-try them just before the election. Their commitment was to stop the violence to conduct a free, fair, and credible election, not to disfranchise the people and the politicians. Going against the corruption is a lengthy process. They can't accomplish the historic problems of last 37 years within the stipulated time.

The over exercise of any issue with biased action against the targeted 4-party could jeopardize the total mission of political stabilization. Is this the way they would like to maintain the fairness or is this another way to accomplish their mission hypocritically?

I think people shouldn't forget the past experience of those horrible political parties they are hideously associated with. They are trying to shackle the leaders of BNP and their collaborators with the violation of rule of law and attempting to carry out the so-called election.

The sensible people are losing their temperament for their distrustful behavior. History will not forgive them either, as it didn't in the past. As a normal citizen of Bangladesh, I strongly condemn this notorious tactic of the CG and strenuously demand the free, fair, and credible election with the profound exercise of democracy – not hypocrisy.

Any attempt to score any goal in the empty field is not only against the democracy but is also an attempt to disfranchise the genuine voters and the politicians.

This is the act of cowards. This is the direct assault on our democracy. It could cause a dire consequence and the CG would be fully responsible for public uprising. If that occurs, people should demand the justice of the interim government.

Finally, I would like to remind the chief advisor and the chief of army staff not to go against the will of the vast majority of 158 million people. If you do, you would be fully responsible for all potential political consternation. You have taken the charge to resolve the problems – not to create the problems. As an independent group, our expectation was too high and we trusted you as the problem solvers. Your immoral and unethical actions are leading our nation toward the political devastation to further extent.

I regretfully acknowledge that like many others, I made a serious mistake in supporting their actions in the beginning. We trusted them without any doubt of fairness and supported their actions – not seeing their mythical actions. But their current exercises are not only distrustful to me but also to the rest of the conscientious people. Once again, they have opened up a darker chapter of the history of our nation. This nation can't afford another one. This nation will not forgive them either.

In finishing, I would like to remind them – please do not be a part of those disgraceful ones of the past. Please don't betray the 158 million people and our nation at large. Please don't do anything that costs our nation for the cause of interest groups like yours. You better follow the philosophy of martyr Ziaur Rahman, the declarer of the liberation of Bangladesh to move forward and tribute the real freedom fighters!

Our Liberation, Banga Bandhu(BB), and Joy Bangla

Recently, one of our politicians made a statement that if there was no Banga Bandhu (BB) there was no liberation. With all due respect to BB, I can't agree with this exaggeration. This kind of statement extremely underrated and undermined the contribution of the rest of the 75 million people in 1971 – especially our freedom fighters and the life and blood of 3 million people. They picked up arms against those barbaric forces to protect rest of us and for our glorious liberation. Many of us lost our loved ones in that horrible war.

Bangladesh was liberated not only for political players, but also for the active unconventional war against those barbaric forces that started genocide and killed all walks of life – men, women, children, students, and intellectuals.

Our liberation had two different phases: politics and war. Of course, BB took the leadership, unified all Easterners, and had monumental success in politics to stand against that evil regime of the West with the unity and integrity. Our people understood that we have to be united and prepared to bear any costs to protect our legitimate rights. But the war criminals Bhutto, Yahia Khan, and Tikka Khan miscalculated the bravery of the East. They arrested BB and started genocide soon after his famous speech on 25th March, 1971.

If we analyze his speech, we can see that he talked about our liberation and freedom – but not decisively. He expected the political solution to take over power as a majority leader of Pakistan. He didn't declare the independence of Bangladesh precisely, rather he put that term as conditional using the term "if" with the hope of the political solution. But the war mongers Bhuttu and Yahya didn't take his speech seriously.

They dismissed the convention not to transfer the power to BB as a majority leader. Instead, they disregarded the constitution of Pakistan and violated the rule of law. They believed that using the evil forces could scare BB and the people of the East. They didn't realize that the people of East wouldn't give up, even their leader was arrested. The people of the East would continue to fight to protect their legitimate rights. They didn't realize that if one BB was arrested, many others like BB would step up until their mission was achieved.

The people of the East took BB's speech as the ultimatum and they engaged in an unconventional liberation war. Initially, people were in despair when BB was arrested and didn't declare independence decisively. But the declaration of independence by Major Ziaur Rahman reinvigorated the spirit of the people to a great extent.

Since there was no political solution, the ultimate option was to fight against those barbaric war mongers. People were despair when BB was arrested and the Pakistani barbaric forces started to kill all innocents of the East ruthlessly. Then in our second phase, the nightmare war broke out in BB's absence. The East did not start the war but the Western uncivilized leaders imposed it on us.

In that terrible moment, Major Ziaur Rahman, along with other heroes, revolted against their military rulers with unmatchable courage and declared the independence of Bangladesh. It was the turning point of real independence. He reinvigorated the spirit of the people with the hope of our victory from the despair in that critical moment. It was very crucial at that time. They fought the war heroically until our total victory on 16th December, 1971. The barbaric forces surrendered to us very disgracefully on that very historic day of our nation.

Despite constant condemnation by the international community, they didn't stop the genocide nor cease the war until they surrendered to us. Finally, they cowardly begged for their lives. But as a heroic nation, we forgave them and made the difference in the history of mankind. Everybody was thrilled and shared the joy of freedom even though it cost us 3 million innocent lives. But their sacrifice was not in vain. They gave us the freedom at the cost of their lives but they have taken an honorable place in the minds and hearts of our people and generations to come.

Their sacrifice will be betrayed if we do not tribute the cause of their sacrifice. They sacrificed their lives fundamentally for two reasons: our liberation and to bring back BB. We got both. *Banga Bandhu* was not his name. He was honored and trusted with that title given by Bangladeshis. Bangladeshis gave this name, meaning the friend of Bangalees. The friend was uniquely trusted as a leader to lead us. We all came under his leadership, with the deepest trust, and our freedom fighters sacrificed their lives for the greater cause of our nation. He was arrested just before the liberation war broke out and we brought him back to our liberated Bangladesh only in less than nine months.

What would have likely have happened if Major Ziaur Rahman and his associates hadn't revolted against those Pakistani savage forces and declared independence? What would have likely happened, if they had surrendered to them because of the political failure? What would have happened, if they had play a timid role against the most sophisticated arms and weapons and become their loyalists? If they hadn't had played their heroic roles, we would never have got back BB and our glorious liberation. Why do some of you do not want to even pay tribute to them? Why are you denying their creditability and misleading the people of all generations to come? We should respect them with a profound gratitude.

What did we see in the aftermath of our liberation war? I have already highlighted this in the beginning. We failed to honor the real cause of the sacrifice of our freedom fighters. They sacrificed their lives for the bright future of our nation, where there will be no injustice, corruption, abuse of power, nepotism, favoritism, discrimination, or undemocratic practice.

Sadly enough, we got all injustice, corruption, abuse of power, nepotism, favoritism, discrimination, and undemocratic practice. All those evil practices took place soon after BB took over the charge of our hard-earned, newborn Bangladesh. Those evil practices took place even before the fresh blood of our freedom fighters had dried up. Our success wouldn't have been possible without their sacrifice. So instead of saying if there was no BB, there was no liberation – better you say, our liberation and bringing back BB were the result of the sacrifice and the contribution of 75 million people in 1971.

In light of the above, it is quite inappropriate to make this kind of statement. It is also misleading with the wrongful message to the generations to come. I believe denying the fact, and claiming unfair credit score is quite egregious. It is disrespectful to the real contributors of the rest of the 75 million people who risked their lives every day and every moment while the war mongers Pakistanis imprisoned him. We should not forget that everybody was a part of freedom fighters in all possible means and their contributions can't be ignored or disrespected.

In fact, an evil selfishness and greediness of power drove our mean spirited corrupt politicians, with no respect to those freedom fighters. As a result, people have been suffering in multiple ways since our independence. Most of their actions were a betrayal to the people.

As a daughter of such a symbolic leader, wouldn't it be wise to take a lesson from history? Wouldn't it be wise enough to correct the past mistakes made by previous leaders and move forward to regain the trust and popularity of the people? Wouldn't it be wise to raise the bar of decency in their behavior? Instead, they have chosen to be one of the most corrupt and violent politicians with obnoxious behavior in the history of Bangladesh. Both of them have been charged for corruption.

I have a similar opinion about the other one as well. Why, as a widow of such great president, she failed to protect the legacy of martyr President Ziaur Rahman, who was not only a great leader, but also a man of glorious personality? His contribution during and in the aftermath of the liberation war can't be faded by our history. He was not only a brave soldier, but also a man of correct vision who tried his best for the peace, progress, and prosperity of our country until the last moment of his life.

Unfortunately, we lost such a wonderful leader by the hand of some horrible conspirators who assassinated him, and the nation was in mourning longer than ever. He left behind his wife and two minor children. Naturally, their lives were shattered and took a horrible turn. The conspirators took the advantage of that tragedy and showed fake compassion to this family. Ultimately, they were the ones who used the image of Zia's family and set up their political goal. They successfully managed to mislead this wonderful family with those little children and injected the germs of corruption.

Today, they are also known as one of the biggest corrupted ones. Wouldn't it have been wise to carry out the glorious principles of martyr Ziaur Rahman instead of being misguided by those depraved politicians or companions? Their lives would have been different if they hadn't lost their father so prematurely. Sadly enough, those conspirators remain untouched. Justice lost its sanctity and the country is in perfidy.

If we deeply analyze the cause of their current crisis, the unhygienic political environment, as inherited historically, affected Begum Khaleda Zia and her sons. The real criminals are those conspirators who successfully managed to lead us to the current crisis. The CG should have gone to the root causes of this problem – not to punish unfairly the martyr Zia's family and his popular BNP. **Even though I have zero tolerance of corruption, considering the reason of their crisis, I strongly demand the immediate release of Begum Khaleda Zia and her two sons unconditionally in honor of martyr Ziaur Rahman.** I certainly support to freeze their all ill-gotten wealth, if any, rather than unfair and inhumane punishment.

Despite all the corruption charges brought against her, she did much better than the other one. She inherited those corruptions historically. There was no magic light to change that depraved political environment overnight. She was repeatedly elected a with wide margin of popularity. She made lots of improvements in security, education, and the economy. She never played any destructive and violent role when her opponent was in power.

The other only obtained power once and left the country in a horrible situation. During her administration, the gangs, donation collectors, kidnapers, and horrible murderers suffocated the entire nation. There was no security of the people. It is undeniable that the corrupt politicians has the stronghold in our political system and needs the total reform with honest and capable leaders. Until then, our sufferings and depression will never be ended.

The CG courageously took some steps to crackdown on those corrupt leaders, bureaucrats, gangs, and other nefarious activists. Now they are trying to politicize their corruptions, denying justice. Now they are talking about the human rights violations. What did they do with the humans when they were in or out of power? How many lives did they take in the name of politics with absolute violence? What was the scale of destruction and murders? If you deny the fact, you can say anything you want – but the reality is already unveiled. You can amplify your noise as loud as you want but you are not the trusted one anymore.

Despite some positive actions by the unconstitutional CG to control corruption, some of their behavior is questionable to one party or another. They are trying to obliterate the most popular BNP in the upcoming election. The chief election commissioner invited some of the fragmented or defector groups of the BNP to divide the most popular party formed by martyr Ziaur Rahman. This is a clear conspiratorial endeavor by the CG to dwindle the BNP. I strongly demand the CG not to make this horrible mistake.

The CG should play the impartial role in order to conduct free, fair, and credible elections. They should invite only the appointed leader by the party leader Begum Khaleda Zia – not otherwise. If the CG fails to do so, they will be fully responsible for the consequences. It seems to be a clear attempt to divide or weaken the strong BNP for their hidden interests. It is clearly against the sanctity of justice. If that occurs, they will lose their credibility and will remain questionable.

Joy Bangla: This was a very powerful slogan before our liberation. We all chanted that slogan against the barbaric Pakistanis before our liberation in 1971. This slogan was very appropriate and effective at that time. We confronted with them, first for our language and eventually for our liberation. Joy means "victory" (in Bangla). We have already achieved our victory for both. We have already kicked our enemies out of our land. They have disappeared. We do not have to confront with bitter Urdu anymore or any other language that could threat our glorious language. We all speak the same language – Bangla.

Secondly, this slogan is ambiguous geographically and inappropriate nationally. If we continue the same slogan that means we are still confronting some other languages. But we are not. Now we are all proud Bangladeshi.

It may cause serious reactions to many but I believe we need to correct something based on time, place, and circumstances. We shouldn't wear the winter suits in the summer or vice versa. We shouldn't wear winter suits in a tropical country. This is a matter of commonsense. We have already corrected something like the spelling of 'Dhaka'. I never supported tyrant dictator Gen. H.M. Ershad as my leader but for this correction, I did. To make corrections is the right thing to do. But to continue any inappropriate form is wrong.

In light of the above, our slogan long live Bangladesh or God bless Bangladesh is quite appropriate, rather than the confusing, ambiguous, and inappropriate "Joy Bangla".

CHAPTER III

FREE CAMPAIGN FOR THE ELECTION OF BANGLADESH – 2008

This campaign was made up prior to the controversial election-2008 based on the political behavior of different parties. All of the major party leaders started with their formal speeches. This sounds like a comedy and is humorous, but the issues are indeed related to the facts. Let's get started.

Awami League (AL):

My dear country people,

It's very much known to you who I am!

You know, it is very painful that despite being a daughter of Banga Bandhu, I was elected not more than one term since our independence. The rest of the time either our country was run by the dictators or by the genetic form of dictatorship, which is BNP.

You couldn't re-elect me and my party AL. I know all of you are very frustrated like me. I understand that my party-symbol boat was sunk. Finding no other ways, I had to choose something I had as a last resort, and used the "poles and oars." The rest...is not unknown to you.

We already showed you how to use the poles and oars. If that was not enough, we will show you what else we can do. My rivals are blaming us for the violence carried out by us. What alternatives did we have when they didn't care about our demands? Maybe my supporters and activists killed some of their supporters, but that was the normal process of our politics. To kill a few out of over 158 millions of people is a big deal! I don't think so! What about you?

You may think we are pretty aggressive. If we wouldn't have been aggressive you would never see the liberation of Bangladesh. Believe me or not, in politics sometimes we need to do something that might not look appropriate. But the success is there. Our activists should get all kinds of support to carry out any type of violence and destruction, if necessary.

As you know, we successfully exhibited the exercise of our strategy. Didn't we? We showed you how to use the poles and oars, which my father didn't do in his entire political life. We did it differently as an innovation. And it works. Is this not a progressive idea? My rivals are saying we are regressive. I think they don't understand the difference between the progressive and regressive. Thanks to the Chief Advisor Dr. Fakhrudin Ahmed and the Chief of Army Staff Gen. Mooen U. Ahmed, they arrested some of my leaders, including myself, with different charges, but eventually they understood our philosophy and favored us in many ways. They deserve some of the credit too. But I can't do everything by myself. I need your help to finish the unfinished agenda. Don't forget that still we have a long way to go.

The emergency was our contribution. If we didn't use our poles and oars against our rivals, you would never ever have the taste of the emergency, which you almost forgot during the continuous regimes of BNP term after term.

The violence in politics is not unusual. Violence is the pillar of success! The caretaker government divided BNP. This is really the good news not only for us but also for you. This is our turn. Their turns are over. Politics is not an easy business. Sometimes, it needs violence and destruction to change the course of the direction. You are the eyewitnesses as to how successfully we managed to get in this situation. This time, again I managed to convince my phony adopted brother H.M. Ershad to be on my side.

I always wanted him on my side. But sometimes he is very unpredictable and slips away. You know who he is! That's not it! We also managed to get other ingredients of Mahajot (the fragmented unknown groups that popped up with new names). You also know about B. Chowdhury who was rejected and ejected from BNP. All of them forgot their own party identity. All of them are trying hard to find my sunken boat.

Rashed Khan Menon is already talking about my boat because he doesn't have any convincing issues to talk about. So he is smart too. Instead of talking about himself, he very proudly talks about our boat. This time we are about to find our lost boat. But we need your help to rescue our boat. Some of them are using the slogan of change. Believe me, we got everything; messages of phony "change and prosperity." Oh, yes, together with my brother, the poet and the dictator H.M. Ershad will lead you in a totally different direction. We know how to make the change. But our opponent four-party doesn't. All kinds of change start from us (fourteen-party and Mohajot) — not from others. Didn't we show you our capability prior to the emergency?

October 28th was a single example only. We know you are also expecting a new style of our actions. We are committed for it. Trust me, we are ready for it. You don't know about our strategy. We successfully managed to get a boost from outside, our neighbor darling country India. I know you can't wait for it. See, I understand what you want. I'm not a poet but my brother is. Check out what he has to say in his poetic style.

Please help me out to find my boat and keep using the poles and oars until and unless we find it. Please! Please! Please!

And yes, don't forget that we were liberated for the last thirty-eight years but still we are not fully liberated. We are still fighting for our language Bangla dominated by Urdu. You know Hindi is okay! We need to make our darlings happy at any cost. We can't change our historic slogan, "Joy Bangla." We have to protect our language from the aggression of any other languages as we are facing in our land. The young generations already started to speak Hindi. Without Hindi, our culture can't progress. Just for political reasons, we will talk about our language Bangla. But without Hindi, our current generation can't even sleep. If we talk about Hindi, our rivals will find another issue. So our slogan should be:

Joy Bangla

Jatiya Party (JP)

Well...I've nothing to say. You know I was not only the dictator of Bangladesh but also known as a genius national poet. I took power from the democratically elected president, pointing the gun but didn't shoot. I'm compassionate and I do care about the lives of our people.

You know what I did with President Ziaur Rahman! My sister used her unconventional weapon oars and poles and killed some out of 158 million. As a poet, I always like to express something as a poetic style. I'm like a football too. If one side kicks me off I go to the other side. If the other side grabs me, I stay with them. If both of them kick me out I get isolated until one of them picks me up. What can I do? I can't do anything by myself. So I'm in the middle of a kicking and grabbing situation.

This time my sister Sheikh Hasina picked me up very tightly and I hope she will not toss me out again. I have a lot of pain when both of them ousted me while I played the role of dictatorship for about nine years only. It was so painful that my normal life was shattered and I became a poet. Now let me say something in a poetic style:

I might have been a dictator
But I managed to off-limit the prosecutors

People talk about the justice
But I know how to establish the injustice

I passionately believe in the rule of laws
I'm very compassionate to the criminal folks

I'm shocked to see the behavior of RAB to those folks
Both of us are committed to protect these groups

They are the one to change the direction
We are always the supporters of their actions

It's our moral obligation to support their mission
That's how we can abolish the indiscrimination

I'm running with my sister Sheikh Hasina again
To show you what we can do with joint campaign

If you elect both of us at least for one more time
We can assure you to revitalize the corruptions and crimes

We will protect the criminal rights
The innocents will not have any capability to fight

The RAB was disturbing for the criminals
We'll end their actions to protect those ill-fated ones

The criminals are also human beings
They should be respected like you and me

The innocents are too weak to fight
Why do they ask for their legitimate rights?

Don't forget us, both brother and sister
Our records are not unknown to you, brothers and sisters

We are both brother and sister
Please vote for us! Vote for us!

And yes, as a matter of principle, here I'm a little bit different from my sister. I believe we are no longer dominated by any other languages. But since I'm tightly caught up by my sister, I've to use both:

Joy Bangla & Bangladesh Jindhabad

Jamat Party

Assalamu Alaikum, (peace be upon you!)

My dear brothers and sisters,

Here you go. They've left nothing for us to say. We must thank them for their brilliant articulation. They already made it clear who they are! Now it is up to you to decide who you vote for and who you don't. We are the party of the people like you. We can't do anything on our own. Our philosophy is your philosophy. We believe in peace, progress and prosperity. Our party Jamat and BNP set the records of progress and prosperity. All credits should go to you because you made the right choice to vote us term after term.

The opponents were always engaged in hostility and atrocity. We are not poets but we have to respond the way they have articulated their philosophy.

We don't believe in weapons of poles and oars
We believe in equal justice for all

We can't do anything alone to move forward
That's why we're running with BNP together

Our success with BNP is not unknown to you
Your valuable vote will help us again to serve you

Please vote for us! Vote for us!
May Allah bless all of us!

And yes, we had been associated with the Pakistanis prior to the independence of Bangladesh, not to divide the country as Sheikh Mujibur Rahman originally wanted to do. Remember that he wanted to be the prime minister of undivided Pakistan! But due to the irreversible circumstances, we continued to stay in our position. That was all about the principle of politics.

Politics is the act of different philosophies only. Now we are all Bangladeshi and Bangla is only our national language. The confrontation of our language between Bangla and Urdu was abolished soon after the independence of Bangladesh. The existence of Urdu almost disappeared right after the independence of Bangladesh. So our slogan should be like martyr President Ziaur Rahman, the one who declared the independence of Bangladesh and fought us for until our victory! **Bangladesh Jindhabad!!**

Bangladesh Nationalist Party (BNP)

Bismillahir Rahmanir Rahim!

Assalamu Alikum,

My dear country people,

We don't want to reintroduce ourselves to you. We are already known to you for last three terms. Our success and failure are not in words; it's on the record. We had been grateful and will be if you vote for us in the upcoming election on December 29th, 2008, for the continuation of the better future of our country.

You must have already tired of vigorous and rigorous corruption campaigns against us, including my two sons. But did you ever hear that they admitted about their own corruptions? How can you hear from them when they were heavily campaigning against us, magnifying of our corruptions with the joint venture of the chief advisor along with his co-advisors using our armed forces. They already got exhausted to magnify our corruption, forgetting their own. You don't have to use the magnifying glasses to find their corruptions. They are already bigger enough to see in bare eyes.

My sincere question is to you is, who laid down the foundation of corruption since our independence? How pure was their administration? Was it better or worse? I don't want to give that answer to you because you know better than me. The corruption they are talking about, we inherited from them. This was the continual process of our culture. It is very hard to change overnight. If they want to blame us they should blame themselves first. But one thing we didn't inherit was the unprecedented form of violence. I think that's the big difference. The nature of their violence denied the civilization.

The caretaker government imposed the emergency for what, and what was their commitment? Their commitment was to you that they would present you a free, fair and credible election within the shortest possible time. Anything else was not their business. Those are the responsibilities of the constitutionally elected government.

But what did you see? I don't want to give that answer either because all of you already know what they have been doing in the last twenty-three months. What was the role of Chief Election Commissioner (CEC) Dr. A.T.M. Shamsul Huda? Didn't he try his best to divide our popular party BNP, abusing his power? Didn't he pick up some of the defectors from our party known as so-called reformists? Didn't he try to prevent our genuine leaders to exercise their responsibilities at the time of political crisis created by the CG? Did you ever see him smile? Rather, he had gloomy and angry faces in dealing with BNP. If this is the attitude, can you expect any fairness from this unconstitutional so-called CG administration? Can you expect to get fair, credible and acceptable election results?

Just about a week before the election, the so-called Anti-corruption Commission revealed a phony report of money laundering of eleven crores of taka (which is yet to be proven) of my younger son to damage the image of our party BNP. They are constantly using the media to mislead the whole nation against my son and our party.

What about the revelation of corruption of the other parties? Why don't they even mention their corruptions? If they were corruption-free saints, why didn't you vote them last term after term?

In one point, CEC apologized for his all unfair behavior toward BNP after the damage already done. Is that enough to deal with such an important issue? Is he dependable to the people? They were also engaged with gerrymandering the certain election areas to facilitate the easy winning of our opponents. These kinds of behaviors are not only against our party BNP but also against the constitution of our country. This is the clear political robbery. This is not the democracy. This is an assault on democracy.

They were animus to us, worked against us and tried their best to divide the most popular party BNP. They've arrested my sons and our leaders and tortured them inhumanely, unfairly and unjustly. This is an unforgivable crime in the name of a credible election. The history will not forgive them either. Their interest is far deeper than you can imagine. They have been unfair with us like a stepmother. But they can't be with you. Don't be misguided by our opponents.

Their propaganda against us is nothing but propaganda. Now it is up to you whether you believe in their propaganda or not. I hope you won't. If you don't, please reject them and vote for us to Dhaner Shish (Sheaf of Paddy) and help us to stay in the course of the prosperity of our country to match with the rest of the developed countries in the world. The fundamental difference between us and them is, they are regressive and we are progressive.

You are also aware of how our opponents got involved in violence and destruction. But they couldn't prevent our progressive movement. They exhibited you the unprecedented form of violence with their symbolic weapons poles and oars. If that's not enough to understand them, what else do you need to see?

We tried to control the murderers, gangs and donation collectors to protect you all and used our RAB forces. Can you deny that didn't work? If not, try to recall their administration. They themselves claim that the era of their administration was a golden period. If so, why didn't you re-elect them? I know you are smarter than them, and you did the right thing voting us term after term. I also believe you will continue to do the same. Since the other parties ended with a poetic style, let me try too.

The difference between our opponents and us are:

They know how to hurt and kill the people
We know how to protect and save the people.

They know to how to scare the people
We know how to inspire the people.

We believe in politics of progress and prosperity
They believe in destruction and hostility.

Their symbol kills the people
Our symbol feeds the people.

Now the decision is yours: who you vote for and who you do not.

Mohammed D. Hussain

I believe you will not make any wrongful choice and this nation can't afford them.

Please vote for us! Vote for us!
Our victory is not ours. It's yours!

And yes, we disagreed with their slogan right after the independence. We not only defeated the Pakistanis, we did their bitter Urdu too. Our victory was for our language Bangla and the liberation of Bangladesh. Our language Bangla is not confronting with any other languages. We are not fighting against any other languages. This is the time to move forward with progressive vision not with the regressive, insensible distortion by twisted ideology. We don't wear the summer suit in the winter and vice versa.

We believe in peace, progress and prosperity as the philosophy of martyr Ziaur Rahman. So he changed the slogan very appropriately 'Bngladesh Jindabad' (long live Bangladesh) and that was the right slogan for all. We don't believe the backdated and confusing politics. We know only how to move forward with optimism and reject the pessimism.

Bangladesh Jindhabad!

Bangladesh Nationalist Party Jindabad!

Note: The above campaign has been designed and made up based on the reflection of their political behavior and some unacceptable actions of the election process carried out by the CG. But my personal support is for none of them because I don't believe in this mafia type of election process at all. As a Bangladeshi, my support will be for **No Vote**. But this is a big **boost for BNP.**

In Response to the Program (Aye Shomoy), NTV

On December 21st, 2008, I was watching an interesting program Aye Shomoy. The participants were Dr. A. K. Abdul Momen, currently residing in USA, Mahmudur Rahaman, Chairman, Amardesh Publications, and the Journalist, Zahurul Alam the moderator of NTV.

Unfortunately, I couldn't watch the whole program, but I watched it partially. The issue of their discussions was about the election process of Bangladesh just a week before the election-2008. Dr. Momen was representing from Mohajot and Mahmudur Rahman was from BNP. Many other issues took place, such as corruptions, election campaigns of all different parties, mainly four-party and fourteen-party along with Mohajot.

During their discussions, it became very clear that Dr. Momen tried to portray himself not on the perspective of the politics of Bangladesh but the western or outer Bangladesh. He was very harmonious with the tone of Indian influence in Bangladesh with AL and other imported and distorted elements blending with old and current history. He failed to highlight the factual issues. He believed that his political ultrasound bite of the Western democracy is quite fit for Bangladesh.

There's nothing wrong in supporting any party or party members, but any biased opinion ignoring the fact to manipulate one way or the other is quite absurd especially in one of the most popular TV stations of international standards, like NTV. Most importantly, this is the election of Bangladesh. The future of the Bangladesh and its people will depend on how this election is going to be held. He acted like being a crow and tried to dance like a peacock.

He talked about the corruption of BNP, especially about the sons of Khaleda Zia and he didn't mention anything about the other parties that he most likely melted with. He complained about the previous elections and tried to beat his drum as hard as he could with negative outcry against the BNP. I didn't want to mention the old history, but his comments forced me to raise the issue about the historical election of 1973 to set an example only.

In that election, did he know what kind of riggings took place? Is he aware of the most controversial figure Knondakar Mustaq Ahmed? Did he know who the actual winner in that election was? It was his opponent, Abdur Rashid Engineer. Did he know who changed the election result and who supported that? Sheikh Mujibur Rahman himself. So when you talk about the history of election to blame, others go back in our history. The genetic flow of politics is derived from their ancestors. The most absurd was that during his lifetime, his son became one of the biggest controversial figures with many scandals. He also used to move around with arms and ammunitions. As a monumental leader, it was his serious moral crisis.

Some of the radical groups of AL always say oh! That was a very minor issue to deal with such a giant leader like BB. They legitimize those corrupt practices just because he was a son of BB. But it was his significant rational and moral crisis.

All sorts of corruption, nepotism, cronyism, etc., took place very nakedly during his administration. As a teenager, I was one of the strongest supporters of him and he was my most respectful leader for the very first time of my life when I didn't know anything about politics. But everything was faded to naught during his lifetime as I begun to know him and I couldn't support him anymore. Until today, sometimes I call him BB with some respect. But many of us even don't want to use his honorable title BB. He lost his popularity and trust of the people with no measure. The reason, it was just because of his greediness of power, moral, ethical and rational degradation.

The greediness of power and the tendency to become the political absolutist were the cause of his downfall to the extreme level. To earn popularity is not easier than to lose. Unfortunately, in his case, that's exactly what happened. He earned the highest scores politically for a limited time until 1971, but he lost his credibility very dramatically soon after he took over the charge of newborn Bangladesh.

Conversely, General Ziaur Rahman changed the course of the direction of the country with the progressive vision and did his best despite the very tough situation after the assassination of BB. During his administration, he didn't allow any corruptions, nepotism and cronyism, etc. He didn't even try to gain anything for lavish life for his own and for his next generations. He left empty-handedly until the last moment of his life. He fought for the country and served the country with glorious revolution and with fullest patriotism. This was the sharp distinction between BB and martyr Ziaur Rahman.

In other words, he was the role model of Bangladesh. Can anyone deny that we didn't see two different scenarios in the reactions of the people right after the assassinations of both of those leaders? The spontaneous reactions of the people from all levels throughout the nation were the clear indication of who was more popular than another. The simple reason is the quality of leadership and their personalities.

Naturally, the question may upraise as to why his widow Begum Khaleda Zia and his sons were corrupted and couldn't carry out the same principle that Zia left for them to follow. You might not have forgotten who took care of this family with fake emotions and ultimately trained those orphans in a very unhygienic political environment. The dictator H.M. Ershad, the most treacherous, corrupt hypocrite used the image of Zia for political purpose and got closer to this family, thus they became infected with corrupt germs.

Besides, the culture of corruption took a stronghold during BB himself in the politics of Bangladesh that was not diminishable so easily by any politicians. As a result, his sons were misguided, derailed and became corrupted. This shouldn't be the acceptable excuse but you can't ignore that totally either. Cultural sickness starts from the environment.

If they would have been taken care of properly, they could have been different than what they are known as today. They could continue the glory and the legacy of martyr Zia. But the politics of Bangladesh is not the right place to pursue the honest agenda very easily. The corrupt bureaucrats and politicians have changed the culture of politics and the way of life of the larger scale of people.

Without any corruption, you can do nothing because the corrupt groups control the whole system as against the honest ones. It is a hard nut to crack to go against those evil corrupt groups and it is a gigantic task for any party or party leaders. Before you blame BNP, you better blame AL, who is the propagator of those corruptions from the beginning of our history.

The current unconstitutional caretaker government is the genetic form of AL and doing everything to resurrect the same, which was mostly controlled by BNP. They are trying to diminish the image of BNP and, in fact, they did that to a great extent. They went against the BNP and favored AL and other so-called Mohajot.

Their crimes were much more serious than BNP. Their actions in the last twenty-three months were a total betrayal to the nation. The history will not and should not forgive them either. I did support this caretaker government in the beginning because I trusted them very strongly. But they lost the trust of the people because of their biased actions to serve their hidden purpose.

They set the date of the election and now they are arresting the supporters of BNP who were trying to campaign for the election. Why did they arrest four students of BUET just because they were distributing some propaganda written by the son of former PM Sheikh Hasina? This is not an election. This is the complete act of forceful selection. This is not an act of credible election. This is the complete act of disfranchisement. This nation spent a lot of money behind the phony caretaker government. I think people should raise their voice to boycott the election and demand the termination of the CG immediately and hold them accountable. The election they are going to hold is totally unacceptable. This could cause us to lead toward Marshal Law. In fact, this is likely to be the case and their whole purpose.

Chapter IV

Farewell 2008 and welcome Happy New Year 2009

Happy New Year to you all with the best wishes for the peace, progress and prosperity from personal level to global level in the upcoming days of 2009!

Our national election was ended up just before the end of 2008 with lots of excitement and it was very crucial for our country. The election of 2008 was a historic in many ways and ended up with lots of questions and concerns. In my last writings, I've already expressed my reaction and opinion the way I viewed the whole process of the election. It might not have reflected the genuine opinions of the voters but we have to move forward.

It is quite normal amongst many parties only one will win and the others will lose. But we have to move forward. The true history is the witness of whatever happened and how it was happened in the last election.

In the election, the most important things to consider is electing the right kind of leaders making a rational choice as oppose to the irrational choice. Similarly, the elected leaders have to think about their commitment to the people and their trustworthiness. Their responsibilities are bigger than the voters.

The winners shouldn't think that they were elected by virtue of their qualities. All major parties were severely disreputable in their administrative histories and as leaders by themselves. It was not an easy ride to get here. Something worked out to achieve beyond the imagination of both voters and the politicians.

The landslide or super slice victory by the Mohajot surprised the whole nation. It doesn't necessarily mean that they got the mandate to do anything they want. They will be watched with high beam every agenda they undertake for our nation.

The politics of twenty-first century will not allow any hidden purpose to serve. Our demand is everything has to be crystal clear and more transparent in this digital era. The landslide or stunning victory is already remained in question to the people. This question could be very costlier one, if they fail to work as their commitment.

The peace, progress and prosperity will depend how our politics and policies will be taken place by the new administration and the oppositions. They have to work for the cause of our country not for their illusion or whatsoever.

As the citizens of Bangladesh we have every right to know what they're going to do. Every step they take for the cause of our country should be transparent to the people.

If they want show something that they have learnt some lessons from their past political failure probably they will be able rebuild themselves for future. In other words, they will be on test from the beginning their administration. It will be serious mistake if they think that they have been elected because people liked them. The whole process of this mysterious election will remain in question in our history and they are the part of it.

The smart move would be to work with all parties with solemn resolution to forget the past disgrace and move forward with the spirit of progressive views for the peace, progress and prosperity of our country and our nation.

Now Is the Time to Pay the Price!

Important: The content of this issue is broader than the past one based on the changing circumstances of the politics in Bangladesh. This may sound like the previous one but is re-edited with very important issues. Please go through from the beginning to end.

Special Tribute: Let me pay my highest tribute to the **martyrs of Ekushey February,** those who have sacrificed their lives to protect our mother tongue "BANGLA," the language we were born with! The language Bangla is not only our language but also our national identity! Our mother tongue Bangla has taken a glorious place in the **United Nations! February 21st is recognized as The International Mother Language Day!**

The controversial election is over. Now is the time to pay the price!

Free, Fair and Credible Election Process!

Firstly, I'm not disrespectful to the verdict of the majority of the people of Bangladesh no matter what outcome I expected. But I can't go against my conscience. I certainly believe the election is all about the honest opinion of the people to choose their leaders through a free, fair and credible election process. The voters should have the free right to choose their fittest leader. If that was the case, I'd have been more than happy to congratulate the winner regardless of any party or party members. But if the whole process remains in question, I don't want to be guilty to support any irregularities whatsoever. Let's hope for the best and move forward.

Indeed, our people demand an administration that is free from corruption, distortion, cronyism, insecurity, injustice, violation of the rule of law, etc., and it is crucial. People also want an administration that is forward looking and capable enough to deal with every issue for the greater cause of our country. Unfortunately, this sounds quite irrelevant to most of the elected ones including their party leader Sheikh Hasina herself (**red alert**!).

The Election-2008 in Bangladesh was historic for many reasons and very crucial for our nation. Most importantly, people suffered a lot for the lack of suitable leaders and interminable corrupt systems as established by the regimes of all those who are dramatically elected (**red alert2!**)! The losers are not immune from the corruptions either. They should learn some lessons that the consequence doesn't forgive anyone whatsoever **(red alert!).**

The Real Red Alert!

The sovereignty of our country is under threat or already unprotected. Our borders are not secured and very often we get attacked by our neighboring country India with the violation of the UN charter. Our sea borders are also under challenged by the international conspiracy. Our border security forces and innocent people were attacked and are getting killed most often. This is no longer a minor concern. This is one of the biggest concerns for Bangladesh.

The election results are clear as to how the bi-national and external conspiracy took place. Their meetings in their living rooms prior to the election with the conspiracy with the CG were quite naked. After all, it was our national election. Any influence from outside of our borders was the direct rejection of the will of the people of Bangladesh.

We have been experiencing the problem of our sovereignty since our independence, during the administration of Sheikh Mujibur Rahman. As a citizen of Bangladesh, we must be prepared to protect our sovereignty first followed by the rest; trade, corridor and transit agreement with any other countries. The sovereignty of our country is bigger than us. If any mean-spirited political party wants to be sold, they may, but they can't sell the sovereignty of our country and our national interest. We should not forget that we earned our liberation at the cost of the lives of millions in 1971.

Undue Roles of India

Soon after the liberation of Bangladesh, (BB) always tried to strengthen the relationship with India very graciously! Meanwhile, India wanted to take full advantage to control Bangladesh and treated it like one of its added states.

I vividly remember on December 16th, 1971, when the Pakistani forces surrendered to the coalition forces of Bangladesh, the Indian forces entered into Bangladesh to conduct the surrender process of Pakistani barbaric forces. That was the conspiracy of Indira Ghandi. However, we the people of Bangladesh overwhelmingly cheered the day of our victory. The Indians were our closest ally and we treated them with great respect. But on their way back they took everything away from our cantonments or even from the street, whatever they liked. The armory and all other military equipment was emptied out from the cantonments. The military installations including communication systems had to be reinstalled. Since India helped us so much during our liberation war, people saw everything but didn't complain.

Some of them were very excited to see the foreign goods in Bangladesh and started to pick up everything they could. Indians are very conservative and patriotic. They hardly imported anything from other countries. In Bangladesh, everything was imported from abroad and those were qualitatively superior quality than their own.

BB was very much loyal to the Prime Minister of India, Indira Ghandi, and didn't disagree with anything; even most of those were against the interest of our newborn Bangladesh in many ways. He almost acted with Indira Ghandi as a capitulator with everything.

First Currency of Bangladesh

As a newborn Bangladesh, we had to change the Pakistani currency with the replacement of our own. We nullified the Pakistani currencies soon after our independence. We must not forget that our first currency was printed from India instead of the U.K. The quality of the bills printed out by India was the most inferior and was designed very poorly and ugly-looking. The paper used for the bills were the cheapest quality that we've ever seen. The currency was printed without any reserve or monetary control and necessary regulation like phony currency.

The forged currency was pumped out in Bangladesh with no accountability. The prices of the general commodities went up on a daily basis. The international aids for Bangladesh disappeared instantly. The comment made by the Secretary of the State of the USA Dr. Henry Kissinger, that *Bangladesh is a bottomless basket,* was not inappropriate in that situation.

The financial backbone of Bangladesh was broken from the inception of our independence by India. It was continued until the currency got printed from the U.K. with necessary monetary control. The financial damage done by India was quite irreparable.

Optimism! As a nation, we are very peace-loving and ambitious. Our country may be one of the smallest in the world. But our population is over 158 million. Moreover, very often we get a catastrophic hit from a natural disaster. We do not want to mess up with the rest of the world. Rather, we want to match with the rest of the world with mutual understanding for the common cause with any other nations in the world in dignity. We want to be one of the partners of global peace, progress and prosperity as we already are!

Struggles: Our history is not too old but very eventful. Indeed, we have seen the corruptions, nepotism, abuse of power and horrible deadly violence carried by those so-called elected leaders. To expect something different from the same groups is quite an over expectation. But who knows if any miracle happens!

Unfortunately, since our independence, we have been experiencing these problems. So who ran against whom? Was it good versus evil? Was it good versus better? Was it evil versus evil? If it was, who was bigger than the other? Was it the same all, same all? I believe everybody wanted to choose their best but they couldn't because of the caretaker gangs, not the government. They brutally tortured and tied up the leaders of BNP prior to the election while they had honeymoon with the most violent party with AL and so-called Mohajot. It was like scoring the goal without any opponent.

The Wishful Expectation

Well, it doesn't matter what we wish for! We already got used to with the same all, same all. My optimism is that it may not be the same all. It could be the best of all as against the worst of all. It is amazing the people voted the same corrupt and tyrant figures that were known historically to disgrace and cause the immense sufferings of the people during their regimes!

Perhaps they are living in a fantasy world. Who were those voters who knowingly voted them? Are these people really caring about the country or our nation? In fact, the young generation, especially the first-time voters, didn't see her regime or forgot the chapter of her gang production also known as the administration of immense corruptions. People couldn't get out from their homes without fear of getting killed. They would be considered lucky if they could return home safely. Donation collectors got free license from her because there was no justice. People couldn't build their houses in their own land without hefty donation. Many of them lost their lives.

What convinced us to believe those who threatened for the civil war and to blaze the country were also elected with a wide margin? The leader who directed her supporters to use the poles and oars as weapons to carry out deadly violence in broad daylight and danced on the bodies they killed also got elected with a huge majority? I really don't get it. Don't get me wrong, the issues I'm talking about are axiomatic. Nothing made up or falsely picked up. If I really want to pick up, I have a lot. So do you. It's the fact.

Their identity is clear. They are the historic worshipers of corruption and violence. They can do anything for their personal interest at the cost of our national devastation. They believe in myths in their words and actions. The real solution was rejecting them all. But the election results are quite matching with the actions of ghosts as recently discovered by CEC Dr. A.T.M. Shamsul Huda during the UZ election.

Hoping for!

I can't wait to see when our farmers will get free fertilizers they need for the whole year as promised by the so-called majority leader prior to the election. The business community will get their expected environment. People will get secured life under their administration. I can't wait to see the reduction of the prices of all necessities, especially food, with the affordable prices of Tk. 10.00 per Kg of rice and so on. I can't wait to see the law, and order can play its independent role. I can't wait to see when the corruptions, gangs and donation collectors will be abolished for good and forever and people will no longer get killed at home or in the street as it was during her last regime. Her single-term administration left all those horrible examples that the history can't deny. If she fails to do as her commitment, this will be the total distortion they are always good at (giant red alert!).

Cautious Optimism!

However, I'm a little bit optimistic about some of the new faces regardless of the party or party affiliations. If those new faces really work for the cause of the country and are courageous enough to fight against their own party leaders with the issues, those are against the interests of our country. If this occurs, our nation could change the course of the direction of our country.

Breaching of Commitment!

The treacherous caretaker government played a very nerve-racking role for the nation. They pretended to protect the interest of our people, our country and our nation. Their commitment was to present a free, fair and credible election at the shortest possible time. We all trusted them even though they had to do something unconstitutional to change the course of our country. But they ended up with the conclusion of devastation with betrayal. The hope of the great number of peace-loving people and their aspiration led to despair. They laid down the foundation of another injustice in our history and widened up the doors of the corruption for both the civil and army level.

The election results itself are quite mysterious. The irregularities as complained by four-party shouldn't be ignored even they became unbelievably minor. Above all, the negative political propaganda was exposed against four-party by the CG very mean-spiritedly. The history will evaluate who they are and what they did for our country.

I certainly can't support the corruption at all for moral reasons regardless of any party. I was always against the corruption in my personal life and I'll remain so. I challenged those evil practices and left lots of courageous examples in my practical life. Being an ordinary person, this sounds pretty big. But I am what I am. It might have been a little early to pick up the arms during our liberation in 1971 but it is not too late to pick up my pen to fight against the enemies of our country.

The Chief Advisor (CA) and the Chief Election Commissioner (CEC) addressed the nation separately and asked for the apology to the people for the mistakes they have made. They also requested the opposition party to accept the outcome of the election results. **It sounds very contradictory — mistakes and acceptance!** This sounds like psychosis. Both of them need immediate psychotherapy.

Why should we accept the mistakes? What would be the consequence of accepting the mistakes? Can we expect any positive change if we accept any mistakes? Aren't they mentally retarded? Should we follow them or forgive them?

We as human beings should forgive them. But the question remains, what kind of mistakes did they make? Are those mistakes willful or unintended? If they were unintended, they should be forgiven. But if they were willful, is this forgivable? Did they treat all parties equally and fairly or had they been biased to one another? If they treated them equally, it was remarkable. But if they didn't, should they be forgiven? Do they know how much cost this nation would have to pay as its consequence? Who will be responsible for betrayal to the nation?

If they didn't make any of those serious mistakes, why should they ask for forgiveness? They should have been proud of whatever they did. Our nation should remember them with great honor. They do have some concerns and those are extremely serious! They may be smart enough to a certain number of people but not too smart to convince 158 million! They may claim the mysterious majority but the reality is quite unrealistic!

They left lots of examples that they would remain questionable in the history of Bangladesh. We may forgive them but the history will not! This nation has every right to ask for the explanations of the questions and concerns as mentioned above. Probably they shouldn't be surprised if they were brought to justice for the crimes they have committed! This nation shouldn't forgive them at all!

Bring them All!

It became imperative to bring them all to justice for the cause of greater interest of our nation. They are nothing but a group of gangs who came with phony jerseys for the just causes to distort the whole nation. Their distrustful activities of the twenty-three months need immediate justice with exemplary punishment!

The so-called Chief Advisor and the Chief Election Commissioner (CEC) betrayed the whole nation with a phony commitment to carry out a free, fair and credible election. Instead, they disfranchised the genuine voters. This is an unforgivable crime and shouldn't be forgiven. The CEC is a total disgrace. He is very much aware of what he did by his hypocritical behavior with BNP. He tried to break the most popular party BNP in pieces with the association of some defectors. He doesn't know how to smile. The criminals can't smile. Their gloomy faces are the index of their identity. He needs to go to the smile therapist to treat his freakish behavior.

And yes, the Chief of Army Staff Moyeen U. Ahmed tried to play his role like H. M. Ershad. He betrayed the former Prime Minister Begum Khaleda Zia as Ershad did with martyr Ziaur Rahman. Any interference of the army threatening to the civil administration is the act of cowards and is a serious violation of the rule of law! He tortured her sons brutally to disabled with the pretext of corruption! As the chief of army staff, he didn't have the guts to defend our borders and our sovereignty. He is a total disgrace as the chief of army staff. His crime is unforgivable! He is a real coward! Does he remember what he swore at the event of joining in the armed forces?

He attempted to snatch power from the civil government. This is an unforgivable crime to take the power from the civil caretaker government. He should be fired and prosecuted immediately. The people of Bangladesh want to see him as the number one criminal behind the bar! The gangs of the criminal caretaker government should be prosecuted without further delay!

His business was in the cantonment and he should have followed the order of the civil government — not to take over the power from the civil government. But his crime along with the whole gangs of so-called advisory groups who snatched the power from the CG is the biggest one in the history of Bangladesh. He failed to serve his purpose to take over the power with the same style as Ershad did with the elected president Justice Abdus Sattar. The tyrant Ershad was successful, but he wasn't.

So as the last resort to survive, he made a secret deal with one of the most violent parties AL and with so-called fragmented destructive groups of so-called Mahajot. They were the ones who caused the **1/11**. Instead of going after the originator of deadly violence and constant destructionists, they arrested the sons of the outgoing Prime Minister Begum Khaleda Zia along with the leaders of BNP with the pretext of corruption. Is corruption is a new word in Bangladesh? Go back to the history of Bangladesh from BB and look at your own criminal faces! Again, don't get me wrong, I'm not in favor of any corrupt of any party. I strenuously demand justice through the legal process, not by brutal means.

Do they know who they betrayed with? She was our national pride who very successfully came to the power with genuine elections, not with the boost of external influence. She came to the power with the genuine popularity. She was the prime minister of Bangladesh term after term because she did much better than the one they were biased with and still she is amazingly popular.

Besides, do not forget the contribution of martyr Zia as a promulgator of the Independence of Bangladesh, as a heroic soldier, as an extraordinary president and as one of the few in the history of human history!

If it was a free, fair and credible election, the result would have been quite the opposite. This is not the result of election. This is the result of robbery. It is quite nonsense to believe that the number of areas people voted 90 to 100 percent, which has never happened and practically quite impossible not only in Bangladesh but also any other developed countries in the world.

Just watch how our nation will have to pay the price for the treacherous actions of their joint crimes with the so-called unconstitutional caretaker government! This nation shouldn't forgive them at all.

Recently, the disgraced CEC in his own statement said that he discovered some ghosts in the UZ election. This is not the ghost Mr. CEC! This is your production! If those are ghosts, I'd like to know who you are! You are fully responsible. I don't find any appropriate title for you whether it should be "ghost" or "producer of ghosts." Maybe you are both. The UZ election is the clear example of how you carried out the MP election and its mysterious results. The whole election process was ridiculous and was quite unacceptable to the sensible people. This nation shouldn't wait for another day to bring you to justice for the crimes you've committed against our nation.

Trade and other Bilateral Agreement with India!

The new controversial administration is so much enthusiastic to sign the trade, corridor, indoor, outdoor — whatever the doors they are talking about — and transit or exit agreement with India! Their deepest honeymoon with India could cost our nation a serious blow.

They shouldn't forget the past history since our independence. I've already mentioned in my writings how they behaved with us immediately after our independence. The people who are over fifty are aware of the behavior of India since our independence. It will be the gravest mistake if they turn back to the same page of our history.

They don't have the guts to raise the issue of our border problems who deliberately carried out the attacks against us by using their BSF and killing our border security personnel and innocents. They came to power with their influence and will capitulate with everything to make them happy at the cost of the vulnerability of our sovereignty. This is one of the serious concerns of Bangladesh. Our national interest is far more superior to their mean-spirited political greed. They are blackmailing our nation.

I'm not against the Indians but their historic behaviors are a serious concern for us. We should not repeat the same mistake as Sheikh Mujibur Rahman did with Indira Ghandi!

Dream of Job Creation and Economic Stimulation!

This is nothing but the fantasy. We are one of the most densely populated countries in the world. The infrastructures of our roads, highways, bridges and culverts are very weak for our own. Our lands are not suitable enough to extend the roads and highways and quite insufficient to deal with our own transportation needs. It will be utter nonsense to allow India to use our roads, highways and ports for their transit. Our ports are also in a similar situation. How can we agree with India to sign the agreement of trade, corridor and transit? There will be no job creation or economic stimulation. It will be an economical, social and cultural disaster. Besides, our borders will be quite opened for in-and-out for Indians. The pressure of a vast country like India on our tiny country Bangladesh will be devastating for us.

However, as a non-politician and having an extremely busy life in foreign land, I have written a lot since June 2006 before they took over the power through dramatic emergency. I strenuously supported the CG in the beginning, but I'm deeply saddened to see their activities of the last twenty-three months.

What about You, the Phony Prime Minister Sheikh Hasina!

Recently, you have made a statement to make a list of the corrupt from the period of BNP and the caretaker government administrations. This sounds very amazing! Everybody wants a corrupt-free government! People can't wait for that kind of government!

May I courteously ask you why you've excluded yourself and your past administration? Why don't you want to go further behind? One of your so-called junior ministers said that to find the criminals; he would go as high as he had to go as low as he had to reach. This is quite a fanatic way to express something he wants to go against the targeted group. Why didn't he say as far behind as he had to go, rather than the period of BNP and the unconstitutional CG only? He is very much aware that would be very surprising because you would be one of the top ones too! Instead of sitting in the office of the prime minister with a controversial election you should have stood behind the bar! Do you really believe you are above the law?

If you accumulate your corruptions and deadly violence, you should have already been in jail without any payroll before everybody else that you are trying to target. You shouldn't try to hide behind the mirror.

And again, if you go further back to our history since our independence, you shouldn't be surprised to see many more of your own. For the greater cause of the country and to protect its sovereignty, you should stop the political absolutism. It is old-fashioned politics and your father was not successful at all. You are trying to play the same old failed game and you will definitely be failed. You may fail but our country can't. Our country is much bigger than you. You are very much aware of how you have come to power!

You are wicked enough to understand that with the genuine popularity, you can't obtain power so you need external boosts. So you made a choice of treason not to care about the sovereignty of our country. You need only the shameful authority. The real patriots are still ready to fight against your ill-aspiration, and they should!

Instead of your dream of fantasy, you better try to do something that at least if you could regain the lost image of your father and of your own. The history is still alive. Please take some lessons from your history and move forward with necessary corrections. My advice may be bitter to you but if you follow, you may get sweeter results.

Finally, I wish the peaceful, prosperous and progressive future of Bangladesh and its people.

Is the BDR Crisis is The Political Issue Only?

I'm deeply shocked to see the horrible rampage of Bangladesh Rifles (BDR) against their officers. I do not have proper language to condemn their behavior. My deepest condolence and sympathy to those officers who lost their lives, their families, their children and their well wishers! In fact, the whole nation is their well wishers. I would like to offer my thoughts and prayer to the Almighty to strengthen the ability of the survivors to overcome such a heart-broken situation. I also demand the justice of those who are responsible and found guilty to carry out such a cowardly attack.

I was deeply thinking about this rampage and was wondering why the soldiers tried to achieve something in such a horrible means. Who misled them and why they didn't think about the consequence of doing so. I was also thinking if there were any alternative ways and means to prevent that deadly clash.

Who are the BDRs? The BDRs are not the aliens. They are our people. This is one of the historic forces of Bangladesh. They are the one who protect our boarders risking their lives and very often get killed by the Indian BSF. In other words, they are protecting our borders and the sovereignty of our country. They are the front liner to face any devastating natural disasters of our country as well. There must be some evil groups within who misled them to carry out such a horrible operation or their wrath went beyond their control for some reasons.

It's the time to find out the root causes with the joint efforts of all political parties, intelligence group and the people in general. It's not the time to play any destructive political game blaming each other for the greater cause of our country.

Historically, we are not immune from such horrible atrocities. We lost our symbolic leaders assassinated very ruthlessly those are; Sheikh Mujibur Rahman, martyr Ziaur Rahman and many other high profiled political and military leaders, intellectuals and many innocent people since our independence. We lost them mostly because of the political reasons, greediness of power, corruption, discrimination, exploitation, mistreatment and jealousy of certain classes of people.

On the contrary, some of them lost their lives just to protect the national interest too. Of course, some of them dedicated their lives for the greater cause of our country and our nation. But the real innocents have had to go through unbearable miseries for the rest of their lives.

In this case, we need to overview the fact very deeply before we jump on the conclusion. We need to figure it out who are against our BDR forces? Who kills our BDR forces? Who do not want our strong defense forces in Bangladesh? How serious threat is this for our national security? Why it's happening now right after our election? What kind of policies could cause such a horrible incident? Irrespective of our political party differences we need to focus on our national integrity and security and the sovereignty first.

We may have different political views, but in question of our national security, we need to be united to protect our national security and its integrity.

Internal Anger and Resentment: Secondly, people do not get proper justice and are being discriminated with no measure. The corrupt politicians and bureaucrats fulfill their evil desires impudently. As a result, very few of the sufferers react very aggressively and caused such horrible atrocity too.

The systematic exploitation and mistreatment could be the leading causes to fuel the flame of anger and resentment. The recent BDR rampage is another clear example that our nation is currently dealing with.

As some statements came out from the BDR forces that they had some demands that they wanted to address to the Prime Minister through their commanding officers or the Director General of BDR. But they didn't get any amicable response rather they were threatened in military style. They failed to reconcile and handle their issues or not to listen to them at all. As a result, the BDR forces might have got angry and carried out such a horrible attack on the officers. Whatever the reasons might have been, the ruthless attack on officers was absolutely unconscionable. They should have followed up the issues patiently and lawfully.

To us both the soldiers and officers are equally important. They are our people. Perhaps to some extent they are interrelated to each other. I do not see any reason to become animus against each other that could lead such a horrible attack. They should have been treated with mutual respect with amity not to make too much difference with any exploitation and mistreatment. If that was the case, the whole ruthless atrocious situation could have been avoided.

Over and over we have been experiencing those horrible experiences since our independence. Our history is not too old but very eventful. We never tried to take any preventive measure prior to worse things to happen. Since our independence we have been experiencing the continuation of the same corrupt system and in some cases even getting worse. As a consequence, we have seen those unimaginable horrible occurrences repeatedly.

We always jump on the conclusion, if and when something happens and blame the responsible groups to punish them. Of course, we should go after those groups. But we hardly do care about the root causes of those problems and fail to take preventive measures. If we do not take any preventive measure with necessary correction, the continuation of the same may not be stopped. It's the time to stop all abusive policies from all departments both in civil and the military administrations.

Rename of BDR! I don't think the renaming of BDR will be the perfect solution at all. Changing the name can't make any difference. The real difference needs a significant rational and moral solution in a justified manner. We all know what is the difference between the officers and the soldiers? We all know there is a huge difference between the officers and the soldiers not only in positions but also the unfair treatment, salaries, promotions, facilities and benefits.

The Moral and Ethical Degradation: Although the civil and military administrations have different form of administrative strategy they should maintain some form of moral and ethical obligations. The army officers in Bangladesh are enjoying the highest benefits comparing to any other developed countries of the world. I'm not jealous to their salaries and benefits. I'm proud of their living condition. But at the same time, I do not want to see any discrimination and exploitation to their service providers, the soldiers.

Most importantly, they are the immediate protectors of our country. I don't care how many luxury houses or cars the officers own. But I do care how they get all those with their lavish life style by the limited salaries. If their wealth is legitimately earned I'm proud of them. But if those are questionable, I abhor them and they must be partly responsible for the consequence too.

It may be nerve-racking to the officers of the BDR in current situation. But I'm trying to figure out the real cause of the resentment of the BDR forces. Most of the army officers change their fortune while they are deputed to BDR for a certain period of time with responsible assignment.

In fact, this is like the department of customs to some officers. They make incredible amount of money dealing mischievously with high rated smugglers and so on. If we carry out a survey of their wealth and resources with their lavish life style we can easily figure it out how they change their fortune.

On the other hand, the BDR forces those who lose their lives to protect our borders and the sovereignty of our country get nothing in their whole life. If this is not the discrimination, what then is discrimination! I certainly respect those officers who are honest and dedicated but those are very few. I knew from my boyhood that army officers were very honest and dedicated that's why I myself was very interested to join in the armed forces. Unfortunately, I was not one of the selected ones.

After the liberation of Bangladesh that perception has been changed. With a very few exceptions, the corruption in the armed forces became overrated. Some of them have changed their fortune with no measure. The difference is clear. If we look at the life style of honest officers - both in civil and military administrations are very simple but honorable. They are not questionable at all.

On the contrary, if we look at the corrupt officers their life style is quite questionable and disgraceful. Despite, there are many honest officers in the army and other forces. Martyr Ziaur Rahman was one of them. I have the deepest respect to him and the officers like martyr Ziaur Rahman. He didn't have any presidential palace but some of the corrupted ones are no longer hidden in the eye of our people. I believe in moral and ethical justification and it is extremely important to prevent such occurrences.

I've seen in Bangladesh and heard some stories from our own officers who came here in the USA for higher training. The life style of the army officers in the USA the most powerful country in the world is quite different than our own. The life style of a Major or even a Captain in our country is way higher than the Colonel or superiors in USA or even our neighboring country India!

Some of the personal services as received by our officers are beyond their imagination. I suggest go to India and see the difference of the life styles of the same ranking officers between India and Bangladesh. They are one of the most powerful countries of the world too. I visited some of the army and BDR officers in Bangladesh too like many of you. We can easily see the difference.

The Preventive Suggestions: We need to determine how far is too far and how much is too much. How the BDR forces are being treated. I think it is too unfair, immoral and unethical in our existing system. We need to change the systematic colonial style abusive and discriminatory custom of services. This is not only immoral but also inhumane.

We need to upgrade the standard of life not only of BDR officers but also others who are really risking their lives during the crisis. They should be treated with respect too. They should serve our country - not to serve as master-like service provider to their officers. We shouldn't follow the customary manual of the primitive ages. We are in twenty-first century and should move forward by rejecting the old fashioned abusive authority.

Their dignity should be ensured. Their children should get equal educational opportunities and other facilities to move forward with high aspiration. This will enhance their dedicational spirit to serve our country rather than their silent resentment and frustration. The frustration leads to anger and anger leads to reckless behavior. I think if we can change the colonial style slavery-like system we can prevent any such reoccurrences in future.

We want them to be happy. The happiness will lead them to serve the country better. I think the rampage on February 25th was not the political only but also the systematic discrimination. It was the explosion of their anger of frustrations. In a nutshell, we need to give up the old abusive style of culture and move towards the modern world order.

The Current Politics and Policies: The current politics and policies of Bangladesh are quite alarming for our border and the sovereignty of our country. They are too much loyal to their master India and attempting to sign the agreements between Bangladesh and India for trade, defense, intelligence, transit, corridor etc. at the cost of the devastating effect to our country.

For the greater interest of our country I'm strongly against those agreements with India but I'm very open to any other countries of the world. The historic behavior of India is the biggest concern for us. All of us especially the policy makers should protect our national interest first instead of their own. The historic behavior of India with newborn Bangladesh is the dangerous signal for us to trust them anymore.

We have seen over and over our BDR forces got attacked and killed by the BSF of India. Our military leaders had some so-called flag meetings to resolve the border problems but they were not successful at all. Over and over our border securities BDR are getting killed including many innocent civilians in the border area. Is this not capitulation to India? As a member country of United Nations why our border securities are under attacked very often with the violation of UN charter? Our politicians never raise this vital issue rather they want to gain everything at the cost of unprotected national security.

The current ruling party was always apologetic to India even our border securities were killed by BSF very unjustly. The army officers who failed to reach any solution with India treating the BDRs discriminately. This kind of behavior is the total betrayal to the life and blood of our freedom fighters in 1971. We were liberated from Pakistan not to get sold to India.

The current controversial administration is always trying to blame their opponent party BNP who are against those agreements. This is not only the biggest concern of the party BNP but also for all sensible and patriotic people of Bangladesh. The controversial prime minister is quite aware of how she came to the power. She is also aware of how popular her opponent is! Therefore, she and her groups are always trying to blame BNP with everything. She doesn't care about the devastation of our country. She wants only the power at the cost of our national insecurity. She believes in the same formula as her father did.

I was surprised to hear from her recent address to the nation about the violence. She said, "Violence begets violence". Well, this sounds a little bit rational I guess, rather than her lifelong destructive and violent behavioral history. Did she forget how violent she was throughout the last two terms until prior to 1/11? Who directed the vicious followers to carry out the deadly violence with the poles and oars in the broad daylight on October 28, 2006 and killed about twenty-eight people and wounded many more.

The scenario of the horrific barbarism of ruthless murders on that day was unprecedented. The whole world watched that horrible violence. They also danced on the bodies they killed? Was it less barbaric than the recent BDR's rampage against the officers?

The sermon of non-violence at least from your mouth is quite a laughable joke madam prime minister! The corrupt judicial department during the Caretaker Government (CG) couldn't bring her to justice. Instead, they made her the Prime Minister of Bangladesh! Is this the rational choice of our people or was it people's choice at all?

She has already made the history of violence, destructions and gang production. Her single term administration left those examples that people could ever forget. She knew that she didn't have any popularity to get to power so she has chosen the violence and external boost to achieve her goal. She got the boost from CG, the betrayer Army Chief and from external sources. It was enough for her to obtain power. The rational voters were disfranchised by the CG in the name of free, fair and credible election.

The whole election process was totally ridiculous and willful distortion by the CG ignoring the genuine opinion of the vast majority of the people. I think there is no difference between BDR's and her brutal political tactics as we have seen during last two terms of BNP. If there was real justice she should have been behind the bar with the so-called CG along with their advisory group.

Remember, Sheikh Mujibur Rahman was not successful with political absolutism and you'll not be either controversial madam prime minister! I use the honorable addressing the word "madam" but you didn't pay minimum respect to the President of Bangladesh. You mocked him dishonorably with his name Iazuddin Ahmed to "Yes Uddin Ahmed". You were never been respectful to him nor your opponents.

In 2006, you made a very mean spirited remark about his health crisis. Instead of wishing him recovery from his health crisis, you made a mockery comment saying that was a politics. You need to behave yourself appropriately, if you want to be respected by others. You better please serve the country for the greater interest of our nation, not yours or your party. Our country and our nation are way bigger than you and your party!!

If I was in Bangladesh it would have been very risky to express the factual issues so courageously. I know lot of sensible people have the similar opinion but they can't express their opinion under the current circumstances. If you and your army loyalists attempt to go against me it will be obstructive to express my freedom of speech with the real issues and you will be fully responsible, if anything happens to me.

Some of your loyalists are already threatening me indirectly. But I will continue to write anything, if and when I see something against our national interest for the greater cause of our people, my country and our nation, no matter where I live. I don't want to see any corrupt and destructive politics and policies in my country Bangladesh.

Circumstantial Issue #1-2010

First, let me express my deepest thoughts toward the Haitians who lost their lives in the recent devastating earthquake – we can never imagine! It is our utmost priority to extend our effort to help them out to recover with all humanely possible ways.

Let's help them out and continue to do so until their full recovery. Our little contribution could help them a lot, and they need it swiftly. I think it is our obligation to do our best to stand by them with generous help as best as we can.

In Bangladesh, we also need to help those are suffering from severe cold and losing their lives for the lack of warm clothes and poor housing conditions. They very badly need our help and we should do our best to protect them from shivering cold.

Honorable Secretary General of the United Nations and World Leaders! I would like to draw your attention to the current political crisis of Bangladesh, where most of the 158 million people are victims under the current illegitimate administration of PM Sheikh Hasina.

I also would like to draw the attention of the international human rights groups to investigate the matter of protecting the people from the current tyrant authoritarians and those who do not care about the lives of the peaceful people of Bangladesh. They are grossly violating the rights of any human being who is against the current sadistic administration.

They should be prosecuted in the international court because they do not respect the constitution and the rule of law of our country.

As one of the patriotic citizens of Bangladesh, I believe it is my obligation to speak out for the greater cause of our people, our country, and our nation. I'm neither a politician nor an activist of any political party, but my real identity is that I am a proud Bangladeshi.

It is not an easy task to express the facts and figures under the current illegitimate administration. They obtained power with a mafia-style election and are acting in same style. They have assaulted the democracy and judicial system just to be the authoritarians that the modern civilized world order denies.

They have managed to regroup gangs who do not care about human rights or the rule of law. They are fully equipped with the necessary evil power, where the majority of our people can't even express themselves. Some of them have been eliminated already and the rest of them are being tortured under their harsh custody.

I myself received some death warnings from their evil dupes and I need protection for my family, the rest of the peace-loving people of Bangladesh, and myself. I didn't threat them with any arms and weapons; I have just written the factual issues that are very sour for them.

During the last administration, they already exhibited how horrifying they are! Their historic deadly and destructive violence are the evidence that true history can't ignore. To take the life of any human being is no matter at all!

The following are the speeches I've written for our both major political leaders in reflection of their actions and behaviors.

Performance Report of the Year-2009 of the Illegitimate PM of Bangladesh

Recently, the illegitimate PM Sheikh Hasina addressed the nation and tried to explain her tremendous success of her first year administration of year-2009. Most of the issues she talked about were quite ambiguous and not the real issues at all. She absolutely ignored the facts and tried to convince the nation with falsifications. She was rambling with the issues of her performance and tried to make a convincing speech to the nation.

I am not a speechwriter, but I would like to volunteer to write the speeches for her and her opponent former PM Begum Khaleda Zia about their real performances based on the reflection of their attitude and political behaviors in the way they should have addressed the nation.

First, Sheikh Hasina

My fellow Bangladeshis,

Happy New Year to all of you! Farewell to the year-2009 and welcome the year-2010.

As you know, we have been in power exactly one year and very successfully accomplished our agendas that our country needed the most.

You must not have forgotten how we obtained power, and how difficult it was to get to power to serve you in a very difficult situation of our nation. Before I talk about our performance, I would like to reiterate some important issues of the past and our outstanding achievements.

You know that being a daughter of Bangabandhu, Sheikh Mujibur Rahman, I couldn't get to power more than once in our history of the last 38 years. You were fully responsible for my failure. It was not very easy to attain the current situation.

We had to struggle and sacrifice much to fight against my rivals, who were the cause of our obstacles. But I was persistent enough to achieve our goals and applied all necessary tools against my rivals to get to power. But it was not an easy business. We applied all necessary tools in the past but could not achieve anything against my rivals.

The year-2006 was the blessing year for us and we managed to horrify not only my rivals, but also the whole nation with our deadly violence and destruction. We earned tremendous popularity not only nationwide but also from our darling neighbor.

We caused the historic **1/11**. As a result, the constitutional CG couldn't hold the election in 2006. If we couldn't have prevented the election, we never could have won at this point. This was the milestone of our subsequent success. Our persistent deadly violence contributed to the emergency that you almost forgot in the history of Bangladesh.

Well, you might have thought that we were very aggressive and played very violent roles during that period. Indeed, it was, but it contributed much to changing the progressive direction of our politics. In politics, there is no such word of 'violence, corruption, and destruction', especially in Bangladesh. These are the necessary tools to change the course of the political direction. We did exactly the same very successfully.

Our rivals continuously ruled us and we didn't have any chance to gain control over our politics. In those circumstances, it became inevitable to engage ourselves in the politics of horror and that was the wheel of fortune for us.

Didn't you see that during their administration, 80 percent of our time we walked out for long- and short-marches and disrupted everything with destructive and deadly violence until all government and private activities collapsed? Didn't we put you hostage in your home to have enough time with all of your family members? The rest of the 20 percent of the time, we planned how to execute those destructive plans. This is called the real democratic movement and the duty as an opposition leader.

The unconstitutional emergency CG was just a political drama. I did it with great success. Fakhruddin and Moeenuddin acted as the villains in that drama. They also played an admirable role in dwindling our opponents with treachery with former PM Khaleda Zia as Mir Zafar and Alibordi Khan did with Siraj-ud-Daula. Their treacherous actions contributed to weakening our rivals and now they are at our mercy.

We do have profound control over those political rivals. I needed some fanatic cabinet members to control them and I did it very successfully. You might have noticed the lunatic behavior of Sahara Khatun, Sajeda Chowdhury, and many other cabinet members. This is very important in our current situation.

Some of our own party leaders became psychotic and tried to tell some truth; but I managed to put them out of power or be almost inactive. I also alleged Abdul Jalil to be a tax evader to keep his mouth shut. The other one, Taz already left voluntarily. If any of my party leaders come out to tell the truth, I will do the same or will take even harsher action.

In real politics, we do have some open agendas; others are hidden. In open agendas, we always say what you want to hear but in hidden agendas, we do what we intend to do. So we are not worried about what we committed to you prior to the election. These were convincing issues only.

We assured you of your wishful expectations: free fertilizer for all farmers at least for the whole year; reduction of the prices of the necessities at the rate of Tk. 10.00 per kilogram of rice; a crime free society where there will be no gangs; and violence, corruption, and re-establishment of an independent judicial system; and many more, just because you wanted to hear about these issues. But our hidden agendas were how to keep control over our opponents and to mislead our people to beat our rivals in the election-2008. We were very successful in our strategy.

Now let me say about our hidden agendas. You might also have noticed that we did something that we never mentioned in our agendas prior to the election and that we are accomplishing one by one.

First, we served an eviction notice on our rival former PM, Begum Khaleda Zia for her house! We are already in the process of removing her from that house and almost pushing her out from politics. She had been dominating us since the assassination of her husband Ziaur Rahman. People made a huge mistake to give her that house in so-called honor of the services of her husband who came to power with military might.

You may have the question of why I am so serious to take the step to remove her from that house. The answer is simple. Why should she get that house? People displayed the wrong emotions after the assassination of that dictator. But they didn't have any emotion when my father was assassinated with all our family members. Many of you cheered too. Some of my supporters tried to allocate me the "Bangabhaban" but you didn't support that cause and I didn't get it. Being a daughter of Bangabandhu, if I didn't get it then why should she?

He was also involved in assassinating my father. I have been waiting for this retaliation for so long and finally I managed to do what I wanted to. My adopted brother Gen. H.M. Ershad did the best job in that regard.

Nevertheless, I put her in trouble in many other ways. I have already put her sons, not only out of politics but also out of the soil of Bangladesh. They do not have any right to live in Bangladesh. We are also formulating charges to diminish their political ambitions in the future. I will keep doing this until they retire from politics voluntarily to clear the way for my next generations as my father failed to do.

I will also manage to keep formulating many other serious charges against their leaders too. I will keep doing this until they look for the exit door from politics. I will obliterate their so-called BNP. In this land, only my party, the AL will be the only party and no other parties will be allowed to exercise their so-called democratic roles.

The BDR case is another successful issue. I am trying to hold them accountable too. Don't think I'm doing all this just because of your support but because of our deep relationship with my lord India. They are committed to support me by any means. In order to do so, you must sacrifice a lot.

We shouldn't complain about the occupation of our Talpatti Island, sea-borders, and the land-borders problem, Farakka Barrage and Tipaimukhi Dam my lord India. My lords are killing some of our BDR forces whenever they like, including some innocent civilians. I believe this is not a big deal. In order to get their support, we need to sacrifice something. We should consider this part of our sacrifice.

In fact, we don't need any defense forces. My lords are committed to degrading or dismantling our defense forces and only 57 officers were killed in the BDR crisis. They are the ones who will take care of us, as the solidarity will remain under their control. We, as a small country, need to depend on our lords and should be loyal to them. This is the only way we will protect our sovereignty.

Second, considering all their contribution, I have opened up our borders, corridors, indoor and outdoor transit trade, and much other openness to make them happy. We are very small country and we should not be too much worried about our sovereignty and integrity.

Third, I managed to nullify the Fifth Amendment with the support of my loyalists. This was the obstruction to carrying out the justice of the assassinators of my father and the war criminals of 1971.

My father was extremely popular leader who liberated our country Bangladesh. May he be tried to be the political absolutist or authoritarian; was it enough cause to assassinate him, including our family members? Bangladesh was liberated just because of my father Bangabandhu, and he had every right to do so. It is long overdue to carry out the justice of his assassinators. Now I'm doing exactly what I need to do.

My rivals are saying that Ziaur Rahman was the declarer of the independence of Bangladesh. If it was so, then what did my father do? Ziaur Rahman was an army officer like many others. Rather, he took power from a very popular leader Khondakar Mustaq Ahmed in an undemocratic way and became the president of Bangladesh by himself. He didn't obtain power through democratic means as Khondakar Mustaq Ahmed did. He came through military might with coups.

We should expunge the so-called legacy of Ziaur Rahman. I don't want to see anything in his name. My next agenda is just that and we are progressing in that direction. I'll remove his name from everything, including from our history.

I have already initiated the process of removing his name from Zia International Airport to something else and am opening up another bigger international airport in my father's name to recover his eroded legacy. I have lot of things to do to control the damaged image of my father.

I have also taken the agenda to re-write our history. In that history, there will be no room for the name of Ziaur Rahman. I will erase his name from the history for good and forever.

My rivals are raising the issues of our deeper bilateral relation with India. They say, I'm surrendering to India and selling our country, Bangladesh, betraying our freedom fighters of 1971 as my father did. Who were those freedom fighters? They were the followers of my father. They sacrificed their lives for the cause of my father not for the liberation of Bangladesh. Whatever he did after the liberation of Bangladesh was absolutely necessary. But the rebellions assassinated my father very ruthlessly.

My rivals are blaming me as a traitor. I think they are out of touch about the nature of our politics. To beat our rivals we could be any. It is within my capability to make a secret deal with outsiders at the cost of our national disaster.

If the people support any wrongful political party and leaders, what should I do? I do not believe in the philosophy that our country and our nation are bigger than my party and me. If the people don't know how to choose their leader, they should suffer.

During the repeated terms of our rivals, they damaged us seriously politically but you ignored me with no rational justification. You kept electing my rivals term after term. But you didn't know the consequences of your unfair selection.

I was elected only once in a very controversial manner with a conspiracy with the dictator Ershad and my regime was the golden period of Bangladesh. But you didn't elect me anymore. Why didn't you? If you choose the wrong leaders, you must suffer. That's why you are responsible, not me. But you made the same mistake so you are responsible for the consequences. Instead of blaming me, you had better blame yourselves.

In the last election, you understood the importance of my past administration and you made the right choice by electing me in such an unprecedented manner. I must thank you all. But it will be very difficult to overcome the damage you did by electing the rightful leader term after term in the past. If you didn't elect me in the last election, you never had any taste of my administration. Now I'm trying my best to serve as you deserve.

I would like to remind you and make you aware that you need to have lot of patience and should be ready for more sacrifice to achieve our goal.

Recently, I attended the summit of "Global Warming" in Copenhagen to represent our country Bangladesh. Unfortunately, Bangladesh is in the most vulnerable situation and could be affected very catastrophically. I successfully managed to raise the issue of green house gases with the world leaders. President Barack Obama called me and assured me that he would help our country to change the climate of Bangladesh. This is one of the biggest successes.

I will continue to pursue this issue to all international communities to help our country to secure enough funds to protect our country from the devastating impact of global warming. If that occurs, we will have lots of opportunities to deal with no-bid contracts to recover our past loses.

But our political warming is gearing up to a volcanic level! It is about to erupt and I must be prepared to deal with this important issue in my iron fist. My rivals are raising democratically unacceptable issues. I must restrain them first, using my full power for the greater cause of my AL party.

As you have seen, I went to participate in the funeral of one of my lords Jatti Bashu of India to pay my final respects, but I didn't do the same when one of our rivals, the finance minister, Saifur Rahman passed away in a road accident. I didn't even send condolences to his family members and to his well wishers!

The PM of India Mon Mohan Singh was too emotional and he sent condolences after he passed away. I'm not that emotional and that's why I didn't. To pay respect to somebody's life is a personal matter and nobody should make any negative comments on this issue!

In conclusion, I would like to say, *"Ask not what we did in the past, what we are doing now and what we will do. Ask how much more sufferings you will be able to endure."*

Thank you, **Joy Bangla, Joy Bangabandhu.**

Second, The response of the opposition leader, former PM Khaleda Zia

My dear country people,

Assalamu Alaikum.

Happy New Year to you and farewell the nightmare year-2009 for Bangladesh!

Well, you have already heard the performance report of your newly forceful selected current PM. She left nothing for me to say. She has covered almost everything on my behalf. You must be proud of her brilliant articulation.

I must agree with her in almost everything as she addressed to you. I don't need to say anything against her. She herself eloquently explained to you and you must be proud of her.

The history is the record of the previous actions and reactions of those leaders. I don't want to re-write the history. But she does. I do believe the history is never written with chalk pencils and a duster that you can easily write and erase. But she does. I do believe people were very rational in the past, are still now, and will be in future. But she doesn't.

In fact, in the last unconstitutional election, people didn't make any mistake. It was the act of the assault on democracy by some gangs, as she mentioned who played the very devastating role for our nation hypocritically. You have already experienced what kind of horrible experience our nation is going through. Her statement is well enough to understand where we are heading.

When the robbers rob you home, you become the horrible victim and you can't expect any legitimate rights of your own, and you have to be at their evil mercy. Fakhrudding and Moeenduddin were the leaders of those robbers and victimized us not only politically but also personally.

They dismayed the whole nation but couldn't apply their minus-two formula. In fact, that was not a minus-two formula. It was a minus-one formula –is my family and me. My opponent has already eloquently explained this to you.

Finally, Fakhruddin and Moeenuddin had to make a deal with the most destructive parties so-called "Mohajot" just to be protected themselves! Now you can't see their disgraceful faces anymore. They are hidden in an undisclosed location with the mercy of our opponents. After all, they are birds of the same feathers.

My opponents are treating us as their enemies and are doing everything that any civilized society can ever accept! They will continue to do so unless you demand an immediate ousting of this illegitimate administration.

Our nation is going through the toughest time it has ever had had since our liberation. Our nation is under the hard squeeze of the powerful octopus from our neighbors who want to exert their wills at the cost of our national disasters.

You have already experienced those elements during the last year under the current illegitimate administration. You need to be concerned what the future of our nation will be if they remain in power for the rest of the term.

All patriotic people should demand very forcefully to oust the current illegitimate administration just to protect our country and our nation from external evil influence. The life and blood of our freedom fighters were betrayed in the past and they are back now.

They not only deny our true history, but they want to re-write the parody in the name of our history.

You know who martyr Ziaur Rahman was. You know what he did for our country and our nation from the liberation war to his presidency. During his lifetime, they didn't blame him as an assassinator of Sheikh

Mujibur Rahman. Now they are. This is a clear act of meanness to mislead our current and future generations.

They know who the assassinators of Sheikh Mujibur Rahman were. Why he was assassinated. But they want to blame martyr Ziaur Rahman to damage his name and the fame that history can never accept.

Since my opponent very eloquently expressed everything on my behalf, I do not want to retouch those issues. But I must mention one thing – the nature of their violence as an opponent during my legitimate administration.

Unfortunately, now we are the victims under the illegitimate administration. You are the witnesses that as an opponent, the last year we have maintained our differences as always. We opposed almost all issues as these were against our national interest but we never went to the streets to collapse the activities of both private and government businesses to scare you with deadly violence as they did during my legitimate administration. We were a constitutionally elected administration but they aren't.

You must not forget what they did during our legitimate administration, causing the historic black day of **1/11**. We made the difference not only in words but also with full respect to human civilization. We didn't burn tires and vehicles in the road, destroy any private and government properties, and didn't take any lives with the horrible violence that they made record in the history of Bangladesh. The style of their violence crossed the barbarism of medieval era.

Finally, I would like to conclude by saying please protect our country and its sovereignty, our people, our nation, and our true history.

May the force be with you to protect our country from both internal and external evil influences!

Long live Bangladesh!

Thank you.

Bangladesh Zindabad, Bangladesh Nationalist Party Zindabad!

An Exhortation to the World Leaders and UN to protect Bangladesh

As an ordinary person, on behalf of the peace-loving people of Bangladesh, I have taken the bravest step to draw the attention of the world leaders, the United Nations, and the International Human Rights group to pay their attention to the activities of the current administration to stop their Stalin-style tyranny in Bangladesh to protect most of the 158 million people and our nation!

The democracy, our history, human rights, justice, and civilization are under assault under the current illegitimate administration.

It is very risky to raise the patriotic and true voice against the current sadistic administration. I need my protection first and foremost from the Almighty Creator and my Sustainer. Secondly, as a human being, I need the protection from the world leaders. But my utmost appeal to them is to protect our country and our people from the evil conspiracy played by some internal and external evil mighty destructionists.

As one of the patriots of Bangladesh, it is my obligation to raise my voice when my country and our people are leading toward the devastating political direction under the current traitor-like deceptive regime.

Our risky neighbor India already attacked our sovereign small country Bangladesh with total violation of UN charter under this administration. They are constantly attacking and killing our border forces and innocents near the border areas and very often enter into our territory with total disrespect to the international rule of law! They also created the internal destabilization in our land in just one year by aiding the current traitors.

The current illegitimate administration is acting as the loyalist and agents of the outsiders at the cost of the unprotected sovereignty and entity of our country peaceful Bangladesh. They are targeting and swooping up many innocents in the name of extremists who courageously raise their voice for the cause of our country. But they don't have the guts to speak out to protect the sovereignty and entity of our country. They themselves are known as the biggest extremists, traitors, and the founder of the paramount corruption in Bangladesh historically.

It is inevitable to investigate by the world leaders and by the international community to issue the stern injunction upon this atrocious administration to protect our country and our nation from the savage groups. The parliament of our country became the epicenter of hostile chamber under the current evil regime. The opposition parties are constantly humiliated by the gang stars of the current administration.

They managed to obtain power by conspiracy with the help of the progeny of historic culprit Mir Zafar; Fakhruddin and Moeen Uddin through the unconstitutional election of 2008.

Stop the Politics of Dead Bodies: Recently, the controversial PM herself made an awful remark about the assassinated body of martyr Ziaur Rahman who was one of the key figures of our Liberation War in 1971. I vehemently condemn her comment she made about such a national symbolic figure. With that comment, she put herself down to the bottom. She started the politics of old dead bodies rather than moving forward for the greater cause of our country. Her phony slogan 'digital Bangladesh' became 'disastrous Bangladesh' under her evil tyranny.

I would like to remind her that martyr Zia's body was not guarded by the limited number of army and law-enforcing agencies under strict security soon after his assassination. People didn't rejoice his assassination. Rather, they paid their highest tribute to his assassinated body with nationwide mourning and outpouring condolences both nationally and internationally!

In fact, as a non-politician, I never could consider her as my leader or PM. She may try hard to damage the image of martyr Ziaur Rahman but she can't cover up the political odiousness and the causes of the abject downfall of her father, assassinated Sheikh Mujibur Rahman.

I didn't want to raise the issue of her late father but tried to pay my respect for his contribution until March 25, 1971. However, she compelled me to respond. She should have been looking back to the true history of Bangladesh from 1972–75 to take some lessons to move forward with necessary corrections before making any provocative, obnoxious comments like this or by removing and dismantling the signboards of martyr Ziaur Rahman.

You can't change the history of the glory and odiousness of those two leaders by misleading our people with propaganda and falsifications of our history. The history of Bangladesh is the history of triumph. Martyr Zia was an unmatchable hero during our Liberation War in 1971.

Millions of people sacrificed their lives and blood for our success while Sheikh Mujibur Rahman was arrested by the Pakistanis on March 25, 1971. It remains in question whether getting arrested by the West was his courageous move or alternative role played to be protected.

The period of our Liberation from March 25th, 1971, to December 16, 1971, was the epoch of our liberation. The declaration of independence of Bangladesh by Major Zia in his absence was the most heroic role at that moment.

The Declaration of Independence of Bangladesh by Major Ziaur Rahman

"This is Shadhin Bangla Betar Kendra. I, Major Ziaur Rahman on behalf of Bangabandhu Sheikh Mujibur Rahman, hereby declare that the independent People's Republic of Bangladesh has been established. I have taken command as the temporary Head of the Republic. I call upon all Bangalis to rise against the attack by the West Pakistani Army. We shall fight to the last to free our Motherland. By the grace of Allah, Victory is ours".

The deniers of his declaration of independence are not only ungrateful to him but also disgraceful. If I, as a teenager, did hear his declaration from Sadhin Bangla Bethar Kendra (Broadcasting Center of Freedom Fighters), why weren't the deniers able to? Our history is not written using chalk pencils and dusters that you can write and erase the way you wish.

Martyr Zia didn't take an easy shelter by surrendering to the West (Pakistanis) and rather revolted against them very courageously and fought in the war-field until our glorious victory.

You have taken the agenda to obliterate the name of martyr Zia from the Zia International Airport and from the history of Bangladesh, but you can't damage his historic triumphal image from the heart of the people. This is the crime against our national history and entity. Do not try to impure the sanctity of our history with any malicious concoctions for the dirty political cause. This will put you down further as it already had. No mighty evils ever tried to change the history in the world, which you are trying to do now.

Most importantly, if you are a real patriot, you are not supposed to deal with the dead bodies of the past — you are supposed to deal with the future of our nation. The malicious provocation with the old issues is the clear act of evils and the modern civilized world should not, must not, and ought not forgive you!

DNA Test Report of Martyr Zia's Dead Body! I didn't want to raise the issue of the dead bodies of those two leaders. It is already several decades. Only the cowards like to engage in the politics of dead bodies. Both of those leaders were assassinated very ruthlessly; whether it was for a good cause or bad cause! But any assassination of innocents is the act of evils and crime against mankind. But the causes of their assassination can't be ignored.

Indeed, it was one of the most horrible histories of our nation. And our giant politicians were fully responsible for their political and moral miscalculations and its consequence. As Abraham Lincoln said, "*Nearly all men can stand adversity, but if you want to test a man's character, give him power."* We have already experienced the quality of the leadership of Sheikh Mujibur Rahman soon after he took over the power of newborn Bangladesh!

Why did Dr. Henry Kissinger say, "Bangladesh is a bottomless basket," during his administration?

If we go back in human history, we can see from the beginning of human beings that there was fierce confrontation between good versus evils. The evils always wanted to establish their corrupt missions by falsification, deception, oppression, exploitation, and even execution of the general people. Amongst them, some of the courageous ones tried hard to fight those evils to protect mankind and ended up with glory. As such, martyr Zia and other heroes played the noble roles to protect the independence and the people of Bangladesh since our liberation war.

To fight against the injustice and exploitation was not an easy business in the past, is not now, and will never be in future unless all of mankind can change their behavior by themselves. But both of those have had an eventual end. They leave the sharp distinction in the history of mankind.

You don't have to go too far to find some examples of those kinds of leaders. Just go back only the last few centuries to check the facts.

Abraham Lincoln, Mahatma Gandhi, Martin Luther King, John F. Kennedy, and many other great leaders in the world were assassinated by some evil intriguers as was in the case of martyr Ziaur Rahman. On the other hand, Hitler, Stalin, and many other tyrants and sadists were also assassinated or ended up too very disgracefully, and are known as the curse of mankind.

You don't have to look for DNA test reports to evaluate the quality of their leaderships; they are already known very differently in human history.

Martyr Zia's coffin was witnessed spontaneously with utmost honor by the whole nation with the attendance of at least thirty thousand people of all levels: children, young, and old when his coffin was brought for a funeral including outpouring condolences both nationally and internationally!

It was a spontaneous unprecedented wave of public attendance to pay their final respect for his greatness; **as a soldier, as a liberator, and as a president, and as a protector of our sovereignty and integrity**. The whole nation mourned for him quite a longer period than any other leaders of Bangladesh. He, Moulana Abdul Hamid Khan Bashani and very few others were one of the great leaders in the history of Bangladesh who did their best for the country — not for their personal gains! But the others, I don't need to mention. The history itself bears the testimony.

The current sadists are having affair-like relationships with the assassinators of martyr Ziaur Rahman but carried out the execution of the assassinators of Sheikh Mujibur Rahman! This is the clear assault on the current judicial system. There is no sanctity of justice under this evil regime.

May the Almighty, Our Creator, grant the souls of those great leaders and our martyr freedom fighters amongst one of the highest eternal peaceful ones! Amen!

Currently, those who are asking for the DNA test of martyr Zia with awful comments, many of them were known as the ring leaders of donation collectors, gang producers and looters to change their disgraceful fortunes during the regime of BAKSAL and caused immense misery of the people. They betrayed the blood of our martyr freedom fighters soon after our liberation just for their selfish gains.

They were the causes of the incalculable number of deaths during the tense history of 1972–75. They were the leading cause of the downfall of Sheikh Mujibur Rahman with a horrible end. They were the cause of his degradation from Bangabandhu (the friend of the Bangalees) and back to Sheikh Mujibur Rahman!

Don't try to reintroduce yourselves as disgraceful ones raising the old odious issues. Let people forget the old odiousness. You didn't have the guts to ask for a DNA test of martyr Zia for the last twenty-nine years! And now you are raising your neck cowardly like a turtle to talk about such an awful issue, denying the true history of Bangladesh!

With the advent of tyrants and sadists in different ages, all of mankind suffered a lot in human history. Unfortunately, Bangladesh was in the same situation during the period of 1972–75 and once again it is now.

Sadly, this will continue to happen most likely until the existence of the last evil and the last human being on the earth.

The parliament of Bangladesh became the platform of throwing rotten eggs toward the opponents with the old disgusting issues mostly dominated by the gang stars of the current regime. The parliament is the place where the solemn decision is made for the country — not to act as political savages.

The recent comment made by the so-called assistant law minister, Sheikh Salim, and many other cabinet members toward the opponents do not have any boundary of incivility and I condemn their comments and behavior with the demand to oust them from the parliament for good and forever. The Speaker Abdul Hamid himself is one of the same.

In response to their outrageous comment, may I ask them and their followers had you been in the grave during the administration of your opponents for the last two terms of BNP? Have you been resurrected by your external lords and by Fakhruddin and Moeen Uddin, the progeny of Mir Zafar to reintroduce yourselves as the disgrace of our nation? We don't want to see the reappearance of those sadists anymore like you.

I completely agree with Syed Ashraful Islam who said, "Sheikh Mujibur Rahman shouldn't be compared with martyr Ziaur Rahman." Of course, nobody should. The true history is the testimony of the qualities of their leaderships. Martyr Zia's name will be dishonored if we compare him with Sheikh Mujibur Rahman.

I would like to quote as President John F. Kennedy said in the

Democratic National Convention in 1960 while he accepted the nomination for the presidency. Maybe this will help you and your followers to break through your irrational and corrupt barriers.

Quote:

'For the world is changing. The old era is ending. The old ways will not do'

'It is a time, in short, for a new generation of leadership – new men to cope with new problems and opportunities'

Unquote:

He also spoke in UN General Assembly, New York City, on September 25, 1961, and stressed the importance of limiting Nuclear Testing by saying, *'Mankind must put an end to war – or war will put an end to mankind'.*

With similar style, for the greater interest of our country Bangladesh and our nation, I would like to say that we must put an end to the deadly violence, enmity, destruction, and corruption from our political and bureaucratic system — or deadly violence, destruction, corruption and enmity will put an end to us with horrible ends as we have been experiencing repeatedly.

The current illegitimate administration is turning back the pages of our history to the regressive tense period and leading toward the devastating situation they were originally responsible for.

The current controversial PM Sheikh Hasina is rebuking her opponents by saying that during the administration of her predecessor, nothing was done for the development of our country.

Well, may I ask her, was it not she who was fully responsible? She is the one who was fully engaged with deadly violence and politics of hostilities and horror with constant destruction during the legitimate administration of her opponent Begum Khaleda Zia. She acted as an obstructionist and full-time destructionist to impede the development of our country. So instead of blaming others, she should blame herself.

Currently, she is trying to deceive the people of Bangladesh with the phony slogan of "Digital Bangladesh." The whole world is already in a digital era and transcending toward the endless explorations. You don't have to use the term of 'digital Bangladesh' — the people of Bangladesh are doing their best on their own. You better stop nefarious activities using your produced gangs and evil power.

Comb Operation: She has started the elimination process of her opponents similar to Stalin-style and scheming to go against the people who go to the mosque for prayer wearing their religious dresses under the direction of her external lords in the name of Shibir members. As a reminder, don't be so hyper to go against your opponents massively. Many of the worshipers are not involved with politics at all. You are eliminating them just because some of them courageously came out to tell the truth.

About 90 percent of the people of Bangladesh are Muslims and most of them are true believers, I believe. You may choose to be any but don't be misguided by your external lords. The people of Bangladesh will not forgive you. You better refrain from this sort of nefarious operation under the direction of your external lords unless you find any genuine criminals with proper evidence.

Most of the horrible incidents are occurring in Bangladesh out of your conspiracy. You are fully responsible for whatever is happening in our peaceful country Bangladesh soon after you took over the power with conspiracy. Do not torture them while they are under your custody. Stop arresting, torturing and killing the innocents in the name of comb operation!

Failing to do so, you will be fully accountable for each and every case. You have already killed some of the junior leaders and activists of your opponent parties and are still torturing many others while they are under your custody.

Your current actions already led our country toward the catastrophic direction! You and your dupes will be fully responsible for the consequence. **Our people should demand immediate prosecution of her administration in the international court because there is no independent judicial system in Bangladesh under her administration.** Our country was in much better shape until the day before you took the evil power.

I would like to demand the current administration; you better apologize to the nation and restore the name of martyr Ziaur Rahman! If you don't, the people of Bangladesh will! You will be fully responsible for all the cost and consequences. Changing signboard and our history was not your commitment to the people of Bangladesh prior to the mafia-style election.

The people of Bangladesh will restore the name of martyr Ziaur Rahman when the insidious will be exhausted by themselves. They will remain guilty in the history of Bangladesh. Do not damage his image by any means.

My Suggestion to The Opposition Parties:

Always maintain the difference with decency and integrity. And in no circumstances get involved with any destructive tactics like the current sadists. So far you have already made the difference and continue to do so to honor the legacy of martyr Zia and for the best interest of Bangladesh. Also try to strengthen the global relationship for the greater cause of our country and our nation to protect its sovereignty and integrity.

The civility makes the difference by itself. But the incivility and insanity lead to deeper odiousness. The behavior of Sahara Khatun, so-called minister is uglier than her vicious looks! It is better to stop reciting the old disgusting issues that led our nation to a horrible situation in the past. It is the time for all of us to reject the regressive evil tactics and move forward for the greater cause of our country and our nation with a progressive and peaceful vision.

Unfortunately, our nation is in the hard squeeze of a powerful evil octopus — not only nationally but also internationally under the current illegitimate administration. Our nation is in a serious threat of protecting the sovereignty and integrity.

From the standpoints of the above allegations, the current illegitimate PM is fully responsible for all those nefarious activities that cost irreparable damages in just one year of her leadership. She should step down from the power voluntarily restoring the name of martyr Ziaur Rahman from everywhere she has removed at her cost; protect our true history, our culture, our country, and our nation. **Failing to do so, a multimillion dollar law suit may follow in due course in the international court against her horrible administration, if the law permits me to do so.**

In closing, I would like to urge all the patriots of Bangladesh, always try to protect the sovereignty, integrity, and entity of our country Bangladesh! Let's remain in force to protect our country first, and move forward for the greater cause of our country and our nation with the highest spirit of our Liberation War in 1971!

Long live Bangladesh!

Mohammed D. Hussain

Conclusion

Well, I have picked up my pen to use as both wisdom and weapon. I acted very tough for the greater cause of our country, our people, and our nation. To the best of my knowledge and experience, I didn't hesitate to express my views in the way I viewed our politicians and bureaucrats and the causes of the misery of our people and our country.

My axiomatic views could hurt the distorted ideologists like a weapon – but to the real patriots, they are courageous and exhilarating. It is very important to act tough as and when the decency fails to protect our history, our culture, and most importantly, the interests of our country, our people, and our nation. Besides, most of our so-called leaders do not have any sense of civility in neither their behaviors nor their actions. They are incompetent to lead us or to represent our country Bangladesh in dignity to the rest of the world.

I believe it is our solemn responsibility to upraise our voices against the corrupt politicians and bureaucrats to protect our country both from the internal and external destructionists. My writings have already agonized those corrupts and external destructionists but to remain silent will strengthen the sadists.

The era of evil atrocity must end now in the twenty-first century and holding these criminals accountable should be our utmost priority. If not, the evil atrocity will end us, as is occurring under the current administration. The recent reports of human rights violations in Bangladesh published by the US State Department are clear evidence of what is happening in Bangladesh!

Justice is the solemn issue for all mankind – irrespective of the religion, color, creed, culture, and so on. Knowledge, power, resources, and abilities can play a very important role in changing the course of our direction. But we need to play our roles with courage and wisdom.

I strongly demand justice in the international court from the current

PM Sheikh Hasina, along with her gang of stars because there is no solemn justice system in our country under her administration. Expressing my bold reaction is to protect our country Bangladesh and its people. None of my family members is aware of my writings. If anything happens in my life or to my family, friends, and relatives, or to any of the opponents of the current administration due to my writings, she (the current PM) and her dupes shall be fully accountable for the cost and consequence!

We need to move forward with compassion and wisdom. Can we do that? Of course, we can. Then where are the obstacles? The real obstruction is our moral and ethical degradation, and our addiction to selfish causes, lack of confidence, no courage to stand up against the injustice. Let's tear down the source of those evil influences and fight against the corruption, injustice, and poverty, instead of gaining anything depravedly to make the real changes in our country.

Many great leaders lost their lives at evil hands just because they wanted to protect mankind in different ages. But they remain immortal in the history of human beings for their greatness.

Similarly, I'm not a leader, but with my writings, I would like to leave something for the cause of our country Bangladesh and its people. On the other hand, mighty evils didn't hesitate to take their lives, cowardly pointing their guns toward those great personalities or by any other evil means and are known as the curse of mankind.

Before I say good bye, I would like to express my best wishes to the peace-loving people of my country Bangladesh and to all mankind at large!

Mohammed D. Hussain